Olivier Assayas

Edited by Kent Jones

Österreichisches Filmmuseum
SYNEMA – Gesellschaft für Film und Medien

A book by SYNEMA ☰ Publikationen
Olivier Assayas
Volume 16 of FilmmuseumSynemaPublikationen

This work is published with support from the Institut français as part of the Publication Assistance Programs.
Cet ouvrage a bénéficié du soutien des Programmes d'aide à la publication de l'Institut français.

Design and layout: Gabi Adébisi-Schuster, Wien
Cover photo: © Régis D'Audeville
Printed by: REMAprint
Printed and published in Vienna, Austria.
Printed on paper certified in accordance with the rules of the Forest Stewardship Council.

ISBN 978-3-901644-43-6

Österreichisches Filmmuseum (Austrian Film Museum) and SYNEMA – Gesellschaft für Film & Medien
are supported by Bundesministerium für Unterricht, Kunst und Kultur – Abteilung V/3 FILM
and by Kulturabteilung der Stadt Wien.

Table of Contents

This book is dedicated to the memory of
Laurent Perrin, 1955–2012

Preface

How do you know? Sometimes you just do, for reasons that may remain unclear. I too felt the "shock of recognition on first contact" that Kent Jones evokes in his introductory essay to this book, at my first encounter with the work of Olivier Assayas. At 21, in Venice, on the last day of my first visit to a major film festival, I saw *Désordre*, his debut feature. A week or so later, writing about the festival for a film magazine in Vienna, I declared that film and its maker to be the one and only reason why a future was still imaginable for cinema. I am deeply embarrassed to read such a grand proclamation today, but one thing is obvious: I felt I knew, and also that the film knew *me*. This sense of complicity only grew stronger over the years: seeing *L'Enfant de l'hiver* with a rather hostile audience in Berlin (and imagining myself as the sole defender of everything they hated about the film); interviewing the filmmaker the next day and being shocked when he singled out "my" favorite North American films of that year (*Colors* and *Dead Ringers*) as his own favorites, too; visiting the set of *Une nouvelle vie* a few years later and getting a more precise idea of his unusual way of making films; seeing *L'Eau froide* in Cannes, in 1994, and immediately writing a 3-page fax to my best friend about the kind of sound a needle makes on the record-player when it is ripped away only to hack into the same chords we just heard, and about the material and emotional music this adds, not just to the opening of that CCR song, but to the experience of cinema as conjurer of (my own) lived reality.

No, this is not a "scholarly book" in the current sense of the word (even though what follows is hardly as simple and unguarded as the above paragraph). It is conceived by its editor, the recipient of my 1994 fax message, in the spirit of critical appreciation and with an intimate knowledge of the subject(s) addressed – but it doesn't aspire to serve as a straight teaching tool for potential "Assayas courses" in the academic field. I should say, however, that this is a characteristic of almost all the film books I have ever enjoyed, scholarly or not. The others – the books whose primary aspiration is to quickly enter the syllabus – rarely go beyond that first wave of "applicability" during the lifetime of a given academic trend. Those which arise from the author's personal need to understand the first shocks of recognition and follow the traces left by certain films, filmmakers, or groups of films (or by cinema itself) on his or her experience of art and life, have a much better chance of surviving the ebb and flow of fashion, as expressive responses in their own right.

I do not know if this is the "right time" for such a book. The fact that it is the first English-language volume devoted to the work of Olivier Assayas, and that it is being published not in the UK, Australia or North America but in Vienna, Austria, should surprise anyone who shares the feeling that he has been one of the defining voices in the past quarter-century of cinema (not to speak of the fact that, were it in French, it would also be the first of its kind…). This is, as art museums usually call it, a *mid-career retrospective,* and it comes at a time not only of major changes in cinema as such, but at a moment when it has become clear that "the film business" and "art cinema" are no longer capable of inhabiting the same planet – or discourse. In certain ways, Assayas' filmmaking has always had one foot in both camps, and it will be quite an adventure to see how, at the age of 57, he will choose (and be able) to navigate this growing abyss. At that exact moment in their respective lives – but under wildly different circumstances, as far as the state of cinema was concerned – Renoir had just finished *The River* and Bresson was preparing *Pickpocket*, the fifth of his 13 features; Bergman adapted *The Magic Flute* and Sternberg was fired from the set of *Macao*; Manoel de Oliveira had realized just one-sixth of his (still expanding) oeuvre, while the work of John Cassavetes was already (sadly) complete. There is no "right time." There is only the will to go on, and keep making the films you *need* to make.

~

Together with Brigitte Mayr and Michael Omasta, our partners in this series of publications, I want to express my deep gratitude to Kent Jones for his unwavering commitment to this project and all its aspects. His writing, of course, speaks for itself. We are equally indebted to all the other writers whose critical dialogue with the films of Olivier Assayas represents the core of the book; to Olivier's longtime collaborators Luc Barnier, Sylvie Barthet, Éric Gautier, Denis Lenoir for their reflections on the actual filmmaking process; to Isabelle Weingarten for enabling us to reproduce so many of her beautiful photographs; and to Regina Schlagnitweit and Gabi Adébisi-Schuster, our most important collaborators in the material production of the book. Their friendship and work ethic – a common euphemism for willingly exhausting one's energies in the service of a beautiful project – can be neither described nor encapsulated in words.

Thanks are also due to several other kind souls who have given their time and support and helped bring the book to life; their contributions are acknowledged on page 253.

Quite obviously, Olivier Assayas and his films are the *raison d'être* of this endeavor. This simple fact does not, however, account for the generosity that he has shown us, while at the same time preparing, shooting and editing his most recent film. He is a friend, and – still, and resolutely – a friend of books as well as movies. It should be noted, therefore, that this is only one of two Assayas volumes to be published in this series. The second book – *A Post-May Adolescence* – is our humble attempt at introducing to English-language readers his other talent, as a writer. It is also his own attempt at explaining to himself how he came to do what he so magnificently does.

Alexander Horwath,
Austrian Film Museum

Kent Jones

Westway to the World

"What interests me in cinema is *not* cinema itself, but what cinema, as an exploratory tool, catches in its nets."

Olivier Assayas said this in 1997, in a conversation with film critic Bérénice Reynaud about Andrej Tarkovskij's *Zerkalo* (*Mirror*), which had been a model for him when he was shooting his 1994 film *L'Eau froide*. The statement reflects a distinction Assayas has always insisted on drawing in the form of an objection. "So many filmmakers of my generation and even generations after me were really concerned with making movies that looked like movies and felt like movies and basically were nourished by their experience of movies," he told me in an onstage discussion at the Walker Arts Center in 2010. "And that's something that always terrified me. To me, movies should not be about other movies. They should be about your experience of life." Such an ambition is, one might think, fairly basic to the creation of all good-to-great art, but it is rather unusual to hear it voiced today, perhaps in cinema most of all.

What is caught in the nets is both personal and global – on the one hand the traces of one's individual consciousness in the form of memories and sensations; on the other hand what Antonioni referred to as "the traces of feeling in men" (albeit without the Italian filmmaker's sense of their impending extinction), meaning: other people, their objects and customs, the landscapes they inhabit. It could be argued that Assayas has thrown his nets wider than many other filmmakers of his generation. "There are filmmakers who define a world for themselves – space, characters, style, genre – and they will make that kind of film forever," he told me. "They somehow manage to put the whole world into their microcosmos... Whereas you have other movies – and I, of course, relate to that myself – in which cinema is a way of *exploring* the world." In both cases, the exploration of cinema is not an end in itself but a by-product of the *act* of filmmaking.

Assayas has no serious objection to cinephilia in the literal sense of the term. Unlike Welles, for instance, he has never refrained from watching other people's movies. He knows cinema past and present and he knows it well. His objection is to the phenomenon of cinephilia as a vocation which has developed its own peculiar energy and flavor over the years and run on a vaguely parallel but never-quite-overlapping course with cinema itself.

Cinephilia as we know it is a brotherhood (sisters are always welcome, however), a loose affiliation of individuals around the world who "get it," and who are forever on the lookout for those who don't. The cinephile has "received the revelation" of cinema, and those who haven't are either pagans or philistines. A great deal of time, energy and ink has gone into the maintenance of these divisions – or, it might be more accurate to say, into the acts of judging, decrying, condemning and sanctifying. The rhetoric of cinephilia has remained consistently polemical – no film or filmmaker can be celebrated without a supposedly opposite number being condemned. In the era of blogs and Twitter accounts, such polemicizing has become all-pervasive.

Partisanship is, of course, a constant in the arts, as is the urge to nullify (see Wittgenstein on the worthlessness of Mahler) or enshrine (see James Agee on *The Treasure of the Sierra Madre*). New strains of thought or approaches to a given art form are judged incomprehensible or puerile by an old guard (which might continue to imagine itself as an avant-garde long after its initial flourishes), and conversely heralded with an evangelical fervor by supporters who violently condemn anyone who hasn't seen the light. Such judgments are almost always couched in moral terms, positioning the critic as a bulwark against impending chaos on the one hand and a weapon pointed at the heart of reactionary aesthetics on the other. In the case of post-war France, which is where modern cinephilia began, something altogether different happened. The avant-garde was a group of critics taking their first collective step toward becoming filmmakers. They were not heralding the new but something pre-existing yet hitherto unacknowledged in commercial cinema, and in the process they re-directed the attentions and priorities of film viewing through the language of discovery and revelation. The collective action of the *Cahiers du cinéma* critics (and of those who followed them at other publications) was fairly wondrous in and of itself, an endless lifting of the veil of surface beauty to reveal what they took to be another deeper and *truer* beauty. There was a great deal of excellent criticism (most of it written by Jean-Luc Godard), but it's the lovely tautologies and proclamations that are often invoked nowadays. Cinema *was* Bresson, Renoir, Hawks, Hitchcock, Nick Ray and Rossellini; and cinema was *not* Autant-Lara, Delannoy, Decoin, Pontecorvo, Kubrick, or Wyler. It was also evidence of a recognition on the part of the filmmaker of the documentary elements within all filmed fictional images, which is to say: the instant of life recorded during the moment of filming, the life of the actor, the life of the set, of the location, of the surrounding air. To reduce every filmed image to its lowest common denominator as a representational unit was a violation, a denial of the actual life recorded.

To speak in grand, romantic terms, to lay down gauntlets and unleash mighty streams of rhetoric is not only customary at the inauguration of a movement, it's *essential*. Reasoned argument and close examination have never been reliable ways of transmitting excitement. And of course, there was a larger and more powerfully immediate circumstance. The groundwork for the *politique des auteurs* was laid by Henri Langlois and Georges Franju and the *ciné-clubs*, and one could say that it was made possible by the flood of Hollywood films that had been banned throughout the occupation. But the moral inspiration lay elsewhere. Cinema had already played a crucial role in the regeneration of postwar Italy, and the example of neorealism in general and Roberto Rossellini in particular created a lasting image of filmmaking heroically engaged in an immediate, raw relationship with the ravaged life around it. The negation of a common humanity in the Shoah was so complete that any artistic impulse *other* than allowing the world to speak for itself seemed suspect and perhaps obscene, a way of dropping one's newly necessary constant moral vigilance. Thus the aforementioned recognition of the documentary elements inherent in every filmed moment; the rejection of elaborate surface stylings, bravura acting and intricate narratives; the dismissal of accepted distinctions between the culturally worthy and the merely entertaining; and the relegation of talent to a secondary level of importance (it was not a question of the filmmaker making a series of good choices, but the one *right* choice). In a sense, the final section of Rossellini's *Paisà*, legendarily made in a surge of inspiration with an absolute minimum of fictional elements, served as a model, its plain, transparent eloquence harmonizing perfectly with the magisterial criticism of André Bazin.

The *politique des auteurs* is a shining moment, but like every shining moment it is bound to a particular passage in time, albeit one around which the maintenance of memory and the question of "pastness" is both haunting and painful. The link between the *politique* and the memory of the camps is neither vague nor indirect, and Godard's *Histoire(s) du cinéma* and Serge Daney and Serge Toubiana's *Persévérance* are only the most powerful manifestations. Certain rhetorical gambits (Luc Moullet's statement in a 1959 text on Sam Fuller that "Morality is a question of tracking shots" and its Godardian inversion as "Tracking shots are a question of morality"; Jacques Rivette's famous condemnation of the camera movement in Pontecorvo's *Kapo*; Andrew Sarris' contention that the worst Ford film was more interesting than the best Henry King film), stark oppositions (Sarris vs. Kael, *Cahiers* vs. *Positif*, Truffaut vs. Godard) and careers (those of Godard, Rivette and, above all, Straub and Huillet, heralded in certain quarters less for their very real greatness than as exemplars of moral purity) have now become mythological touchstones, and what began as an immediate response to a human catastrophe has slowly devolved into a system of moralizing judgmentalism. Of course, this narrative has been revised and diluted throughout the years as all such narratives usually are, yet it retains a potency that informs the attitudes of writers on film to this day. Moral absolutism is a tough habit to break. To speak the language of polemics has an obvious appeal (for young people in particular) in that it makes everything clear, certain and urgent. But to speak such urgent rhetoric on a habitual basis is, finally, to cultivate a kind of complacency.

Over the years, some astonishingly persistent prejudices have set in. Satirical filmmakers from Billy Wilder to the Coen Brothers invariably come out on the losing end of the auteurist equation, dependent as they are on courting cruelty and the cultivation of extremely stylized performances. Acting in general is sidelined, and commonly spoken of in iconographic terms when it is spoken of at all. Directors like John Huston and William Wyler are vilified to this day because of their adherence to literary sources and their presumed lack of a "consistent" visual style. There has been a fairly constant and reflexive (if extremely selective) distrust of filmmakers who enjoy a measure of power within the industry. And perhaps most damaging of all, there is a general lack of understanding in film criticism of how narrative films are made, based on a refusal to abandon the appealing but erroneous notion that a great director is a divinely inspired being who can make a great film out of any source material – in this light, "editing" amounts to nothing more than the *evidence* of editing, and "writing" almost always means dialogue. Finally, the individual film counts for less than the elaboration of any given filmmaker's "themes."

For a first-time French filmmaker in the mid-1980s, then, the question was: how do I go on? Is it possible to embrace character and narrative complexity without appearing retrograde? If one diverges from the post-war idea of cinema and the post-'68 urge toward a greater asceticism and reflexivity (still vaguely present at the time), is one violating the memory of the

Olivier Assayas, Self portrait, 1995

past? During this period, the sheltering coziness of a cinephile-based cinema was very much in evidence, from good to not-so-good films by directors as diverse as Jean-Jacques Beineix (*Diva, La Lune dans le caniveau*), Luc Besson (*Le Dernier combat, Subway*), Leos Carax (*Boy Meets Girl, Mauvais sang*), André Téchiné before *Hôtel des Amériques* and Benoît Jacquot before *La Désenchantée* (in fact, these last two filmmakers were once given to recounting their careers as before-and-after narratives of pre- and post-cinephilic inspiration). First-time directors were all but expected to mill in the shadows of the Nouvelle Vague lest they be accused of reverting to the scourged past, former *Cahiers* critics (as Assayas had been in the early 1980s when Daney and then Toubiana were editing the magazine) most of all. But this particular first-time director, with a couple of "naïve" shorts already under his belt, took a wildly different path.

~

Assayas was born in 1955, the son of Hungarian fashion designer Catherine de Károlyi (and the grandson of the celebrated painter Tibor Pólya) and the screenwriter Jacques Rémy, who was born Rémy Assayas to a Greek Jewish family from Milan. A staunch anti-fascist, Rémy worked as an assistant to Ophüls in Italy and then followed him to Paris, fled France for South America after the occupation, and on his return worked on many films associated with the "tradition of quality" defined by François Truffaut in his notorious invective "Une certaine tendance dans le cinéma français." Assayas received training from his father in the rudiments of elementary screenwriting (he and his brother Michka actually ghost-wrote some episodes of the *Maigret* television series when their father was ailing), but this was not what inspired him to make movies. "There were always filmmakers around, but not modern filmmakers from the Nouvelle Vague," he told me. "They were directors from another generation. To me, as a kid, they were very nice old men, but certainly not connected to whatever I wanted to do with my life in the future, specifically in terms of my art."

"I always knew that I would make movies someday. I don't even dare use the word vocation, because it's weak in terms of the certitude I had as a small child. But what nourished me during those extremely important years when you're discovering the world and trying to make sense of your relationship with it, wasn't movies. Because in the '70s, movies were not at the center of the culture." Assayas began his artistic life in painting. "When you're a teenager,

Szolnok művésztelep, Hungary:
Grandfather Tibor Pólya on the far left,
Nicolas Sarkozy's grandfather, a local administrator,
on the far right

Catherine de Károlyi

Olivier Assayas, early 1960s

it's very difficult to get a hold of the tools of cinema. The process of learning about movies is long, difficult, laborious, whereas art is immediate. So, I think that for some reason that is mysterious even to me, I kind of had this *need* to practice an art. It was *essential*, and much more important to me than whatever I was learning in school, which I hated. I think I learned through painting what art was about for me. When you're creating an abstract canvas, you arrive intuitively, very quickly, at solving extremely complex questions, like: what is it exactly that you're doing, why are you doing it – that's the difficult one – and, ultimately, when is it done. At some point you have to decide, 'This is *it*.'"

Like most teenagers of the time, he was not looking for a refuge from contemporary reality but a way of engaging with it. He paid a brief visit to the Cinémathèque française but was never a habitué like Jacquot or so many others. "What I was attracted to were the experimental films, the radical films, modern American films, which, to me, connected with the art, what felt like the zeitgeist of my times." He was also attracted to the radical politics of the post-1968 era, a theme he began exploring in his 2002 memoir *Une adolescence dans l'après-Mai.** He examined it from a wildly different angle in *Carlos* (2010), and further refined it in *Après-Mai* (2012). "The political 1970s were *defined* by the fact that people believed in a coming revolution, which was really based on the initial impulse of May '68 in France and similar movements all over the world," he explained. "There was this conviction that the purpose of this generation was somehow to make that revolution happen. It was *always* about to come. You had a lot of empty ideological talk, the rhetoric became more and more wooden and more and more disconnected from real life. To me, the mid-1970s are about the *agony* of that idea. The rhetoric was lacking any relevance, and everybody was living in some abstract world, completely cut off from reality. Because they were – *we* were, because I was part of it in my own way – projecting whatever we were looking for into the future."

Many of us found ourselves in this kind of dilemma. From varying distances, we had witnessed and even been caught up in the spirit of upheaval that had swept through the '60s, but we were born too late to have actually *been*

* The English-language translation of *Une adolescence dans l'après-Mai* has been published in 2012, as a companion to this volume and including two further essays by the filmmaker: Olivier Assayas, *A Post-May Adolescence*, Vienna: FilmmuseumSynemaPublikationen Vol. 17 (distributed internationally by Columbia University Press).

Olivier Assayas, early 1970s
and summer 1980

there. The afterimage of the recent past burned brightly through the mid-70s and beyond, *so* brightly that, for a time, it camouflaged the exhaustion, fragmentation and acquiescence that surrounded us. We found ourselves in a state of suspended animation, recognizing that the moment had passed yet secretly harboring a magical belief that it would, indeed *had to*, live on as an indefinitely extended present. The violent rift between the old left and the new left would never be repaired, the gap between the rapturously romantic vision of Mao's China and the terrifying reality was closing fast, and the operations of the Weather Underground, the RAF and the RZ, and the Red Brigades seemed disturbingly disconnected from any form of effective political action. Most disquieting of all, we watched as the desire for order and stability was relentlessly milked and exploited, as the "failure" of the Movement became the dominant narrative, and as "the '60s" was alternately neutered, discredited and memorialized as a series of fashion choices, iconographic touchstones and guitar solos. It was an odd moment to be young in the western world. For anyone with aspirations to self-knowledge or enlightenment, it was not simply that there was no longer an "us." There was also the stingingly poignant knowledge that we had *just missed it.* We found ourselves, as we all do but perhaps with more than usual bewilderment, on our own. "We were alone," begins one of the most eloquent passages in *Une adolescence dans l'après-Mai,* "all of us trying to reconstitute some connection with the world, to find a path on which we wouldn't betray ourselves."

For Assayas, there were several artists and writers who provided the tools that allowed him to map out such a path. There was Orwell's *Homage to Catalonia*, then little read in France. There was the example of Warhol as both a painter and a filmmaker. There was the punk movement, which hit like a furnace blast. Most crucial of all, there was Guy Debord. "I instantly identified situationism as the party of truth," he writes in *Adolescence,* "especially welcome at a time when truth, more than anything else, was lacking. There did, then, exist an idea of revolution that articulated its theory based on the world as it really presented itself..." Situationism was a bulwark against the most dispiriting currents of the moment. It stood for individual thought as opposed to blind acceptance, for articulation as opposed to Maoist baby talk, freedom as opposed to self-subjugation, and for immediate, as opposed to systematic, responses. For a budding filmmaker with slogans about art-as-petit-bourgeois-diversion still

Olivier Assayas, Self portrait, 1973

ringing in his head, situationism also stood – movingly – for the romantic and the creative. For this young man, Guy Debord and the Situationist International meant "poetry, a possibility for re-enchantment of the city and of life itself."

And in cinema, there was Ingmar Bergman. "The whole generation of the Nouvelle Vague considered themselves as children and didn't want to be fathers," Assayas told me in 1997. "And they especially didn't want to be fathers to the following generation – they had no connection with them, they didn't help them. So the father the post-Nouvelle Vague filmmakers chose was Ingmar Bergman. I mean, the common influence they *all* share is Bergman, to one degree or another." This is true for Téchiné (who gave Assayas his start as a screenwriter on *Rendez-vous* [1985] and *Le Lieu du crime* [1986]), for Jacquot, for Arnaud Desplechin, and certainly for Assayas, who conducted a book-length series of interviews with Bergman that was published by *Cahiers du cinéma* in 1990. On a practical level, one might say that Bergman's movies gave these filmmakers the license to think about contemporary situations, conflicts and characters in dramatic terms, to render the world around them in narrative form. This is an important point within the context of French cinema, where the question of representation has so frequently trumped the question of what is actually being represented. By choosing Bergman and Truffaut, equally important, as models, a post-Nouvelle Vague filmmaker was essentially saying: I'll bet on fiction and character, and against the constant interrogation of the image – a dead end. For certain critics, this commitment to narrative and artifice makes Assayas a retrograde melodramatist... Which is itself a retrograde assertion: this is not an artist who has resorted to or calculated his aesthetic moves but fully embraced them. If the complications between Assayas' characters seem overly melodramatic to a certain strain of film culture, it is, I think, largely attributable to the twin vogues for minimalism (Pedro Costa, Lisandro Alonso) and "strategic" excess (Gaspar Noé on the one hand, Park Chan-wook on the other), which both serve as critical safety nets.

Bergman once described Max von Sydow's character in *The Passion of Anna* as "the kind of person who doesn't really exist anymore," a man whose frame of reference and way of being have started to betray their temporal shaping, who is beset by doubts and dilemmas and torments that have become uncommon. From the beginning, such a precise delineation of the relationship between character and contempo-

Après-Mai (2012)
Carlos (2010)

rary moment has been extremely important to Assayas. In the first four films – *Désordre* (1986), *L'Enfant de l'hiver* (1989), *Paris s'éveille* (1991) and *Une nouvelle vie* (1993) – all of which feature characters in their late teens or early twenties, there is a powerful sense of what can only be called "lostness," very much rooted in the era. The characters in those films are somewhat like children cast adrift, looking for one last, elusive element that will allow them access to real adulthood. They are directly related to a telling passage in *Une adolescence* in which Assayas explains that like many others of his generation, "I maintain the air of someone much younger." I am from roughly the same generation as Assayas (five years younger), and I can attest to a shock of recognition on first contact with his films, with the characters and the lives they led, with their private senses of themselves in the world and in relation to "adults," and on a subtler and more elusive level, with the speed of life as they experienced and perceived it. Here was the world as I knew it and as I had never seen it rendered in cinema.

By alluding to the "speed of life," I am referring to an unusual quality that extends well beyond the matter of pacing. It has to do with the sense of personal agency shared between characters, the phantom awareness of how one measures up against other people, within society, as a citizen of the world. To a certain degree this is, of course, an existential element that only begins to haunt cinema in the postwar era, which, as Gilles Deleuze put it, saw the collapse of "the sensory-motor schema which constituted the action-image of the old cinema"; or, as Manny Farber put it, when "the spatial threads seamlessly knit together for the illustrative naturalism that serviced Keaton's *Navigator* through *Red River* simply broke apart." Deleuze's "sensory-motor schema" and Farber's "illustrative naturalism" were made possible by characters with a uniform idea of their own worth, dignity, and ability to effect change, which started to de-materialize in cinema in the 1940s. This reconfigured idea of exactly what it means to be a human being, up for grabs with every new movie, affected all aspects of filmmaking, and more or less obliged the filmmaker to re-knit spatial threads (per Farber: physical space, psychological space, and shared "experiential" space) and re-think sensory motor schemas with each new story. For certain filmmakers, like Scorsese or Téchiné or Assayas, this is in large part a gestural matter. In Téchiné's films, for instance, one often has the impression of ongoing life moving one or two beats ahead of the characters, always breath-

On the set of *L'Enfant de l'hiver* (1989, right) and *Désordre* (1986, below)

On the set of *Paris s'éveille* (1991)

lessly catching up, which Téchiné himself attributes to his irregular heartbeat. In Assayas' films, there is a close attention to the rhythm of life and its alignment with the individual lives of the characters, which he continually adjusts and re-adjusts with small cuts, shifts, jumps or even ellipses according to the emotional upsets and intrusions felt by those characters. This is an elusive quality that is difficult to describe or even name, perhaps for the filmmaker most of all – it's a little bit like asking a singer about her approach to a melody, or a writer about the rhythm of a paragraph. Assayas addressed the question with a fairly basic tenet: "I believe in trying not to be boring." Then, he re-framed his answer: "I believe in concision. I think I function adding layer upon layer of concision...I suppose it's also the reason I like the pop song format, which is also about concision. So the way I film has to do with the energy of the music and the concision of Bresson. Those are the two elements that are at the root of whatever I've done in film."

In 1999, Assayas wrote a piece for Film Comment magazine about the experience of watching Robert Bresson's *Le Diable probablement* (1977) with his friends when it came out and laughing it off the screen – "We were that clever, sneering public which, placed before the risks taken by artists and the dangers they face, adopts (to its detriment) the most comfortable point of view." When he saw the film again years later, he received the same kind of shock I did when I saw *Paris s'éveille* for the first time, the uncanny sensation of seeing one's younger self caught in the net of another artist ("How is it that I see it now as the most faithful mirror of the teenager I was?"). Indeed, many of the characters in his first few films might be the younger brothers and sisters of Jacques and Marthe in Bresson's *Quatre nuits d'un rêveur* (1971) or Charles and his friends in *Le Diable*.

But how did the world change between the late 1970s and the late 1980s? Perhaps the sense of being lost changed, as 1968 in particular and the '60s in general receded further from memory. The kind of political and spiritual disillusionment felt by Bresson's Charles was no longer possible because the very notion of political or spiritual change had come to seem like something from an irretrievable past. Everything appeared to exist in an eerie timelessness, through which those disinclined to celebrate the yuppie revolution either drifted or raged. Assayas never dealt with yuppies (one had to wait for Desplechin's *La Sentinelle*, 1992), but with young outsiders of nascent artistic temperaments, blindsided by life. From the very

Le Diable probablement (1977, Robert Bresson)

Désordre (1986)
Paris s'éveille (1991)

With Claire Denis,
Théâtre de l'Odéon

first shot of *Désordre*, he was given to dropping his characters and his audience *into* moments, sensations, and actions without explanation or preparation. Of course, ellipsis was in the air when Assayas began making films, and one could point to a variety of antecedents – Godard's entire body of work, Nicolas Roeg's early films, *Muriel, Nicht versöhnt, Two-Lane Blacktop, The Shining*. In the more immediate vicinity, ellipsis was integral to the cinema of his friends Claire Denis and Atom Egoyan, in the work of Wong Kar-wai, David Lynch and others. But in Assayas' movies most of all, there is a persistent feeling of life as a succession of dislocations and displacing shocks. This tendency is taken to an early limit point in the hypnotic *Une nouvelle vie*, in which the audience must regain its bearings again and again throughout the movie. The original cut lasted over three hours, and Assayas found his way through his material by creating a trajectory that seems to operate according to a mysterious governing logic, yielding a finished film with the potency and magical simplicity of a tale by the Brothers Grimm.

In all those early films, the strategy of ellipsis is acute, perhaps even severely so, but as the years have gone by Assayas' use of this particular tool has become increasingly subtle and refined. Many of the key dramatic events in his films – the deaths of Nadine in *Une nouvelle vie*, Adrien in *Fin août, début septembre* (1998), Lee in *Clean* (2004) and Hélène in *L'Heure d'été* (2008) – happen off-screen, as does Emily's withdrawal from heroin in *Clean*. On a more local level, narrative information is imparted to us as if in passing, and we seem to *happen* upon moments within a rush of time. Again and again in Assayas' cinema, from scene to scene, image to image, action to action, we are plunged, often violently, into a new texture, mood, or state of being. For instance, one of the most beautiful passages in his work – Gilles' walk through the woods in *L'Eau froide* (1994) – derives a lot of its potency from the fact of its suddenness within the narrative. All at once, we find ourselves deep within the muted colors of the natural world (a misty forest near twilight…or is it dawn?) and the hypnotic unfolding of a stroll through a private pathway, the uncanny beauty of a solitary teenage ritual (the recitation of Ginsberg's "Wichita Vortex Sutra" in broken English while smoking a Gauloise and pushing a bike through the forest) ending with Gilles climbing on his bike and riding off into the fog. Immediate sensation is given primacy. And as we happen upon such spells or interludes, we become attuned to the reality of time's passing, of characters who seem to catch the evanescent beauty of the moment – for instance, Adrien and Jenny's walk through a very similar landscape in *Fin août, début septembre*, or Pauline and Jean's mountain idyll in *Les Destinées sentimentales* (2000).

Assayas' storytelling has an abstracting effect, removing characters as much as possible from either expository time or the "magical" temporal suspensions of the bravura interlude, the better to hold them in the light of their proper humanity. With rare exceptions, the story and the movement of forms are one (the odd film out is *Les Destinées sentimentales,* his one adaptation of someone else's fiction and his one pre-modern period piece, necessarily structured like a 19th century epic). There is an overriding perception of people *as* action, beings who can be seen fully only when they're in motion, which is indeed Bressonian. With *L'Eau froide* Assayas abandoned the relatively heavy stillness and sculpted action of the first four films (which reached its apex in *Une nouvelle vie,* with its grave and hypnotic choreography between camera and actors) and began to cultivate a syntax of continuous motion. This commitment to flux and mobility, far from the trendy affectation it has been taken for by some of Assayas' critics, seems to me less a matter of style than philosophy. In the end, it is a commitment to the oneness of thought and action, to a conception of people as sentient creatures whose every utterance and step and touch is both a leap into the unknown *and* an affirmation of consciousness and existence. It is hard to recall anyone in a state of repose or stillness in Assayas' collected body of work, which tends to re-play in the mind as a series of diagonal criss-crossings, of people moving forward and never stopping through bustling houses and offices and parties, sometimes by car or moped, sometimes darting toward or away from one another in close-quartered spaces. And it is telling that one of the rare exceptions – Hélène (Edith Scob) in *L'Heure d'été* sitting quietly alone after her children and grandchildren have departed – is an eloquent and near-wordless depiction of someone mentally preparing herself for death.

There is also a painterly side to Assayas' moviemaking, manifested in a lyricism of motion married to a tremendous fluency with color – the airport arrival in *demonlover* (2002), a dazed re-entry after a flight from Japan blurring into a fantasia of clicking numbers, money

L'Eau froide
(1994)

dispensed and exchanged, and quick balletic movements, may be the most spectacular example. What is so unusual, and impressive, is the linking of the freedom of motion of the actors and the characters with the always-decisive color values, achieved through an acceptance of chance and the workings of the moment that have a great deal more in common with modern art and music than with cinema outside the avant-garde. Assayas has an uncommon understanding of movement and its visual effect once it has been inscribed on film and he knows how to "paint" with motion and color (in that regard, he is without peer), but I think that the most direct link between his painting and his filmmaking lies elsewhere. The question of how much or how little importance a background in visual art holds for filmmakers like Assayas, Bresson or Maurice Pialat has been frequently discussed over the years, usually with a misplaced emphasis on the composition of individual frames. In the case of Pialat, there is a strong impression of the *values* of painting woven into the fabric of the entire film. In Bresson's case, an atemporal arrangement of images and sounds frequently adds up to a multi-dimensional rendering or portrait of an event both in and out of time. In the case of Assayas' films, it's the layers of concision he attributed to the influence of Bresson but that, I think, he initially discovered during those years when he obsessed over his brushes, paints and canvases. "You work in different layers, layers on top of layers, and it evolves," he said of his process as a painter. "Something structures your canvas, you decide to get rid of it, and all of a sudden something else seems to be emerging, it might be the beginning of something that you did not have in mind and that ultimately will become the painting… The process can go on and on, and at some point you have to decide, this is it. And why do you decide that? It's a *certitude*, a certitude you have within yourself. Ultimately, that's *exactly* what art is about… You can't put words on it. So that kind of structured my relationship to art in general, and somehow, in mysterious ways, to cinema."

Such fluidity is, of course, possible in cinema only when and if one is prepared to either dispense with or circumvent the crushing burdens and ungainly appendages of industrial moviemaking. "Films should be light," Assayas once wrote to me, and he more than fulfills his maxim on a number of levels. In this sense, *L'Eau froide* was a pivotal work. The film was made for an Arte channel series developed by producer Pierre Chevalier entitled "Tous les garçons et les filles de leur âge," named after the once-popular Françoise Hardy song. The

Une nouvelle vie (1993)
demonlover (2002)

concept was simplicity itself: give filmmakers extremely low budgets and Super-16mm cameras to make films about when they were 16, with the stipulation that they include a party scene and make use of contemporary pop songs (in this case, by Roxy Music, Leonard Cohen, Creedence Clearwater Revival, Donovan, Alice Cooper, Bob Dylan and Nico). The TV versions of the films were an hour or under, and only Assayas, Téchiné, Cédric Kahn and Patricia Mazuy expanded their films into features. "I did not imagine doing something that would just end up on TV. I said, 'Okay, let's try and do something challenging' – take the *very* little money I had to do a 45-minute film and see what would happen if I turned it into a feature. The maximum I could have was, like, a four-week shoot – 24 days, including Saturdays, four weeks. And it was the first time I was working in super-16. The idea was that I could do something which would be semi-experimental, made the way Philippe Garrel made his films in the 1960s, or the way some of the experimental filmmakers I admired made their films."

This marked the initiation of what has since become common practice for Assayas: to work quickly, decisively and constantly. When all the moving parts of a big project take time to cohere (as was the case with *Les Destinées sentimentales*, which he originally planned to make in the mid-90s) or fall apart altogether (a fate which befell *Moins une*, a film noir he co-wrote with his friend Emmanuel Bernheim, and *Sang versé*, an ambitious gangster saga), there is always another smaller project ready to go. "I'm not dependent on getting money here or getting money there, because shooting in four weeks with no stars and a small crew, you can always manage." This has given him an extraordinary mobility in harmony with the movement of his characters and his films, a level of ingenuity to rival that of a B-filmmaker of the '40s (that the 5.5-hour 3-part *Carlos* was made for $18 million remains a source of astonishment), and an artistic freedom that eludes filmmakers in pursuit of big budgets, particularly here in America. "To me, the major problem that you have to overcome when you're making films is the weight," he said. "It's such a *heavy* art form. That's not just anecdotal. You have all those trucks, and all those people, and this heavy machinery, stuff it takes four guys to carry…and those are the tools you're going to use to try to create something as fragile as poetry? The problem is to transcend all that weight and to make it light. But not just in terms of the images you create. It's also on the set, you have to help everybody forget the weight – your actors,

On the set of
L'Eau froide (1994)
and *Irma Vep* (1996)

technicians. And help them forget the rules." Many filmmakers I know have alluded to this crucial element of filmmaking, and described it in their own personal terms. For Claire Denis, it is a matter of having something to fight against, whether it be the producer, the weather, the actors, or even the film itself. For Ulu Grosbard, it is a question of relaxation: "A director who can manage to convey a sense of play on the set, even though he knows the clock is ticking and even though he is under pressure with budget and schedule [is at] an enormous advantage." Assayas' approach to the problem is very close to Brian Eno's approach to working with studio musicians: the job is to throw everyone off-balance. "Ultimately, in one way or another, you have to go on the set and create chaos. *Some* kind of chaos. So that people lose their reference points and just use their brains, and don't just go through the motions. Ultimately that's what movies are about. Because they don't *need* you to make the film. They need you to create confusion." This is also, finally, a spiritual matter. At the end of *Une adolescence*, Assayas likens a film shoot to a "situation" in the Debordian sense, an ongoing collective act of "conscious creation in the domain of everyday life" which is "inextricably entwined with reality." This one-to-one relationship between actor and character and immediate and depicted reality is present in the first four films, but it does not fully flower until *L'Eau froide*. Because the low budget, the tight schedule, the singular focus of the commission and the lightweight equipment gave him the freedom to experiment, Assayas was able to open the door to fleeting intuitions and inspirations that tend to run and hide from the pressures of big budget moviemaking.

"What you see [in *L'Eau froide*] is fairly close to my experience at that age," he told me. "You see my Hungarian nanny who was the person I loved the most in the world – she was my mother, grandmother, everything at the same time, and she was very Catholic, and every evening she would read and say her prayer in Hungarian and I would also say my prayer in Hungarian...I spoke Hungarian with her. And I lived in a house in the countryside, and I have so many memories of just escaping from the house, getting my bike and riding off through the woods to go wherever I would be going, and it had this kind of Tarkovskij feeling to it, specifically *Mirror*. I just didn't realize that I would recapture something that was so deeply embedded inside me. I had no idea. So I was a spectator of my own film. I was watching this kid be myself, and all of a sudden the whole *thing* just came back to me so powerfully. You

L'Eau froide (1994)

can imagine, when we were shooting the long party scene with all the music I was listening to, which was what defined that age for me, and just being around the kids, and going to the set to shoot that party scene every evening, finding myself in the middle of the woods, in that house, in those old ruins, with those kids smoking grass and then half dancing and burning furniture in a big bonfire…you know, to me it was like *living* those times again. It was an extremely fascinating and disturbing experience. It kind of made me realize the power of cinema in a way I'd only had an intuition of before. Here, I had it before my own eyes. There was this extraordinary dialogue between my present and my past, and the line was blurred. And when we finished shooting the film, I had this incredibly melancholic feeling of having once again left my teenage years behind, that I had had the privilege through one movie to relive those years. Briefly. In a glimpse, but still, in a very relevant and powerful way. I had no idea that movies could go that far, and be as disturbing as that."

~

It is very common in film culture to see a director's body of work systematically broken down and sorted into manageable units such as themes, common motifs, visual style, and levels of political awareness and moral "fitness" (meaning how much or how little they "love their characters"). The last two extremely problematic categories aside, what is sorely lacking in this Freshman English approach to aesthetics is an idea of the *action* of filmmaking, the movement of thought, the peculiar ongoing relationship between artist and art form, the unfolding or shutting down or expansion of an individual consciousness as reflected in cinema – such considerations are usually confined to quotes or breezy observations in Sunday Arts and Leisure profiles, or else plucked from interviews and inserted into directorial studies as evidentiary support.

In the case of Assayas' body of work, it is common to take strictly autobiographical projects like *L'Eau froide* and *Après-Mai*, group them with the fictions partly drawn from autobiographical elements such as the four early movies, *Fin août, début septembre* and *L'Heure d'été*, and contrast them with what are now commonly referred to as Assayas' "Debordian thrillers," *Irma Vep* (1996), *demonlover* and *Boarding Gate* (2007). The idea is that Assayas operates in two registers – people talking in cafés and people chasing each other across the globe with guns and expense accounts – and enjoys some

Fin août, début septembre (1998)

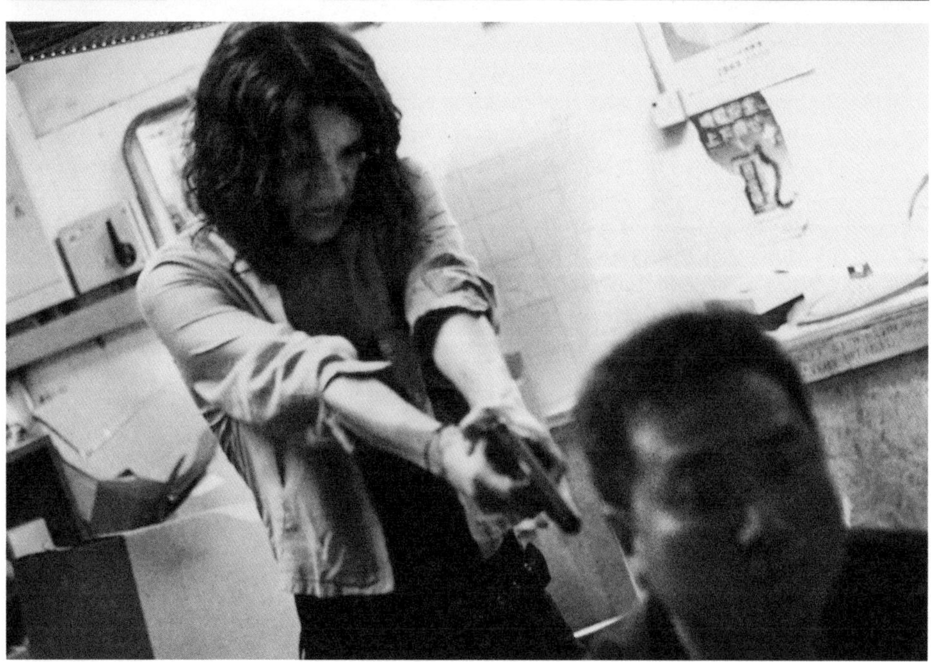

Boarding Gate (2007)

kind of artistic double life. Of course the whole idea of dueling aesthetic registers (which I admit to perpetuating myself on occasion) falls apart on even cursory inspection. "All of my movies are as good as whatever I was at the moment of making them," Assayas said by way of explanation. "There's not one movie of mine where I didn't have a sense of throwing absolutely *everything* of myself into it, and I've always made my movies as if they were simultaneously the first and last movies I would ever make. So when you finish making a film, you don't want to go back into the same territory because you're...spent. When I make a movie like *L'Heure d'été* which deals with the loss of my mother, with very intimate emotions, I'm not going to do the same thing all over again. I don't want to touch it, and I'm perfectly unable to find something as essential and emotional to me. Obviously I have to move on to some other place. I believe in the dialectics of reality. I believe that in art you can move from the intimate to the universal. You can make movies that deal with what is going on within yourself, which is part of commonly shared human experience, and simultaneously you can make movies that are open to what happens in the big world around you, that deal with history, with the geo-politics of your time. I think the intimate films make sense because they are connected to movies that deal with the broader picture, and the movies that deal with the broader picture are legitimized by the fact that they're connected with movies that deal with the essence of human experience."

Filmmakers are driven to this or that project for all kinds of reasons – desire, pressure, a need to maintain a certain status within the industry, an impulse to explore or to be playful, an urge to work with a certain actor or to recapture a certain moment. What Assayas is articulating, and more importantly enacting, is a link between the rhythms of attention in art and in everyday life. When you've just finished traveling, you want to stay home. When you're done with a Tarkovskij retrospective, you usually want to follow up with something diametrically opposed. A mood properly exists only in relation to an opposing mood, clarity only makes sense in contrast to confusion, the depth of a blue sky can be most fully appreciated only when it is dotted with clouds. In Assayas' case, each new project feels humanly rather than industrially motivated, and the same is true of Hou Hsiao-hsien or Philippe Garrel, Stan Brakhage or Nathaniel Dorsky. In each case, it is never a simple matter of systematically following a project with its tonal opposite, but of

On the set of
L'Heure d'été (2008)

pursuing intuitions, following leads, piecing things together and, more often than not, pursuing multiple lines of thought and tying them up in one film.

Irma Vep, for instance, is a film of obviously autobiographical elements based on Assayas' own adventures in the feverish world of low budget moviemaking; a pointed reflection on the Babel-like conditions that are never very difficult to find in contemporary experience (film crews tend to offer a perfect microcosm), in some ways anticipating the hectoring solipsism of the blogosphere by half a decade; a tender comedy of human awkwardness and lurching attempts to connect; a gossamer journey through the looking glass; and a snapshot grabbed on the run from a particular moment in time. *Les Destinées sentimentales* is a historical saga which benefits enormously from the freedom Assayas found with *L'Eau froide*, a lovely character study of a man who is trying to be good, responsible and free all at once, and an affirmation of the artisanal and a rejection of the mass-produced, the lasting solidity of the one vs. the instantly consumable flimsiness of the other (within the immediate context of the year 2000, Assayas saw *Destinées*, in tandem with Wong Kar-wai's *In the Mood for Love*, as an "anti-Dogme 95" movie). *demonlover*, made in reaction to the long, weighty adventure of *Destinées*, is a relatively single-minded film unlike anything else in Assayas' body of work, in which he reversed course from the previous project and looked at the problem of institutionalized avarice not by rejecting it but by making a film infected by its energies. "It was inspired by the images of those years, the proliferation of *layers* of images," he said. "Movies had a different style that had to do with the special effects. There was the internet, the comics... So I was trying to absorb the crazy manifestations of the subconscious of those times, and not to be scared by them. Not reject it, not discard it, but try to absorb it and do something with it and comment on it." He would later visit similar territory with *Boarding Gate*, a film with a solid human core (in the person of Asia Argento) necessarily missing from the earlier movie. *Clean*, like *Paris s'éveille*, is involved with heroin addiction (both are based on Assayas' experiences with friends and acquaintances), but unlike the earlier film, where addiction is secondary to the longing that summons it, the later work stays fixed on regeneration and, more unusually, on its acceptance by others as a reality rather than an abstract idea. It is also a film about life as experienced from the perspectives of different ages, a framework that has evolved

Irma Vep (1996)

Les Destinées sentimentales (2000)

and deepened over the years for Assayas. In his first four films, parents tend to be monstrous and forbidding figures, and their relationships with their children range from mutually uncomprehending to coldly divisive (Jean-Pierre Léaud's Clément in *Paris s'éveille* is an exception, an adult who wants to remain a teenager and relinquish the responsibilities of parenthood). In this area as well, *L'Eau froide* marks a shift. In contrast to Philippe Laudenbach's imperiously indulgent father in *Désordre* or Bernard Verley's terrifying patriarch in *Une nouvelle vie*, László Szabó as Gilles' father is exasperated with his son's frustrations and confusions but realistic about the pain of adolescence, the fact that it can only properly be understood by adolescents themselves.

As he has grown older, Assayas' understanding of generational divides has grown increasingly nuanced. It is even present in *Carlos*, where Ahmad Kaabour as Wadi Haddad plays the stern father figure to Édgar Ramírez' Carlos, an overgrown precocious child. Ten years after *L'Eau froide*, there is Nick Nolte's majestic Albrecht in *Clean*, a man who loves the grandson he has been obliged to raise but who is weary of the effort it takes to understand children, who knows that he can't afford to harbor a grudge against his daughter-in-law and that he has no choice but to bet on her ability to change, who can not afford the time to grieve for his son or his dying wife because he must prepare for the future. Nolte's performance is grounded in a wonderful economy of gestures, in watching carefully and speaking his measured words slowly and clearly with a saddened composure that finally communicates genuine nobility. The gracefully contrasted and fitfully harmonizing perspectives of Albrecht, Maggie Cheung's Emily and James Dennis' Jay, rather than drug addiction, are at the core of *Clean*, to my mind Assayas' most underrated and mischaracterized film.

There is a nice exchange in *Conversation avec Bergman* in which Assayas questions the older filmmaker about the somber character of his early film *Fängelse* (*Prison*). "My dear friend... Olivier...couldn't one say the same of your film *L'Enfant de l'hiver*?" answers Bergman, who had just screened a print. "When you're young, you're pessimistic. You enjoy it... It's even more than that: 'le plaisir du pessimisme.'" Throughout the first four films – four stories of young people by a young man, four reflections of a young consciousness – "winter" is a constant state of mind, almost an affliction of the soul. In *Fin août, début septembre* the principal characters are in their thirties and forties, dissatisfied but pensive, aware that their youth is

Ahmad Kaabour in *Carlos* (2010)
Nick Nolte in *Clean* (2004)

over but still imagining life as an orderly process. In *L'Heure d'été*, the characters are in their forties and fifties, more serene, accepting of their dissatisfactions as realities of life. Both films deal with the shock of mortality and the acceptance of loss, as well as the bracing realization of *others*, the strange sensation of having your world picture suddenly re-adjusted (as in the scene in *Fin août* where Gabriel is stunned to hear his recently deceased friend Adrien, who he always thought of as a writer of great promise, pronounced a "genius" by a younger man). But the two films are also very different precisely because they were made at two distinct junctures in Assayas' life. *Fin août* operates somewhat in the manner of *Irma Vep*, offering an assembly of individuals who frequently collide and occasionally cohere. By contrast, *L'Heure d'été* is about a family that imagines itself as close-knit but that is in fact far-flung, whose members must measure the cherished image of past intimacy against a colder and more pragmatic present.

"One wants to consider the imagination on its most momentous scale," wrote Wallace Stevens in 1948. "Today this scale is not the scale of poetry, nor of any form of literature or art. It is the scale of international politics and in particular of communism." Replace "communism" with "global corporate power" and you have a perfect description of the shadow that has been hovering within the collective imagination of the west since the collapse of the Soviet Union. Assayas has always had his eye on this phantom presence, and he is one of the artists who has most devotedly transmitted and chronicled its effects on individuals. In the first films, we feel it in the painful confusion shared by the characters, all of whom seem to experience a terrifying sensation of smallness in a big world, which provides each of the films with its center of energy. But as Assayas has progressed, he has left behind the undiluted existential weariness of the early work and become increasingly adept at creating dramatic structures and cinematic canvases which keep the characters and the world in which they live in a delicate balance of attentions, and afford us an ever more heightened awareness of the economically determined equations which hang over our lives, businesses, and governments. "The stripping away of humane constraints to liberate great 'natural' forces, such as capital flow or the (*soi-disant*) free market, has acquired such heady momentum that no one even pauses to wonder whether such forces are indeed particularly 'natural,'" wrote Marilynne Robinson. One objective of contemporary

Fin août, début septembre (1998)

On the set of *L'Heure d'été* (2008)

fiction, written or filmed, is to mirror the feeling of living in a world deep in the thrall of this absurd but generally accepted idea. Few have done a more thorough job of realizing this objective than Assayas.

The "new world order" was in the process of cementing itself when Assayas began as a filmmaker. As I mentioned above, he had no access to any collective movements but considered himself part of a loose affiliation of filmmakers without artistic father figures other than the ones they selected individually. "I did not really experience myself as a French filmmaker," he wrote in a piercing reflection on the artistic legacy of his late friend Edward Yang, who he met along with Hou Hsiao-hsien, Chris Doyle, and Wu Nien-jen on a trip to Taipei in the mid-80s when he was still a critic for *Cahiers du cinéma* – indeed, he was one of the first western critics to draw attention to their work (a little over a decade later he would make *HHH* [1997], a documentary portrait of Hou). Assayas considered himself a "Western cousin to the key figures in the New Taiwan Cinema, who were given a chance I never had, a chance to begin their careers with the collective energy of a shared faith." The Taiwanese filmmakers, after half a century of Japanese rule followed by four decades under martial law, had a chance to remake their national cinema from the ground up and re-define the image of their country around the world, like the Italian neorealists after the war. Moreover, Hou and Yang, the greatest of the Taiwanese and two of the finest filmmakers of the late 20th century, quickly understood that there would be only a brief interval before Taiwan would, in Assayas' words, start speaking the "language of commerce" and "absorbing the habits, values and even the imaginary that are the universal language of the west" – in a word, globalization.

When the opening for a global economy arrived in the west, it was interpreted, as Robinson wrote, not as an opportunity but a natural outcome, an overdue correction, the happy "end of history." One became used to an ever-increasing unreality, a convergence of round-the-clock entertainment in an ever-greater selection of delivery systems, the relaxation of trade barriers and "excessive" financial regulations, the regular cooption of anything spontaneously generated (so regular that "popular culture," "commercial culture" and "consumer culture" came to be thought of as one), and, in America, a triumphalist spirit that merged seamlessly with the "upbeat" aura cultivated by the advertising industry. The net effect was a grand and constant effort to achieve consensus

Cover of *Cahiers du cinéma* Special Issue *Made in Hong-Kong*, 1984

Olivier Assayas at the Shaw Brothers office in Hong Kong during research for the Special Issue

With Edward Yang and the cast of *A Confucian Confusion*, Cannes, 1994

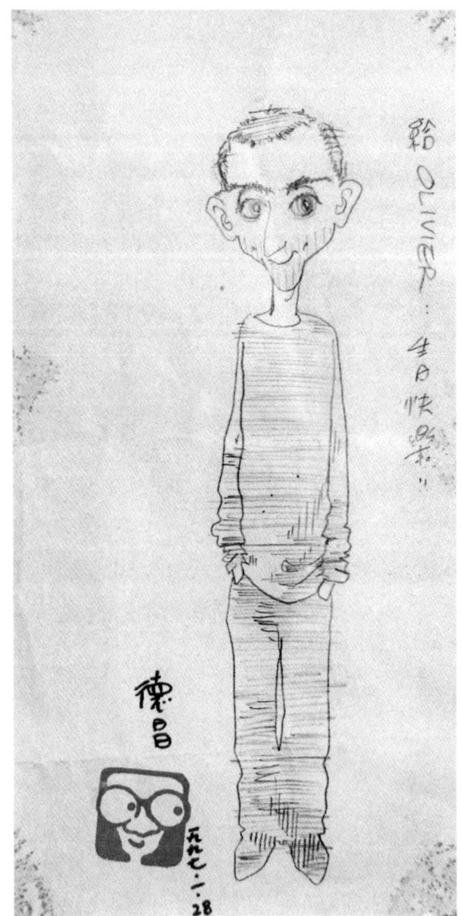

Edward Yang's drawing of Olivier Assayas

at all costs, reconfiguring large swaths of the newly globalized planet as a nervously conformist environment akin to a massive American high school ca. 1952. If you weren't happy, you were odd, a downer, a naysayer, artsy, esoteric, and so on.

In cinema, this arrived in the form of a temptation to look away from the present and take what Assayas refers to in his appreciation of Yang as "the easy path of postmodern mannerism." On the one hand, there was the aforementioned overwhelming pressure to embrace commercial culture. On the other hand, there was the pull of a leftist cinema engaged in, to quote Assayas, the "umpteenth rehash of the class struggle and the enduring contradictions of capitalism," appealing only to those blinded by May '68 nostalgia. The third point in the triangle was an intellectual culture which chose to see reality from an aesthetic remove, a "spectatorial left" as the American philosopher Richard Rorty named it, which ceased to be interested in genuine political change (or indeed, to admit that such a thing was still possible) and chose to focus exclusively on a project of cultural change from the inside out that was and still is unrealizable.

As it was for Hou and Yang, who were experiencing historical change at their front door,

With Hou Hsiao-hsien, during production of *HHH* (1997)

Assayas' course was clear – a belief in cinema not as an abstract essence but a historical continuum; a belief in fiction and character not as outmoded or retrogressive tropes but as precious tools; and a belief in oneself, one's own experience as witness and participant in life and history, one's own perceptions, observations and conclusions, as opposed to an aesthetic or interpretive system. Assayas operates according to his own intuitions, desires and his own shifts in perspective over time. Among all the filmmakers at work around the world today, it's in his films where I feel the frisson of life in the present most sharply, as sharply as I did 20 years ago. Sometimes it occurs in the overall shape of a film, as is the case with *L'Heure d'été* (per Larry Gross, Assayas' "most Chinese film") and *Carlos*, where the insane movement of geopolitics at the end of the 20th century is pitched at exactly the right rocketing rhythm and giddily unhinged tone. Often it occurs on a scene-by-scene level, in certain pointed exchanges (the hilarious conversation between Maggie Cheung and Antoine Basler's aggressive reporter in *Irma Vep*) or revelations (Gabriel's dumbstruck realization at the end of *Fin août* that the heartbroken teenager played by Assayas' future partner in life, Mia Hansen-Løve, has already left the memory of Adrien behind and fallen in love with a boy her own age) or in the agitated motion of certain characters (women in particular – Nathalie Richard in *Irma Vep*, Connie Nielsen in *demonlover*, Maggie Cheung in *Clean*, Asia Argento in *Boarding Gate*). And sometimes, it is felt at a moment-by-moment level of acuity within a scene itself.

Late in *L'Heure d'été*, there is a scene of enormous complexity in the service of the greatest simplicity. If someone wanted to get a sense of life in the west 100 years from now, they couldn't do better than to watch this meeting between three siblings and their spouses after the death of their mother in which they discuss what will be done with the family house and its contents. The scene is built on an extremely subtle insight, which is directly linked to the specter of consensus at all costs evoked above: that almost every face-to-face interaction today is governed by a mortal fear of conflict. When the conversation begins, Charles Berling's Frédéric (a temperamental cousin to Mathieu Amalric's Gabriel in *Fin août*) imagines that everyone is in agreement that their mother's house should stay in the family. Slowly, unassumingly, without any overt disagreement, Jérémie (Jérémie Rénier) and Adrienne (Juliette Binoche) steer things in another direction – he and his family are living in China, he has just signed a new contract with Puma, and they have no plans to return to France anytime soon; she has a design business in New York and is planning to marry her American boyfriend. No one actually states their point of view until they have to, and the wives of Frédéric and Jérémie (Dominique Reymond and Valérie Bonneton), say little but encourage or offer solidarity with their husbands through glances, shifts in posture, movements toward or away from the area of conflict. When Adrienne announces her marriage plans, she prompts a round of kidding from her brothers about her disastrous first marriage. What is so poignantly true here is the relief that comes with the break in tension, the willingness of all parties to obliterate, for one last moment, the cold realities of the situation.

Assayas and his actors and cameraman built the scene little by little. "I had written this long scene," he remembered. "Basically, there was a scene in the living room, and then the food came and they sat at the table and started having dinner, and then having that discussion. And during the process of preparing the film, I got completely bored with the notion of seating the characters around a table. You know, I just could not *picture* it, it felt wrong. And then, when we found the flat where we ended up shooting the scene, I said, 'You know what? Let's shoot the scene in the kitchen and use the

Maggie Cheung in *Clean* (2004)

Connie Nielsen in *demonlover* (2002)

Nathalie Richard in *Irma Vep* (1996)

balcony,' because there was this small balcony. Then came the day of actually shooting. In our schedule, I had two days. I never plan ahead *how* I'm going to shoot, I do it in the morning before going on set. Sometimes it's difficult and it takes time, but I kind of figure it out and end up having a structure for the scene which I can follow or not, but I know I have some kind of safety net: I have my plan, I go on the set, and then I adapt my shots and turn it into whatever will be in the film. Usually it's difficult, but I manage. I handle it. The morning of shooting that scene, I woke up, I looked at the plan, and I thought, 'What got into me, deciding to shoot this absurdly long scene in this absurdly small space where there are basically two angles?' When I walked into the kitchen with my cameraman Éric Gautier, I said, 'Éric, let me introduce you to angle 1 and angle 2.' I just *could not* figure out how to do it, so I ended up improvising it on the set. Whatever the scene was about would be defined by the way the characters were moving closer, further, re-grouping – it was this choreography within this absurdly small space. Really, I had to invent it on the spot, because I had no idea how to design it. It's something I very rarely do. And it involved shooting many different versions with many different movements, and I patched it together with Luc Barnier, my editor, from a mountain of material. It's very simple in terms of what goes on, but in terms of how we shot it, it was like a nightmare. It's a film where I used a lot of improvisation but here…there are lines, here and there, that are basically what the actors tried at a specific moment, or lines that I invented on the spot, to kind of patch things up. Because I had to invent all the movements, it was taking shape in front of me, so what I was *seeing* would inspire new ideas, add a line here and add a line there. Ultimately the scene grew into something fairly different from what was on the page." The memory may be harrowing, but the outcome is a seamless whole which encompasses a vast amount of social, political, behavioral and spiritual territory, and stands as a perfect example of Assayas' earlier contention that the job of the filmmaker is to create confusion on the set, to leave technique behind and respond directly to *this moment* – or, to quote one of Brian Eno's most frequently cited Oblique Strategy cards, to "trust in the you of now." Which is to say, oneself.

~

L'Heure d'été (2008)

This book originates with my first encounter with Olivier Assayas and his films. It was Alexander Horwath, the co-publisher of this series, who encouraged me to write to Olivier in 1993, the beginning of a correspondence and a long friendship, now covering many years and a lot of ground, which has played no small role in the evolution of my own relationship to cinema. It will undoubtedly be noted that all of the writers included in this book are American, spanning generations and disciplines. This was a conscious decision, less polemical than reflective of a key factor in Olivier's career and his recognition as a filmmaker. Just as France once helped America to re-examine its own cinema in a fresh light, so American writers, critics, programmers and distributors have cultivated and transmitted a special appreciation for his films back across the Atlantic. "Every ship is a romantic object," wrote Emerson, "except that we sail in." We tend to long for what we don't have and scorn what we do. If not, Olivier would never have sought out Bergman, Hou, Yang, or the grand open world of which he has incorporated so much in his films. I think that's what I prize most of all in his uniquely gestural filmmaking, with its nets cast so wide – an embodied sense of cinema as an act of endless exploration, illumination and exaltation.

Location scouting for *demonlover* in Tokyo

① Départ gare St Lazare

train au bout ~~du quai~~ de la gare sur la dernière voie : c'est le dernier départ grandes lignes de nuit.

Peu de monde sur le quai.

Un contrôleur à l'entrée du quai.

Wagons anciens. Fauteuils en skaï beige. Allée centrale.

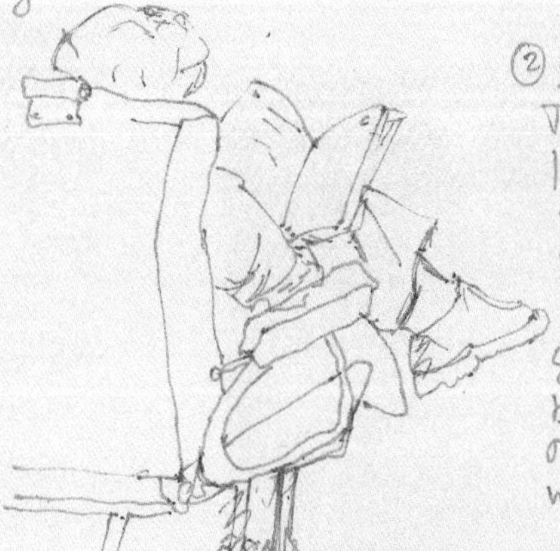

② Dans le train

Très vite les gens qui dorment.

les wagons sont pleins.

Sacs, sacs de sport, sacs à dos.

Voyageurs jeunes.

Plusieurs en train de prendre des notes

genre journal de voyage.

buée sur les vitres.

Dehors : obscurité totale.

WALKMANS.

▯▯ ▯▯ etc....

etc.... ▯▯▯▯▯▯

bagages et voyageurs dans les extrémités des wagons. Assis sur leurs sacs.

A première vue, il n'y a pas de bar.

Un peu plus de lumières à l'extérieur à l'approche de Rouen.

(pont de fer : on traverse un fleuve)

Au bout d'un peu plus d'une heure les gens dorment.
Des filles recroquevillées sur leur fauteuils.
Des types étendus, pieds sur le fauteuil d'en face. Un s'étant couvert le visage avec son manteau.
Des couples enlacés.
Confirmation après exploration systématique du convoi : il n'y a pas de bar.
Beaucoup d'anglais. Un groupe de toutes jeunes filles bavardant non stop.

(12h45) Arrivée à Dieppe : grève surprise.
Le train reste bloqué et ne peut accéder à la gare maritime.

C'est une dame genre cheftaine scout qui l'annonce à la cantonnade : une heure d'immobilisation en attendant un prochain bateau.
Tout le monde dort à moitié.

(3h10) Le train s'est remis en marche. On arrive sur le quai de la gare maritime.
On descend, les gens se massent dans le froid devant un bureau où l'on présente son passeport et donne le coupon d'embarquement.
Pas vraiment de cohue. Juste la queue.
Bateau : le <u>CHARTRES</u>.
Extérieur OK.
2 ponts supérieurs.
2 plateformes arrière. On n'accède pas à l'avant.

Intérieur du bateau : nul.
Cafeteria/self cafardeuse.
Une boutique duty-free.
Des magasins. Un arbre de Noël.
On fait la queue pour les passeports.
Un bar avec des jeux vidéos. Un juke-box à clips. On croirait une salle de MJC à Sarcelles.

Je fais quelques photos.
Ext. + Int. généralement au flash : aucune idée de ce que ça donnera.

À l'intérieur des escaliers. En particulier ceux qui descendent au stationnement des voitures.

lumières allumées : néon.

En fait, à l'arrière, trois plate-formes superposées.
Une avec les machines, au-dessus de l'entrée des véhicules, assez abritée du vent.
Une seconde au dessus, latéralement exposée à un vent très violent.
La troisième, encore au-dessus et un peu plus petite, abritée, dominant les deux autres ainsi que les deux coursives superposées.

les 3 ponts.

les 2 coursives.

Les deux coursives sont étroites. De la supérieure, on peut voir l'inférieure. Entre les deux, à peu près à mi-hauteur sont suspendues les embarcations de sauvetage.

Au fur et à mesure de la traversée, des gens ivres déambulent. La plupart des passagers sont étendus tant bien que mal sur les banquettes.

6h45 Heure française : une voix annonce que l'autorisation ne nous a pas encore été donnée par la capitainerie d'entrer dans le port de Newhaven.

Finalement on parvient à Newhaven.
(Après être passé à la douane, c'est obligatoire, sur le bateau)
Les gens se massent devant les portes.
Descendent la passerelle. En ordre [illegible] et se retrouvent
dans un hall où l'on fait la queue : c'est l'inspection des bagages.
Puis le train anglais : les compartiments, ce sont les premières.
Les secondes, c'est :

Il fait noir.
Les gens se sont réveillés. Moins de dormeurs que dans le train français.

Four pages of notes and sketches for *Désordre* (1986)

Glenn Kenny

Black Boxes

"You must be waiting for things to happen / expecting something to happen / but nothing ever happens."

The Feelies, "Original Love"
(*Crazy Rhythms*, Stiff Records, 1980)

The opening scene of Olivier Assayas' 1986 debut feature *Désordre* seems designed to keep the viewer off balance. It's an awfully rainy night in what immediately looks like not even a one-horse town. Inside a car parked outside of a nondescript, and closed, shop, sit three young adults, two men, one woman. In near-claustrophobic close-up, boy and girl kiss, ardently, and the rain and their passion and the insistent closeness of the camera might bring to mind the opening of Nicholas Ray's *They Live By Night* and its depiction of innocent, ingenuous, only-have-eyes-for-each-other passion. Except that a few seconds later the girl is making out with the other guy, perhaps with slightly less enthusiasm than she had shown for the first fellow (the performances in this film, the particularity of the gestures, have this kind of constant intense detail, inviting a scrutiny that can only lead to frustration). Okay, so these are sort-of kids, and it's the 1980s, and this is a French film, but nevertheless, it's a slight shock, being thrown headfirst into what was and still is a mildly unconventional arrangement. The trio is practically giddy as they rush forward and break into the shop, a musical instrument store. One of the guys, the lanky black-haired one with high cheekbones that practically shriek "New Wave front man" picks up a bass, of all things, and it's clear that the kids are anticipating a happy, no-consequences raid on the place when suddenly a sleepy older man enters, and he's annoyed, and he has to be subdued. Or more than subdued. Never ratcheting up the soundtrack, Assayas cuts with due deliberation through a few disturbing images: the sickly slight smile on the face of the other male would-be looter (this one of smaller frame, with kind of a Dee Dee Ramone haircut) as he approaches the man who caught them in the act; the steel string he twists in his hand; and a bit later, the strangled man's face on the floor of the shop, the combination of blood and froth dribbling from his mouth made all the more awful by the reflection of the shop's green neon front sign. The kids flee, they make off with nothing, they rush back to their rehearsal space and peevishly chastise the friends who they find crashing there. And they wait for something to happen. But nothing ever happens.

That's not quite true, of course. Plenty happens. The rock band to which the two males of the trio, Yvan (Wadeck Stanczak of the high cheekbones; he had previously appeared in

André Téchiné's *Rendez-vous* and *Le Lieu du crime*, both co-written by Assayas) and Henri (Lucas Belvaux) belong, play a couple of gigs, even crossing the Channel to London for one of them. The band's drummer Xavier (Rémi Martin), disgusted by the crime committed by his bandmates, quits and joins the army. Henri and the girl, Anne (Ann-Gisel Glass), who, as it happened was officially his girlfriend, break up. Most consequentially, one band member hangs himself. Everything falls apart, and then sort of comes back together again, but not in a way that any of the players had wanted or envisioned.

But the one thing that they're all afraid of, that they will be found out by the law and made to account for their crime, never happens. The eventuality just hangs there, it could drop any second, and it never does. Nothing ever happens, but nothing has to happen. One of the maddening puzzles suggested by the film is the question of whether this band could have actually *been* anything had Yvan and Henri and Anne not committed this initially reckless and finally, well, evil act. Artistic genius is hard to simulate in cinema, as is actual artistic process. I once knew a painter who told me that she didn't much care for fictional films about visual artists and that every movie about a painter she'd ever seen, with the exception of Scorsese's *Life Lessons* in *New York Stories*, got the actual act of painting completely wrong. As far as music is concerned, it's not for nothing that Clint Eastwood largely stuck to Charlie Parker's own saxophone solos for his fictional biopic of the musician, *Bird*. It is no fault of Robert De Niro that he doesn't quite convince as even a journeyman sax player in Scorsese's *New York, New York*, whereas his counterpoint Liza Minelli is exactly right playing a singer of the precise dimensions and talent of...Liza Minelli. We do not hear enough of Yvan and Henri's band to come to any musically-based conclusion about them (their sole song is the invention of an actual combo called Les Avions). It is pretty clear that Yvan does have a post-punk charisma but a style that's about four or five years out of date by London or New York standards (albeit cutting-edge for the Continent). We learn that the band does have some major-label interest, and Assayas is pretty casually accurate about how the tendrils of corporate rock reached down via seedy managers and indie record stores to scoop up talent; the viewer never gets into the corridors of real power, the high windows and the prestige and the money are all tantalizing rumors, like those of the afterlife. (Even in Assayas' 2004 film *Clean*, whose protagonist is the one-time manager and now widow of an overdosed rocker, the "industry" is seen from something of a remove, in this case an inverted Eden from which its protagonist has been expelled.)

But back to the act that, it would seem, throws everything into disorder: it's significant that the viewer is never made privy to the actual logic behind it. Yeah, it's clear in a sense; if you're in a band, you need gear, and stealing gear is kind of a rock and roll, and particularly punk and/or post punk tradition; Sex Pistols guitarist Steve Jones more than once jocularly bragged about how his own setup fell off a truck after a Faces or Roxy Music show. But these aren't such street kids, all that needy; Assayas makes a point, not very long after the botched robbery, of depicting an exchange between the band's keyboardist Gabriel (Simon de La Brosse) and his father (Philippe Laudenbach). Gabriel has tried to steal some cash from dad, much in the style of Patrick in Truffaut's *Les Quatre cents coups*, and here it's kind of pathetic rather than shocking/cute because Gabriel's a young adult; in any case, Gabriel's dad finds him out, and barely taking a break in his toilette, gives him a little talking to, imperiously offering to write the kid a check as he strips down to enter his bath.

~

"The big guy and myself had been huddled over bean soup and coffee long enough to watch two sets of customers come and go. It wasn't that we weren't hungry, and the food at the Kettle doesn't disappoint you even if you are looking for nothing more than ballast; we just took our time. He stubbed out Winstons in an ashtray that looked full of gray-white worms, sipped his double-cream coffee, bringing it to his lips with pale, nubbed fingers that shook a little in the transit… […] I felt as wide awake as possible on an after-hours morning like this. The big guy's nerves were infectious… I was wired, all of a sudden, on some organic frequency that seemed to take hold of my motor responses and transmit 'you are not fatigued but simply passive…use your muscles, your brain, your tissues NOW! MAKE A MOVE!'"

Peter Laughner, sleeve notes for Hearthen HR101 45 RPM ("30 Seconds Over Tokyo" b/w "Heart Of Darkness," Pere Ubu, 1975)

"Rock music is mostly about moving big black boxes from one side of town to the other in the back of your car."

Attributed to various individuals in the orbit of Pere Ubu, including lead singer David Thomas and record art designer John Thompson

Soundtrack cover

Dead rockers haunt *Désordre*. Not just the obvious one, Ian Curtis, whose suicide by hanging is directly echoed in the film. Joy Division's founding member and lead singer was a depressive, an epileptic, and a possibly too-young husband and father who took his own life after viewing Werner Herzog's film *Stroszek* on television, a detail much contemplated or morbidly appreciated by certain enthusiasts and/or cultists. When the somewhat Curtis-like Yvan – who has no marital attachments, nor, it would seem, outside interests, to speak of – does himself in a little past the midpoint of *Désordre*, there's not much in the way of interesting peripheral detail to the event. It's not just the guilt; in fact, it might not even *be* the guilt. Still, the viewer understands his sense of frustration and rage at being, as Johnny Rotten once put it, "in suspension," of waiting for something to happen but nothing ever happening but at the absolute same time not being able to MAKE A MOVE. Or rather, not being able to make any move but the self-obliterating one. By means of careful but purposeful pacing, aided greatly by Stanczak's tight performance, Assayas makes what cannot be articulated palpable, whether or not one "sympathizes" with the character. What finally comes across is the feeling that Yvan's act, like Curtis', is such an awesome accomplishment of self-negation that its ostensible motivation is practically beside the point, and *Désordre* wants us to feel that horror, on behalf of Yvan and Curtis both (and, retrospectively, on behalf of Simon de La Brosse, who committed suicide in 1998). There are no Joy Division songs on the soundtrack, but there are two by New Order, the dance-music inflected band formed by the surviving members of the prior outfit. As big a cult icon as Curtis was/is, New Order and its music wound up being loved by people who had never heard of Curtis, a pertinent notion to chew on when considering *Désordre*'s final quarter.

Also heard on the soundtrack of *Désordre* is Pere Ubu, the Cleveland, Ohio-based band that formed in the mid-'70s well before the terms "punk rock" and "new wave" entered the cultural lexicon, a band whose impetus was nicely summed up by founding member Peter Laughner in the above-quoted sleeve notes to that band's first single. Laughner was a vora-

cious reader and, among other things, a deft, mercurial writer, and the tone he picked up from both Kerouac and Hemingway rings even more resoundingly in the full text of those notes. But it's also worth remembering that the brilliance of founding members Laughner and David Thomas notwithstanding, the band was, in fact, made up of American provincials. David Thomas has long taken pains to explain that the title and catchphrase of the early Ubu song "Final Solution" (one of *Désordre's* two Ubu selections) did not make reference to (and hence, he insists, was not making light of) the planned extermination of Jews from the Reich, since this was an area of history of which he claimed total ignorance at the time.

Laughner and Thomas were the animating spirits of Pere Ubu, as Yvan and Henri are the animating spirits of their band. Laughner essentially drank himself to death in 1977 before he had lived even a quarter of a century, prompting this rueful observation from Thomas: "He was a genius and a fool, and the fool killed him." The thing about *Désordre* is, while the film keeps viewers on the hook with respect to the work, it makes it pretty clear that neither Yvan nor Henri are geniuses, even in the most loosely-defined sense of the word. And an interesting aspect of the film's structure is the way it flits from character to character; the early scene focusing on the strained home life of keyboardist Gabriel; a sojourn with Yvan as he ditches his bandmates en-route to a gig in England, runs off to sleep with a British photographer and hangs around a cold beach; after Yvan's funeral, stopping off at record shops and other hanging-out joints where real business may or may not be under way; and finally a decisive trip to New York with Henri. But the film doesn't finally rest on him. *Désordre's* final shot is of Anne, teary eyed, having traveled across an ocean to reunite with Henri only to learn that he's gone.

While the film tells a very definite story, its tendency to shift focus from character to character makes its ostensible "through-line" seem kind of elusive; it's almost as if Assayas himself is looking for something to latch on to, someone to believe in. There are a number of ostensibly failed creators in Assayas' oeuvre, or at least people whose approach to their work embodies a painful contradiction. *Irma Vep*'s Vidal is supposedly a washed-up director. Frédéric in *L'Heure d'été* is an economist who professes not to believe in economics. Is the dying Adrien of *Fin août, début septembre* an overlooked genius or a justly neglected mediocrity? Is *Clean's* Lee a Cobain or Cave-like genius laid low, or just another aged alt-rock wasteoid? And of course not

On the set: Wadeck Stanczak, Ann-Gisel Glass, Lucas Belvaux

only does the title character of *Carlos* fail to bring about world revolution, but he abrogates the job before he even starts it. But none of the characters in *Désordre* have achieved the level of self-definition that those figures have, befitting a film about young people, one could allow. Still.

The film's most quietly crushing irony is saved for the final scenes. Turns out that the one person in the band's circle to actually score a record deal is the little twerp who was fooling around with his girlfriend in the rehearsal space when Yvan, Henri, and Anne returned from their disastrous adventure. For whatever reason, he found the older fellows an inspiration, and here he is, on his way to New York to make a record and he asks Henri to come with him, lay down some guitar tracks. And in the studio, Henri can't hack it. Watching the recording process, we are reminded that music-making in the age of mechanical reproduction isn't a matter of turning it up to eleven and letting it rip; it involves sitting quietly, calmly, and trying to conjure some musical magic in the sterile environment that is a recording studio. And Henri, who inflicted enormous suffering and subsequently suffered greatly as a result, can conjure...nothing. And the further punchline, if I may be so crass as to call it that, is that the guitar part he fails to pull off isn't that big a deal; I could probably do it, given a couple of hours. But Henri can't, and when he shows up at the studio the next day, the kid who was once his most devoted fan has brought in a studio pro to do the part. The youngster understands the reality of Henri's situation more clearly than Henri himself, leaving him definitively adrift. *Désordre* can be seen, from one angle, as a film about how not to become an artist. All that lugging of black boxes has been for naught, and we know why and we don't know why, which is what makes Assayas' debut so naggingly disturbing.

Jeff Reichert

Cold Comforts

It might take some time for viewers of *L'Enfant de l'hiver* to recognize the film as the handiwork of Olivier Assayas. It begins with a very pregnant Natalia (Marie Matheron) in bed, alone. She's in pain, and calls out to someone named Stéphane, who isn't there. Worried that her child might be in distress, she gets out of bed, grabs her telephone, lies down on the floor, and calls for a friend, who calms her down. The next morning, Stéphane (Michel Feller), the father-to-be, comes home. Natalia demands that he continue preparations for their upcoming wedding. He balks, childishly (he hates doctors, lawyers, and, apparently, Natalia) and storms out in a huff. Throughout these opening sequences, the camera moves with, rather than "on," the actors, and the emphasis is on performance and character rather than visual flourishes, save for one mannered composition that pits Natalia and Stéphane against each other at opposite ends of the frame. Assayas' primary objective is to precisely capture the dissolution of the couple's romance in their cramped Parisian apartment.

Immediately after Natalia is left, wounded and alone, on the stairs leading up to their flat, the camerawork suddenly goes handheld, rickety; we're hurtling backwards through a narrow hallway filled with people, many of them in costume, suggesting the backstage area of a theater. Stéphane searches amidst the hustle and bustle for someone, eventually revealed to us as the production designer Sabine (Clotilde de Bayser), his new lover, a brunette with severe bangs (Natalia is a dirty blonde). As Stéphane peeks into a series of rooms, the camera peeks with him, then comes unmoored from his perspective entirely, entering and exiting spaces, approaching the escape velocity we've come to associate with the roving, voracious camera movement in Assayas' better known films. Eureka! one might think – here is the filmmaker who conjured whirlwinds of activity from film production offices in *Irma Vep*, the arrival area at De Gaulle airport in *demonlover*, the Hong Kong import / export storerooms in *Boarding Gate*. There is that long track down a hallway, a disorienting cut to a car, then to driving at nighttime; we're initially unsure who's in the vehicle at first, the edit is jolting, the angle reveals little. Much has been made of the mobility of Assayas' camera, but his mastery of cuts that sever time and space and continuity have become just as central to his cinema.

Sabine later scales a wall (as Maggie Cheung does in *Irma Vep*) to put a knife to her former lover Bruno's throat (one recalls the sex act as locus of violence in *Carlos*, *demonlover*, *Boarding Gate*, *Une nouvelle vie*, and *Fin août, début septembre*). Stéphane's overbearing father (an-

other in a lineage that includes the similarly forbidding fathers of *Désordre, Paris s'éveille, Une nouvelle vie* and *L'Eau froide*), played by actor/director Gérard Blain, has just returned from a business trip to China (the looming presence of international commerce, central to *Les Destinées sentimentales, Boarding Gate, L'Heure d'été*), and his sudden death later in the film sends aftershocks through the lives of his children (as in *Clean* and *L'Heure d'été*). Attractions between men and women wax and wane but never quite evaporate, as the characters share an acute and aching realization that time is passing ever-so-quickly (see also: *Fin août, début septembre* and *Paris s'éveille*). There's even a climactic show-stopping, youth-dominated extended party scene (as in *L'Eau froide* and *L'Heure d'été*).

Given the fact that most U.S. viewers only became aware of Assayas with the release of his sixth feature, *Irma Vep* (only a lucky few were able to see *L'Eau froide* and its predecessors), there's a temptation to view his virtually unknown early trio of Parisian dramas through the prism of his more mature and prominent later works. Taking a fresh look at early Assayas put me in mind of the newfound availability of *La signora senza camelie, Cronaca di un amore* and *Le amiche*, which complicated my thinking about later Antonioni. I may prefer *Il deserto rosso* to the earlier films, but I appreciate the evolving creator of all four titles; he's far more interesting to ponder than the predominant image of a revered, fully formed master. Similarly, the regal *L'Heure d'été* becomes even more meaningful and resonant with the knowledge that it was preceded by *Une nouvelle vie*, which might still be Assayas' most formally radical film, and *L'Enfant de l'hiver*.

The frenetic cult that worships at the altar of bold, cinema-shaking debuts likely had little room for the modest, coolly assured *Désordre* (it did win a prize at Venice but never got any traction in the U.S. beyond a few screenings and an invitation to MoMA and The Film Society of Lincoln Center's New Directors / New Films Festival). *L'Enfant de l'hiver*, even quieter, with even fewer obvious rough edges or odd angles, remains even less known. The film appears to be a small, frigid fable of young Parisians in their late twenties (a prelude to the mad reshuffling of *Fin août*'s principal characters, older by roughly a decade), as they fall in and out of love, unleashing acts of physical and emotional violence, small and large, along the way. The film's intimate focus and claustrophobic interiors, alternated with quick trips to various lush countrysides (here Italian) should be familiar to anyone acquainted with French romantic melo-

drama. Despite the trappings of youth, there's even a kinship between Assayas' film and Woody Allen's middle-aged icebox dramas of the same period, especially in their focus on how people move through (and are moved by) their surroundings. There's more at stake here than straight melodrama, though. Assayas' time as a critic and screenwriter is perhaps even more obvious here than in *Désordre* as he pokes and prods the boundaries of his genre.

Like the people in Allen's films, Assayas' characters careen into and off of each other like supercharged subatomic particles, grasping at happiness and comfort, pivoting away from instability and possible ruin. Sabine steals Stéphane from Natalia, but she is repelled by his weakness and remains dangerously obsessed with the egotistical stage actor Bruno (Jean-Philippe Ecoffey), who pushes her in turn back into the arms of Stéphane. An uneasy detente holds for an interval, but Sabine's obsession with Bruno lingers, flares up, leaving Stéphane in the lurch. For his part, Stéphane longs for Sabine, recognizes that his treatment of Natalia might have been a mite indelicate, and finds himself compelled to make some kind of amends with his ex-lover so as to forge a connection with his child. Something like a year passes in the lives of these lovers. Unlike *Désordre*, where an accidental murder sparks a Dostoevskyan narrative of guilt and paranoia (another link that recalls Allen), in *L'Enfant de l'hiver* the vagaries of passion give rise to remorseful acts, and the focus is on the damage caused by heedless and immature behavior – tricky waters for a young filmmaker.

L'Enfant de l'hiver is a curious film. It is Assayas' first attempt to deal with the ebb and flow of lives as they are lived, and less successful in this regard than *Fin août, début septembre* or *L'Heure d'été*. But it's a far more assured and engaging film than the bulk of its now-forgotten contemporaries. Jumping in and out of multiple lives over a lengthy span of time without losing the individual threads of character is no mean feat; Assayas was fairly fresh off his apprenticeship to Téchiné, and his deftness in this area signals time well spent. There is some dramatic clutter. A bereft Natalia attempts suicide, Stéphane's father dies, Sabine is fired from several theatrical productions because of her increasingly destructive behavior towards Bruno. In what might be the film's heaviest scene (emotionally and cinematically), Stéphane sneaks into Natalia's house under cover of darkness to introduce himself to his child and determine its sex, and wakes up the next morning in the nursery with the baby in his arms. Daring as it is, this central interlude doesn't hit quite as hard as the film's epilogue in which, years after the principal action, Stéphane is reacquainted with his now toddling child.

In *L'Enfant de l'hiver*, Assayas is building his command of cinematic language, and realizing the preoccupations he began to develop as a critic in the pages of *Cahiers du cinéma*. It may well be his least *immediately* exciting film and its short running time aside, the film has its laborious stretches (even the lengthy period piece *Les Destinées sentimentales* is a lighter and fleeter experience). Michel Feller is a distracting, awkward presence, acting with a tilting of his head, down, then up, to suggest a shiftiness and inconstancy that a flicker of his eyes might have accomplished with greater economy. His Stéphane is the purported hero but he is never fully convincing, in either his lack of passion for Natalia or his headlong fixation on Sabine (for her part, Sabine is the film's most full-blooded, fascinating, creation, rich in contradictions even when Clotilde de Bayser hardens her face into a mask.) Except for Gérard Blain, most of the actors were at the beginnings of their careers here, and on occasion they appear, well, *actorly*.

If *Désordre* passes before our eyes in a chilled rush and *Paris s'éveille* blasts off into the future

of a justly-lauded career on the back of Joey Santiago's epochal guitar riff from the Pixies' "Debaser," *L'Enfant de l'hiver* now seems like a necessary stepping stone. It's hard not to think of the three films as one breath. *L'Enfant de l'hiver* is the mildest of the trio but it features the most ambitious set-piece, the previously mentioned party sequence that brings the film's central quartet into rotating contact, tying up every complication. As Assayas the restless image-maker (and, let's not forget, rock music omnivore) skips through spaces, he gaudily changes up the color palette of his images. The sequence progresses something like this:

1. White – Natalia/Stéphane bump into each other at what appears to be an upscale cocktail party. They discuss Natalia's new lover, who is now a father to Stéphane's son. 2. Yellow – Stéphane passes Sabine, wearing arty glasses in a low-key club atmosphere. 3. Red – a punk show…on a rooftop? Natalia and Stéphane again, she's drunk and falls, they share a kiss while the Ramones' version of the Heartbreakers' "Chinese Rock" blares. 4. Green – Natalia and Stéphane start to make love in a bathroom and then stop, choosing instead to enact the more adult breakup that should have happened earlier in their relationship. 5. Blue – in the light

of morning (maybe?) Bruno and Stéphane, who have never met, cross paths but don't interact. 6. Grey – a stairwell in which Sabine and Bruno have their final confrontation.

The movement between spaces is as obviously cinematic as the conceit is literary; Assayas attacks melodrama head-on, drags it into a filmic register. As Stéphane crosses the different thresholds of the party, each cut takes him further and further into some kind of shared interior "wintry" reality. Is anything that happens here real? Who knows? At the film's end, after a shocking act of violence, we find Sabine wandering in the snow with Stéphane behind her. It's winter, again.

Looking over his career, Olivier Assayas' decennial seasonal films, *L'Enfant de l'hiver* (1989), *Fin août, début septembre* (1998), and *L'Heure d'été* (2008) feel like dispatches, markers from a series of given times and places. In the first film, a filmmaker in his early thirties is eulogizing the end of his twenties with a surgeon's concentration, absent in most films about young adults. In *Fin août*, a filmmaker in his forties looked back on his thirties, injecting it with an intimation of mortality all too easy to ignore at such a young age. In *L'Heure d'été*, a filmmaker now firmly in his fifties looks ahead through middle age to death. Even after seeing *L'Heure d'été* a half-dozen times, the first melancholy cello chord reduces me to a puddle of tears, in anticipation of all the deaths to come, in the film and in my life. And now that I'm the same age as *Fin août*'s hero Gabriel, I find that I am also experiencing the feeling of a coherent life path tantalizingly out of reach (but it's there!). I feel more removed from the headlong passions of *L'Enfant de l'hiver*, but, at thirty-three, how could I not be? There's a sense of recognition central to the special place Assayas' work has always held for a core group of cinephiles – the feeling that, here, finally, was a director, emerging in the wake of May '68 (our own generation!) using images and films and music we also hold dear to try to make sense of the changing world around us in an accessible fashion as opposed to struggling in isolation to attain some kind of aesthetic purity. His films all function on the cerebral plane, but they explode at the gut level – each new Assayas film of the past decade at least has been, simply, a fucking blast to watch. They've always, even from as far back as *L'Enfant de l'hiver*, been recognizably his. But they've always been ours as well.

Alice Lovejoy

When You Leave, You Want Time to Stand Still

In the penultimate scene of *Paris s'éveille*, twenty-year-old Louise (Judith Godrèche) pays a visit to the home of her former lover, the much older Clément (Jean-Pierre Léaud). The apartment has changed radically since she left it, and with it, Clément: his new lover, an interior designer, has knocked down walls and widened windows, creating a bright, open space in place of the cramped, mazelike corridors that were there just a year or two earlier. "I'd have preferred it to stay the way it was," says Louise, "when you leave, you want time to stand still."

It's a charged statement for Clément, who is painfully preoccupied with the passage of time: earlier in the film, he laments to his son Adrien (Thomas Langmann) – who's returned unexpectedly to Paris on the run for a crime committed back home in Toulouse – that he's not the man he was. This resonates beyond the film and the character at hand, for in *Paris s'éveille*, Léaud (as is the case in so many of his later films) seems to not only be performing the role of Clément, but also the role of Jean-Pierre Léaud. Clément speaks in the measured tones of Emile Rousseau in *Le Gai savoir*, his dialogue almost declaimed; his face is steady, serious, much as Antoine Doinel's is in the final freeze-frame of *Les 400 coups*.

Louise's words also echo a central metaphor in *Paris s'éveille*, which draws equivalences between the architecture of space and the film's emotional architecture. The love-triangle narrative, indeed, is fundamentally geometric (Louise leaves Clément for Adrien), and its relationships play out in distinctive spaces: Louise and Clément's tortured affair in his dark, rambling flat; her relationship with Adrien in the utopic doll's house of an abandoned building – built with found materials, electricity "borrowed" from the neighbors – in which Adrien's friends Victor (Antoine Basler) and Agathe (Ounie Lecomte) are squatting "until there's a demolition permit."

But the film itself is also more formally architectural than much of Assayas' other work. It's paced by Clément's practiced dialogue, by the rhythmic strings and repeated themes of John Cale's minimalist score, and by visual motifs that mark time, giving the sense that there is a larger temporal scope within which the story plays out. We see this most clearly in the still long shots of Paris that appear throughout and that give the film its title. At times, the city is laid out in grey early morning tones; at times, we see a time-lapse progression from dusk to dawn, street and apartment lights shimmering, then extinguished. Beneath the dramatic arc shared by these characters, there is a sense of time which is both linear and cyclical.

The cinematography is equally structured, stylized. In place of the dynamic handheld camerawork that defines so much of Assayas' work – and that, in films like *L'Eau froide* and *Fin août, début septembre*, pulls the viewer squarely into the vortices of its characters' emotional lives – here, DP Denis Lenoir largely stands back from the drama that unfolds between the characters, framing them instead in still or moving portraits that position them, like puzzle pieces, relationally. At times, we see Clément, Louise and Adrien alone, their faces lit by passing taillights, by the moon. More often, we see them in meticulous over-the-shoulder or two-shots that highlight, at once, the isolation of and interdependence between Clément's aging countenance and the young faces of Louise and Adrien.

The precision with which Assayas and Lenoir compose these images is important, for throughout the film, the characters, too, are composing themselves, in ever-new attempts to bring order to lives that are fundamentally in disorder: Clément, early on, confesses that he feels as though he is not in control anymore, and his relationship with Louise – a woman young enough to be his daughter – his new lover and new apartment all seem to be responses to this need. The police finally catching up with him, Adrien adopts a false identity, leaving Louise, Clément, and France behind for a new life in Argentina. And from the moment that we first encounter her, Louise, the daughter of a suburban hairdresser with a beautician's degree and ambitions to work in television, is continually composing herself, and always for others: she dyes her hair, wears wigs; we frequently see her in front of a mirror, trying on clothing for an audition or for the pornographic photos (or movies, it's never clear) with which she pays for her drug habit.

The film plays its own role in Louise's story, matching her attempts at self-composition with an almost fetishistic focus on her face, capturing it in tight, near-restrictive framings in which she, paradoxically, seems to find a degree of self-realization. At one point, we see her auditioning for a gig as a television game show host, uncomfortably fixed under hot TV studio lights and forced to smile at the camera as she's cruelly interrogated by the director. When she and Adrien sleep together for the first time, she's framed in an overhead shot, Adrien's hands around her neck, as she pushes him to squeeze harder. Assayas comments on all of this implicitly with the Pixies' song "Debaser," which plays at a club where she waits for her dealer – who will, later that night, leave her passed out in a city park.

In this sense, the film's most interesting relationship is that between Louise and Agathe. Where Louise's dealings with Clément, with Adrien, with her mother, with her dealer are heavy with expectations, with Agathe, they're refreshingly unburdened. Agathe – played with calm possession by Lecomte – has been disowned by her Chinese parents for living with the French Victor, and is studying to work in set design for the theater: that is, she's a character who, like the others in this film, is concerned with composition and image, but in her case, it's for others, not for herself. And the few scenes that Louise and Agathe share alone – laughing as they drive back to the squat at night; a conversation in the courtyard – are points of relief in a story that is so often overtly dramatic, even melodramatic; moments at which the film seems to escape its characters' pathos.

It's with Agathe, in fact, that *Paris s'éveille* ends. In the film's final ten minutes, Louise visits Clément in his renovated and shockingly brightened apartment, where we learn that it's not only this flat that has changed; the squat, too, has been demolished. And in keeping with the parallels that the film draws between relational and spatial architecture, Clément refuses to give Louise Adrien's address in Argentina, and exclaims, as she leaves, that he does not love her anymore. His protest – too pitiful, too late – signals, of course, the opposite, and when we follow Louise to her new job in a television studio (having coupled off with the director who so demeaned her earlier in the film – she's now doing the weather), it's clear that the uneasy links between her ambition and her degradation remain firmly in place. We've watched and heard about her posing for cameras throughout the film, but here – finally on the air – her disembodied face seems grotesquely large on the studio monitor, then, via a cut, blurry and unsteady, its color faded, on an old television set. Then, a hand reaches up and abruptly switches off Louise's forecast.

The hand is Agathe's, and we are in a Chinese restaurant, where she works as a waitress: she's traded in her leather jacket and jeans for a *cheongsam*. She, too, seems to have lost in the game of ambition, and Victor is now in prison. Yet if this appears tragic, the brusque dispatch with which she turns off the TV also signals that she has none of the sentimental attachment to the past that haunts Louise and Clément; that her time is more the cyclical time of dawn, constantly renewing itself, to which the film's title refers. And oddly, it's with this gesture that, in its final minute or so, the film itself suddenly changes course. As the syrupy Chinese pop music in the restaurant crescendos from diegetic to non-diegetic and the camera tracks backward as Agathe walks steadily and impassively towards us, Assayas cuts to the credits and the driving rhythms of Birdland's "Paradise" – replacing all of the pathos and melodrama of the previous ninety minutes with something more vibrant, pulsing; something that is, for this film, uniquely hopeful.

Michael Koresky

Moving On

"The outer edges of the screen are not, as the technical jargon would seem to imply, the frame of the film image. They are the edges of a piece of masking that shows only a portion of reality. The picture frame polarizes space inwards. On the contrary, what the screen shows us seems to be part of something prolonged indefinitely into the universe."

When he wrote this in his essay "Painting and Cinema," André Bazin was talking about the inadequacy of film to convey the work, and by extension, the life of the painter. But the observation resonates, as so much of Bazin's writing does, well beyond the subject at hand – all the way past the limits of the frame and into the infinity of the universe, in fact. It's a basic tenet of film-making and -watching: we see only what the director wants to show us, and our minds, fired by his or her imagination, fill in the rest – not only what's lingering on the periphery of the frame, but what's happening in the greater world outside. Painting and cinema are thus perhaps intrinsically different forms, philosophically and naturally: while the painter may also encourage us to wonder what's beyond the confines of the frame, film, which is contingent on the passage of time, always gives the impression that there are a thousand other possible versions of itself. This is what makes the work of such painterly post-New Wave filmmakers as Olivier Assayas, Maurice Pialat, and Philippe Garrel all the more impressive – they're not simply treating the film frame as a canvas (ontologically etching, if you will), but rather they are brushing the screen with forward motion, moving so swiftly yet so elegantly through space and time that what's left outside the frame inevitably becomes tangible. It's subtly perception-altering – and you barely sense the radicality of the gesture as you're watching it, so invested are these filmmakers in the actions and interactions exploding onscreen.

Assayas has been refining this approach over the past twenty-plus years, moving from one perpetual-motion machine of a movie to the next with such grace that one might not notice the similarities between such vastly different films as *L'Eau froide, Les Destinées sentimentales,* and *Boarding Gate.* There's nothing overtly abstract in Assayas' films (save certain purposely pixilated passages of *demonlover,* perhaps), but they pass by in such a rush that the impression is of having viewed something like a Clyfford Still color field. There is often the sense that something outside the frame is also *in* the frame. It's not a simple matter of Assayas and his DP – whether Denis Lenoir or Éric Gautier or Yorick Le Saux – appearing to be everywhere at once. Rather it's an instinctual brand of

art-making that's so sensitively attuned to performance, character, environment, and location acoustics that you feel like you're in the midst of a work of art as it's coming to life. *Une nouvelle vie* (1993), never released in the United States, could be credited with launching Assayas on this path; it's a work he later called "consciously a film where its shape is very much part of what it's about," and the film with which, following three very personal, close-to-the-chest features, he seems to have gained sufficient confidence as an artist to dare his audience to keep up. There's furious motion here, but there are also frustrating ellipses: it's a film that, like its protagonist, always seems just out of reach.

With this not-at-all simple tale of a young woman who lunges into her long-lost father's world after the death of her eternally lost mother, Assayas did not set out to make a provocation. Something happened in post-production: he shot a three-hour film, then in the editing room, he removed a third of the narrative. This was not just a matter of "streamlining" or cutting out the chaff, but of ripping right into the fabric of the thing. By leaving out much of what an average filmmaker would consider important information, *Une nouvelle vie* challenges the viewer, right along with its protagonist, to make sense of the world it presents. There's nothing scarier than being confronted with the *new* – that the film will grapple with this fear is right there in its seemingly innocuous title. Assayas' turning-point movie is a study in alienation, a theme the director would return to time and again; in *Irma Vep, demonlover,* and *Boarding Gate,* such alienation manifests increasingly as the malady of an emerging global consciousness, in which drama blossoms out of a network of international communication – all of these later films at one point plunk their main characters down into frenetic or forbidding foreign landscapes that the director leaves deliberately decontextualized. (A more benign but no less disruptive instance of this would be *L'Heure d'été*'s three grown siblings, who by film's end have taken up residence on three different continents.)

His most radical gesture in this regard comes less than a half-hour into *Une nouvelle vie.* The eternally glowering early twentysomething Tina (Sophie Aubry) – burdened with a physically demanding supermarket job and a day-sleeping mother who requires a lot of care and attention (even more than the many children under her watch, all from different fathers than Tina's) – has been summoned during the work-day. "The boss wants you. He looked grim," a coworker states ominously. After an abrupt fade to black (the film's first), we're suddenly somewhere else. Not in the boss' office. Not back in her mother's teeming flat, piled high with scattered papers and wafted with cigarette smoke. Not with Tina's "down-and-out" boyfriend, Fred, whose part-time job as a truck-driver doesn't bring in enough money to keep his hopes of marriage alive. Instead we're in a disconcertingly clean, almost antiseptic space decorated minimally, with chairs and tables of wire and glass; and we're looking down at Tina, curled into a fetal position on the floor, as she stirs awake. We soon learn, after the markedly sinister arrival of the elegant Constantin Normand (Bernard Giraudeau), that Tina is in the palatial apartment of her father, whom she has previously known only from a crumpled photograph, and that she is not at all welcome. And as we later discover, much has transpired in the black space between these scenes.

The dramatic ellipsis has less to do with Assayas' disinterest in how his characters get from here to there than in creating a puzzle for his viewers to tease out, as well as his penchant for cinema as experience: he seems to want his viewers to feel as bewildered as the people onscreen. There is something *avant la lettre* Dardenne-ish about this furious identification

Denis Lenoir (left), on the set

with such a difficult character; hard to read and even harder to like, Tina is something of a proto-Rosetta in the single-mindedness with which she ploughs through life and work. Her drive is given form in the very first images, under the opening credits: Denis Lenoir's camera is hypnotized by her, relentlessly focused on her agitated movements as she motors a forklift through the back of the supermarket (she is first seen from behind the machine's wire grates, a prison of sorts from which she will soon extricate herself). One gets the sense that nothing could come between this young woman and whatever she strives to accomplish, except perhaps a self-defeating obsessiveness. This is why her vulnerability following that sudden fade to black – this force of nature is now a rag doll on an unfamiliar floor – is so jarring. Yet as we gradually come to realize, the transition represents more than just a sudden narrative leap. This is a film about an adult who is frantically trying to be born.

After Tina's reawakening, there are revelations, but they provide more questions than answers. Constantin claims to be her father Ludovic's former lawyer, who still handles his personal affairs, which for years had included overseeing regular deposits into Tina's mother's bank account. There is foreboding talk from Constantin about Tina's half-sister, Lise, who must never know about Tina's disruptive visit. Yet is this man to be trusted? Giraudeau's glower is disconcerting, and Assayas' narrative schism has left us wary. He tells her to forget she ever came, but Tina is not so easily swayed. When we finally meet Lise (at a bowling alley, where she has come to find Fred and tell him that Tina has shown up at her father's house and ingested an excess of sleeping pills), she is hardly the vengeful, potentially jealous creature Constantin has made her out to be. Rather, as embodied by the steely yet vulnerable Judith Godrèche, her hair shorn to boyishly beautiful Peter Pan length, she is a lost soul much like Tina, if more tremulous, a similarly incomplete person seeking wholeness (and perhaps destined to find it in the near-mirror-image of her half-sister). A former dancer who never regained her footing after a car accident, Lise now works part-time as a secretary in Constantin's law office, an atmosphere as bustling in its own way as Tina's former, blue-collar place of employment. Like Tina, Lise seems to be carried aloft by some mysterious current; it's unclear where either of them is going.

Une nouvelle vie would have to be regarded, simply, as a film about the bonding of these two young women, but its creator doesn't telegraph anything, so there are few easily identifiable plot points or pivots, no crystallizing "eureka" moments. Assayas, ever the roaming chronicler of people in states of transition, is too invested in depicting the quake of youthful experience to be able to regard it with ruefulness or detachment; he never fails to capture the state of being young and alive in the *moment*, like a rude smear on a blank slate. The insight of this extremely wise film, as is the case with so much of Assayas' work, originates with his innate knowledge of where best to put the camera in order to harness the tremors of youth and visualize its aftershocks. (Right after *Une nouvelle vie*, Assayas would uncork *L'Eau froide*, a brilliant convulsion of a youth film that would one-up this movie with its powerful combination of energy and melancholy; given the fact that it's about teenagers and is set in a more outwardly tumultuous historical era – the early seventies – *L'Eau froide* has freer license to detonate).

It soon becomes clear that Tina is trying to thrust herself into a situation that Lise is desperate to get *out* of, as illuminated by their respective erotic relationships with the married Constantin, who, more of a constant presence in both women's lives than Ludovic, is clearly father surrogate as much as lover for both. He has a sadomasochistic relationship with Lise, one would presume of lengthy duration given the intuitive familiarity with which they initiate their first on-camera encounter. Early in the film, as Tina spies from the safety of a balcony window, Lise stuffs a scarf into Constantin's mouth, removes his shirt, and with his belt ties his hands behind his back before pushing him face down on the floor; later, Lise will confess to Tina that she can't stand the touch of a man. Is Constantin merely complying with Lise's phobia? Are his fetishes and her aversion to men conveniently compatible? When he and Tina become lovers in the film's second half, they have a more intimate, open exchange. This is

not to imply that Constantin and Lise's kinkier relationship is merely clinical and passion-free: sex in Assayas' films is often, without judgment, based on submission and domination, occasionally supplemented by bondage (*Fin août, début septembre; Boarding Gate;* and at its most demoralized, *demonlover*). The power games Lise (seemingly) initiates in *Une nouvelle vie* feel like an innocent's hesitant stabs at adulthood: S&M as an expression of immaculacy rather than a mere refusal of affection.

The most refreshingly intimate romantic relationship in the film is also the most severely cracked: Constantin and his television-host wife, Laurence (Christine Boisson), have genuine chemistry, the kind of bond that can only result from domestic familiarity, which allows them to veer from amicable to vindictive and back again without batting an eye. Laurence is aware of her husband's affairs, but as shown in a scene where she confronts Tina in a shopping mall, she remains confident that he'll always come home to her. Boisson's performance and the way Assayas positions it as an unexpected emotional anchor for the viewer – but never a crutch – are sublime. She is as emotionally transparent as Tina is hard to read, the Truffaut-esque counterpoint to Aubry's Bressonian protagonist. Her gaze is penetrating yet serene, and it's not difficult to see why Constantin feels so comfortable in her scrutinizing presence that he is able to admit to her, in one of the film's occasional curtain drops, how despicable he feels when he carries out Ludovic's bidding.

Constantin and Laurence's relationship may be fractured but their future is not uncertain, making them an island amidst the film's ever spinning emotional whirlpool. But the stasis is also frightening in its marked contrast: if it's a film that is wary of slowing down, then maybe Constantin and Laurence represent its greatest fear.

The most cataclysmic coupling, on the other hand, is Tina and Ludovic. The film is nearly half over before these two meet, and it's one of Assayas' most exquisitely staged scenes, shot through with an erratic, intimate violence similar to the volatile family fights in Pialat's *À nos amours*. The father (Bernard Verley, surveying the world as if he had conceived it himself and despises his creation) arrives at his apartment, finally; initially he addresses only Lise, keeping his back to Tina – out of focus in the back right of the frame – for such an extended, uncomfortable period of time that you wonder if he knows she's there at all. Ultimately he tells Lise to leave him with Tina; he addresses her with coldness, and it's the first time we learn of her mother's death, a suicide, which had been elided by that abrupt fade-out. Almost spectral, he stands by a light-drenched window, callously pragmatic as he tells Tina that he never loved her mother. Later he commands her to take off the clothes she's wearing, which belong to Lise and which he finds disconcerting; boldly, she undresses in front of him. During this extraordinarily painful scene, the camera is everywhere, but Tina still moves so fast that it barely registers when she grabs a vase and smashes it against her father's forehead, instantly drawing a pool of blood. The aftermath is awkward, forlorn; she doesn't run out immediately, but instead tentatively tends to his wounds, and Assayas keeps his camera rolling on them for more beats than most directors would allow, soaking in Ludovic's new vulnerability and Tina's momentary, shaky triumph.

There's so much destructive behavior in Assayas' film that its final, wordless grace note comes as a genuine surprise, and a balm for all that's come before. Lise has left the city to be alone at her family's summer home on the island of Noirmoutier; eventually, Tina extricates herself from the city and follows, a welcome change of scenery. A measure of peace blankets the film just as it does the two women. Lise might even be letting a young man into her life,

a houseguest and fellow student. After what seems like a final goodbye between the half-sisters, Assayas upends expectations with a silent gesture. In one extended take, filmed from what seems a significant distance with a telephoto lens (there is a hushed voyeurism to the shot, as though the cameraman is perhaps crouched in the forest that surrounds the house), we see Tina get in a car and take off down the driveway; the camera stays on Lise as she walks back into the house, unaware that Tina has already returned, entering and taking off her coat. In a remarkable moment, Lise opens the back door to let in a vision of the rustling green trees beyond – we are looking *through* the house. It's the world outside of her world. The air feels clear, the world transparent. Finally Lise sees Tina. Again, Assayas has made us aware that, while we're only privileged to see what's in the frame, we know that we're being directed to something beyond its boundaries. The image is masked on all sides, yet is infinite. Tina and Lise won't be contained. The universe is theirs.

L'une de mes idées de départ, l'une de mes envies était de poser ce microcosme hongrois avant tout : de présenter Gilles dans ce contexte, qu'un moment on ne sache pas où l'on est, etc…
D'un côté l'intemporalité campagne/Hongrie/Roumanie et de l'autre la moyenneté contemporaine de l'adolescence au lycée.
Est-ce possible dans le cadre d'un récit court comme celui-ci ?
En tout cas je suis convaincu qu'il faut dans un premier temps développer ce prologue, le vrai est de ce côté là. Quitte à réfléchir ensuite sur la structure d'ensemble.

Je tourne autour de ce bloc depuis déjà un bon moment et c'est celui qui dramaturgiquement tient le mieux. Le problème est qu'il ne se relie qu'assez mal au reste.
J'y vois encore deux problèmes majeurs avant d'en envisager la rédaction.
1) La mise en place de Gilles. Commencer par le vol est dramatiquement bien et conventionnel par ailleurs. En tout cas ça le banalise durant toute la première partie.
2) Qui est Christine : elle aussi doit avoir son histoire. Et par ailleurs Gilles et Christine doivent aussi avoir le leur, il faut la poser.

Il doit y avoir quelque chose de fort entre Christine et Gilles : ils s'aiment, comme on s'aime à cet âge là, très fort. Il faut une séquence, aussi pour le poser avant le vol : oui, à condition qu'elle soit très forte.

Christine est l'enfant de parents divorcés, comme Gilles, le père a une quincaillerie, elle est élevée par une belle-mère qu'elle déteste, elle a déjà fait des séjours en psychiatrie ? Sa mère vit aux Ulis, elle fait des ménages.

L'autre hypothèse pour faire exister cet épisode en rapport avec l'intrigue serait de recycler l'usage des explosifs dans un usage politique : genre très infantile, attentat contre une gendarmerie ou quelque chose de cet ordre ?

Évidemment cet épisode est essentiel, mais pas pour ce qu'il raconte, d'ailleurs il ne raconte rien. Mais pour montrer Gilles dans la forêt, les courses dans les sous-bois, le feu, la peur : et la foi – le souvenir de m'être agenouillé pour remercier le ciel lorsque le feu que nous avions mis s'est éteint alors qu'il menaçait le bois tout entier. De même le trajet sous la pluie, la nuit, en vélo, qui est le pendant de cet épisode, aussi vain dramatiquement. Puisque dès lors que l'intrigue est portée à travers la disparition de Christine c'est ce volet qui devient moteur.

C'est vraiment la limite de mon écriture dramatique de buter toujours sur l'économie du récit, sur l'utilité des séquences. Qu'il y a un moment gratuit est-ce que je serai capable de le construire ? Il faut l'assumer frontalement tel que.

Marianne et Maxime ont vraiment trop des utilités si les choses sont racontées ainsi. Faut-il les dissocier du lycée ?

Kent Jones

Revival

"Nothing can bring you peace but yourself."
Emerson, *Self-Reliance*

L'Eau froide, an expanded theatrical version of a television commission made for Arte's spectacular mid-90s television series "Tous les garçons et les filles de leur âge," shot on super-16mm for very little money and on a very tight schedule, is a sustained poetic mapping of the terrain of western adolescence in the 1970s, when to be young was to be continually reminded that you were too late. Too late for the Great Depression, too late for the cataclysms of WWII, and just a little too late for the global effort to turn reality upside down in the '60s. To be young was to experience two realities – the glory of the counterculture, a big bold epic narrative, slowly dissolving to (yet still superimposed upon) a more diffuse and exhausted present. For the most fortunate among us, it was to be reminded again and again that we were lucky to be safe from war and plunder, with plenty of everything; to be told and re-told, lovingly, that we would never have to endure the horrors of the past, a knowledge we absorbed as something like a curse because it implied that we were destined to float along through life. We tried, during those phantom years, to remain connected to the spirit of the recent past, by then officially written off as a youthful folly – we were reminded, in a million different ways, that it was time for the adults to step in and take over again. The principal grievance of the young – that the western world their elders had fought for had immediately devolved into a voracious, over-consuming and politically opportunistic quagmire, hardly worth the effort of preservation – was written off as an impossible demand for perfection in a world of contingencies. Not exactly an incorrect diagnosis, but rather than recognize the demands of '60s activists as a building block, a stepping stone to a future that might be fashioned from a recognition of past errors, it was systematically employed as a damning final judgment, a rationale for an all but officially sanctioned historical amnesia, inaugurating a parade of economic brutalization that even a threatened world financial collapse has not drawn to a halt. At the time, the great retrogression had yet to arrive, but it was in the air, darkly hovering.

By some miracle, Assayas caught it all – not the facts but the tone that contained and was formed by them, the clothes and the haircuts

Notes during the preparation of *L'Eau froide*

Polaroids of Cyprien Fouquet and Virginie Ledoyen during the preparation

but also the people who wore them, the body language (between kids, between kids and parents, between kids and teachers) and what it enacted, the undertones but also the social music from which they sounded, the destructive impulses and the world which received them, the fierce privacy and what it was intended to lock out. If *L'Eau froide* has precedents in cinema, they can be found in Tarkovskij's *Mirror (Zerkalo)*, Garrel's *L'Enfant secret* (both films frequently acknowledged by Assayas) and Scorsese's *Raging Bull*, all of which move not according to narrative logic but wayward fluxes and currents of remembered sensations (it's also possible to see Hou Hsiao-hsien's *The Puppetmaster* [*Xi meng ren sheng*], made just one year before, as a kindred work). They are wondrous films with distinctive visual palettes meant to evoke memories, home movies, or snapshots, for the most part situated within dank, harsh atmospheres punctuated by flashes of freedom and beauty. The power of these films can be found in their respective creators' connections to their painful pasts, of which they carefully elucidate every crevice and corner. Indeed, *L'Eau froide* gives us adolescence not just remembered but summoned back to life in all its searing *now*-ness: every slight, betrayal, wound and twinge of guilt is felt once again. But for each of these filmmakers, re-creation and avid attention bestow a measure of grace, hatred is converted into something like love, dread into exaltation.

Like *Mirror*, Assayas' film moves through states of being linked by nothing but his own personal and poetic associations. It is precisely the lack of any connective tissue other than that afforded by memory, coupled with a narrative so simple and uncluttered that it hardly even qualifies as such, that allows nearly every scene to open out to wide swaths of experience, rendering each interaction both typical *and* specific. Assayas gives us a sensation, the way the sensation played out under particular circumstances, and the space in which it occurred, cumulatively forming a vivid fresco of adolescence

forty years back, with its attendant variations of hopelessness, recklessness (common sense was out of fashion), and terror in the face of oncoming adult responsibility.

Amidst the chaos and clamor of a shoplifting episode gone bad, from which the teenage hero, Assayas' autobiographical surrogate Gilles (Cyprien Fouquet), takes it on the lam while his girlfriend Christine (Virginie Ledoyen) is held by store detectives, there is a sudden dissolve to a tracking movement over the hieroglyphic graffiti patterns on a row of school desktops (not unlike Tarkovskij's shots of objects underwater) in a dully lit classroom full of murderously bored students. This is followed by a countervailing movement of stolen LPs passed from hand to hand (and money passed back) over the drone of a teacher's voice. But not just any teacher's voice. This character with villainous eyebrows, clad in a tweed jacket and turtleneck over a paunched belly (the adult middle class uniform of the period, also sported by László Szabó as the father a few scenes later), is not just reading aloud from Rousseau but hectoring his students with a show of his own emotional bravura – a theater of vanity conjured by a great actor (Jean-Christophe Bouvet) rising to a surge of self-satisfaction as the character gets off on his own reading of the words "extravagantes *manoeuvres,*" repeated to the pounding rhythm of his chalk marks as he writes them out on the blackboard.

The specificity of detail in this scene is hair-raising: the desks, the fluorescent light, the clogged air (it appears to be Assayas' own high school, the Lycée Blaise Pascal – a poisonous homage), the pricelessly exact rendering of a public school teacher-class relationship of the era (global boredom, unspoken antipathy, rote authoritarianism, neither expecting much if anything from the other), the sense of everyone off in his or her own world. Just as specific is the *action* of the scene, the perceived and anticipated humiliation by the paranoid teacher begetting the humiliation of Gilles. The teacher catches the money passing into Gilles' hand from the corner of his eye, his eyebrows flare when he realizes that his masterful performance has been ignored, he calls on Gilles only to discover that he has left his copy of Rousseau at home (he pretends to be thumbing through another book), and then performs his own extravagant maneuver by picking Gilles up by the scruff of his neck and literally throwing him out of the classroom. Compounding the terrible embarrassment is the fact that the passage in question from the *Confessions* is about sexual longing and self-exposure, duly incorporated into the teacher's rant.

Scene after scene has a similar force. For instance, the Hungarian nanny (Ilona Györi) with the weathered, pillowy face in the film's opening images, recounting atrocities perpetrated by the Soviets to Gilles and his little brother. It's a surprising, unexpectedly touching way to begin a film about teenagers, and her monologue climaxes with a tearful exclamation that "There's no way I can explain it to you." She is cooking dinner, speaking in Hungarian, and even if you don't know Assayas' personal history ("All throughout my childhood, her stories were a kind of continuous radio program," writes Assayas of his own beloved nanny Margit Toth in *A Post-May Adolescence*, "spiraling endlessly around the misdeeds of the 'rotten communists' [*rohat communistak*]"), you know immediately that this kind of interaction has been repeated many times before – you see that the woman becomes easily drawn into the web of her own memories, that the boys love her and remain only half-interested out of habit and respect, in full knowledge that they will be hearing the same stories repeated in the near future; you feel the enormous gap between the world in which these traumatic events have transpired and the more immediate and less sensational present; and you have an acute understanding of the fact that interchanges ending with someone old telling someone young that they'll "never be able to understand" are as fulfilling for those delivering the news as they are defeating to those who hear them.

There is the scene in which Christine's father (Jackie Berroyer, whose face all but pronounces "working class") picks her up from the police station and gets right back on the job at his hardware store ("One hour it took me," he complains to his smiling employee before he starts prioritizing the day's delivery route), leaving his taciturn daughter to retreat to the back of the shop with nothing to do but twirl a carousel of nails, screws and brackets in plastic packages, which she will send toppling to the floor. What is so sharp here, and utterly true to the era, is the wide gulf between many teenagers and the very rhythms and responsibilities of labor. In her army jacket and ratty hair, her slouch and dismissive half-smiling withdrawal, she is 100% alienated from her father's profession and from the mundane idea of work itself, like a video gaming freak stuck in a screening of *Shoah*.

Even more minimal but equally evocative is the passage in which Assayas goes from Gilles slicing open the seat cushions on a city bus to black, and then places us at an angle looking up at an old television set placed high on a shelf. The image on the small screen: the clean-cut, well-scrubbed, middle-aged-or-thereabouts Swingle Singers doing an acapella version of "Spring" from Vivaldi's "Four Seasons" on an early '70s French variety show. They stand in orderly diagonal rows, the women and then the men, wearing suits and ties and evening dresses, their vocal gymnastics sadly echoing through what we quickly understand to be the institutionally appointed waiting room of the Beausoleil Clinic, where Christine sits with her enormous luggage on her lap. Listlessly slumped in a chair, dressed in a big sweater, army jacket and jeans, playing with strands of her unwashed hair, she is everything these people are not, the epitome of the "Problem Girl" ca. 1972 (the fresh-faced Ledoyen is formidable as a psychically wounded girl apt to shift to self-protective mode at the slightest provocation). She is stuck listening to these strange creatures from a dreaded universe of clever repartee and delightful virtuosities, emanating from an out-of-reach television.

There's László Szabó as Gilles' father, leafing through a book of expensive reproductions separated by sheets of tissue paper (which Assayas later realized was an unintended echo of *Mirror*). He is looking at Caravaggio's "Death of the Virgin," and calls his son over to look with him. "Few images of suffering move me more than this. And you?" he asks. "Does it move you like that, or not?" It's a ridiculous question that only the frustrated parent of an adolescent would dream of asking, and a prelude to a more unpleasant encounter about another disciplinary letter from school ("Do whatever you want but don't get caught at it – I'm sick of having to go see that director and make 'salaam alaykums'..."). Gilles' response is to stand up and walk away *and* to stay in the room, carefully placing one foot before the other within the border pattern of his father's Persian rug as if it were a balance beam. This is an extremely refined representation of adolescent withdrawal – refuge from danger within the immediate environment, tuning out the parental signal, postponing the inevitable yet staying within reach. We know immediately that father and son have a shared appreciation of art which the son no longer wishes to recognize, and that the father is at the stage of making vain attempts to recapture their former ease of communication by command; that they both realize that their conversation will end in frustration; that no matter how antagonistic they become they will never reject one another outright. The father knows what his son is going through and he knows equally well that there is nothing he can do to make it any easier.

In the end, this behaviorally intricate scene, played out in the comfortable home of an aesthete, the varicolored walls decorated with paintings, is about a father betraying his son: Szabó has to pour himself a whiskey before explaining to Gilles that he simply can't put up with him anymore, that he has finally agreed with his ex-wife that he should be shipped off to a "very correct" boarding school in the south. What makes the scene so heartbreaking is Szabó's exquisite real-life bewilderment, speaking every measured word in a quavering voice with the greatest care and delicacy, like a first-time altar boy handling sacred objects – you feel the accompanying pain and regret behind every outburst. Assayas works wonders with the young, inexperienced Fouquet, matching him gesture for gesture with Szabó, and carefully fashioning a good, straightforward representation of a sensitive kid trying to act tough and backing himself into terrible perplexities. The scene ends, unforgettably, with the father calling the son back to his side and putting a hand on his shoulder – two comrades at an irreconcilable impasse.

If one considers the film closely, one recognizes elements or figures from one passage echoed or answered in another. Gilles' father questioning his son about his degree of emotional transfiguration before the Caravaggio reproduction is a gentle variation of the dreaded teacher trying to hector his students into a rote acceptance of Rousseau's greatness. The emotional violence of Gilles' destruction of the bus cushions (anyone who grew up in the era with an ounce of rebellion in their soul knows the sensation of the vinyl ripping open and the satisfying wound left behind) is carried by electrical current into the Swingle Singers' vocal wizardry, hanging like a storm cloud over Christine and summoning darker energies inside her. The nanny tells Gilles and his brother that she can't explain the Soviet atrocities, the father reminds him how lucky he is that he's never lacked for money, Christine's stepfather Mourad (Smaïl Mekki) screams in his face that "Mom and dad can get you out of trouble or cough up if they have to" – three variations on the same "what a lucky boy you are" message. Berroyer as Christine's father and Jean-Pierre Darroussin as a juvenile crimes cop, with their big rounded heads and softened features, are like two sides of the same working class coin. And throughout the film, music is the lifeline, the secret language carrying the promise of refuge, from Gilles and his little brother tuning in "Virginia Plain" on a transistor radio to the records stolen from the Prisunic (including *Pendulum, Exile on Main*

Street and *Machine Head*) which we later see passing from hand to hand in the classroom, to the film's visionary final section which begins with the nanny winding her clock, telling the boys to turn off their lights, and reciting her bedtime prayers. This Christian prayer seems to summon forth an altogether different kind of invocation.

The camera tracks alongside Gilles as he escapes from his house, grabs his bicycle, lights a Gauloise, opens a copy of City Lights' Pocket Poets edition of Ginsberg's *Planet News* and starts reciting "Wichita Vortex Sutra" in broken English. We are plunged deep into a teenage ritual, and the damp verdant forest, Gilles' full-throated rendition echoing along with the birdsong and crackling wood, becomes enchanted as rock formations and trees pass before our eyes in the foreground and planes of vision start to assume magical properties, as in a Magic Lantern show. When Gilles reaches the road and rides off into the fog, a spell has been cast.

What has this private ritual invoked into being? A community of shared privacy, a cocoon of freedom within the greater unforgiving world – in a word, rock and roll. A lot has been written and said about the party scene at a deserted chateau which immediately follows:

about the extraordinarily fluid choreography of bodies and camera, the momentum, the unearthly visual texture (made possible by the "skip bleach bypass" Assayas and his cameraman Denis Lenoir used on their first five films together, which deepens blacks and, in night scenes, creates an effect of free-floating movement). But just as important is the quiet, the guarded solitude. We enter the party not with a wide shot of teenagers in frantic motion, but on Christine alone. We are aware of the fact that there are others beyond the frame, but we remain situated within her own "headspace," as they used to say. Someone somewhere puts a 45 of Janis Joplin's version of "Me and Bobby McGee" on the sound system, and it becomes Christine's private soundtrack. We stay tightly locked on her face while she roams, produces a pair of scissors and starts to cut her own hair. The impression, finally, is not one of communal energy but of safety in numbers, of multiple subjectivities free to exist side by side without fear of correction or humiliation. The scene's most telling detail: when Christine's girlfriends find her with chopped hair, they go into an enactment of maternal caring, a typical adolescent move, building to one girl's gentle plea to give up the scissors; "Donnes les moi, chérie," she says in her most adult and unconsciously condescending manner, prompting Christine to stab her in the arm. Solitude is not to be violated.

With the help of a group of game '90s kids unleashing their own energies, Assayas finds – or re-discovers – the rhythm of a real '70s party, the obsessive playing and re-playing of records ("Knockin' on Heaven's Door," "Virginia Plain" again, "School's Out," "Cosmic Wheels" and "Up Around the Bend" among others), the expectation of Dionysian release meeting the reality of a series of ever-thinning peaks and ever-deepening valleys as the night wears on, the discordant intrusion of adults, and the cold, punishing morning after, which begins with kids running to the rolling lawn and squatting to relieve themselves under stark, overcast skies caught in long shot by the camera tracking with ominous formality past the chateau picture windows in sync with Nico's mournful "Janitor of Lunacy" (already wedded to another film, Garrel's *La Cicatrice intérieure*).

From there, we shift into a different poetic register, perhaps a bit more high-flown , for the film's brief final stretch. Throughout, Christine has planned to run away to a commune, and as she and Gilles hitchhike to nowhere in the starkest pastoral landscape imaginable – wintry, rocky, damper than the forest and harsher than the teacher's stare – they could be a pair of

runaway children in a fairy tale. As they find shelter by a river, the discrepancies between feigned experience and practical inexperience and sophistication and naiveté become darker and wider. Gilles' desire to be the good, caring, supportive boyfriend and perfect bad boy is checked by his common sense questions about the commune and how they'll get along, perhaps too probing for Christine's essentially private vision (or is it a fantasy?) of a perfect life. In the end, this is a boy's story. Gilles wakes up to find himself mysteriously alone and deserted by the river. Christine has left a parting message alongside a pile of her clothes: a blank white page of folded paper. The final image of this one-of-a-kind film, this fierce cinematic poem, is, on reflection, oddly hopeful, imparting the kind of lesson that would soon be obscured in an oncoming era of relentless good cheer. The blank white page speaks to the recipient in a voice of rushing cold water which fades into silence, and says: "You and you alone must write yourself into being."

to : EDWARD YANG
from Olivier ASSAYAS
3 pages.

August 27th 1995

Dear Edward,

This letter is bound to make you laugh.
As my other projects are stalling I've been writing these last few weeks a screenplay for a film I want to shoot very fast, here's the premise :

A french film director (Jean-Pierre Léaud) is commissioned by a TV company to film a remake of a classic silent serial, LES VAMPIRES, originally made by Louis Feuillade in 1915. It's not about vampires at all, but about a gang who call themselves the "Vampires". The central character is a woman, Irma Vep, she is part of the gang, wears a black catsuit, prowls on the roofs of Paris, gets into apartments, or hotel rooms passing through the windows, or the chimneys, etc... Basically, she is the original *catwoman.*
And this slightly weird director has decided that if he were to do a remake of LES VAMPIRES he absolutely would have to use a chinese actress he has seen in a martial arts movie : for him it's the only way to make it a) modern, b) to avoid confrontation with the original Irma Vep.
To make a long story short he convinces his producers. And the film begins with the arrival of the chinese actress in Paris two days before shooting begins.

It will definetely have comedy undertones, but I hope it will be a little more than a film about a film : it's about fiction, and work, and cinephilia blending with reality.
And many other things.

The story is seen through the eyes of this chinese actress. She is not completely sure of why she's there and what she's doing but
~~And many other things~~

~~The story is seen through the eyes of this chinese actress. She is not completely sure of why she's there and what she's doing but~~
progressively gets interested, in her own strange way.
Too late : the director who really turns out to be a very confused mind has a nervous breakdown.
He won't finish the film. Then the production calls another director for help.
Only condition : he wants another actress for the part.
End of the story (more or less).

So you understand the purpose of this letter:
I'm urgently looking for an actress for this part.
Ideally :
- she has to have done leading parts in action/fantasy/or martial arts movies. (There is a clip of one such film that I would like to include in my movie, involving her).
- she has to be famous, or have some kind of notoriety. (There is an interview included in the film, with a movie journalist, I'd like it be a real interview involving real movies, real parts, etc...)
- she has to speak english, but not perfect english as the idea of the film is that everybody speaks english but it's nobody's mother language : the whole film is in broken english. Or slightly broken.
- she has obviously to be a good actress as the part has very subtle shades (I hope), but also she has to be good looking and have something special that makes believable the fixation of that director for using her.
- she has to be someone who understands independant filmmaking as this movie will be shot on a modest budget, in something like five weeks and I haven't decided yet if it will be super16 (like COLD WATER) or 35.
  but :
  The film might be co-produced by UGC (who produced SHANGHAI TRIADS, etc...) , will definetely have major exposure in France and hopefully in Europe. Also the english language will certainly help...
- she has to be free minimum five whole weeks between november and january...

I know this isn't the moment to bother you with this kind of stuff, you have plenty to do with your movie, but if you could spare a few moments of your time to discuss this with Sylvie, and counsel her on this matter I would be very thankful.
This is urgent and Sylvie will take the first contacts so I can come myself to Taipeh/HK and try to figure out the possibilities.
To give you an indication, the kind of actress I had in mind, obviously because I've seen her the most often is Maggie Cheung, do you think it's worth it to contact her ? And if yes, how ? Do you imagine Marco Müller ~~do~~ to be a good recommendation ?

You see, all this is very unclear yet, but I count a lot on Sylvie's stay to make things a little more realistic. This was an opportunity not to miss. Thanks to you.
(Actually this is a project I've been thinking about for a long time now, and it's ironic that it's the fact you had a similar idea on the reverse side that ends up helping making it happen...)

So, thank you very much for your patience on this matter. And I hope that your shooting goes as you wish.
All the best,

Olivier Olivier

PS : Can you show this letter to Sylvie becuse I haven't had the time to give her the outline of the story before she left.
Also : tell her my fax functions normally (she thinks it's out of order)

Letter to Edward Yang about the *Irma Vep* project

Howard Hampton

The Strange Case of Irma Vep

Breaking free from the dog-end of the 20th century with chameleon stealth and resourcefulness, *Irma Vep* employed an exceptionally inspiring array of mix-up-and-match guises: kicky homage to the movies' first great pop-pulp-sort-of-modernist epic, Louis Feuillade's cunning, sinisterly circuitous *Les Vampires* of 1915; director-screenwriter Olivier Assayas' dashed off/mashed-up love letter to Hong Kong film star Maggie Cheung, gracious ballad notes hurriedly scrawled on Hotel Truffaut stationery; unfussy evocation of the bygone (the Silent Age to the Nouvelle Vague, May '68 to *Batman Returns*) in the midst of the here-and-now (the postmodern defined by how quickly everything slips into the past tense). All the while *Irma* outlined the 1,001 pseudo-underhanded, semi-disreputable acts, compromises, blind inspirations, mistakes, feints, feuds, jealousies, and blissful accidents that go into the making and managing of cinematic utopias. Assayas fashioned an exultantly melancholy salute to the craftspeople and crackpots who perpetrate or delegate the aforementioned acts with harried assurance or neurasthenic abandon, those women and men who make movies concretely possible and not just hypothetical.

Watching the film today, close to fifteen years after its release, I find if anything I love it more than I did at first sight: the years have added rueful luster to its heightened, dreamy verisimilitude. Initially, the speed and energy were its most attractive aspects, coupled with the emotional aplomb with which it casually assimilated rock & roll, diverse strands of Nineties Asian cinema – from poetic action fables to Wong Kar-wai, Stanley Kwan, and Hou Hsiao-hsien – and even a touch of Hawks-Sturges playground atmosphere into a highly specific French sensibility/sensitivity. All of which remain relevant as entry points into the picture, but are not necessarily so viscerally compelling now – the sense of *Irma Vep* being at the forefront of some nascent international tendency in hindsight seems more like wishful thinking, a gold rush that didn't pan out. Olivier Assayas didn't blaze the trail here for a new movement, youth or otherwise, any more than Wong did with *Chungking Express* (*Chung Hing sam lam*).

More's the pity that Assayas' exquisitely integrated and invigorating use of Sonic Youth's "Tunic" for Maggie Cheung's latex-encased midnight prowl through her hotel and Luna's cover of "Bonnie and Clyde" woven into a wondrously convivial dinner for the film crew (a double recontextualization of Serge Gainsbourg, and all the more captivating for it) never managed to cross over the cultural divide and capture the insular hearts of the indie rock crowd. (Or maybe there just wasn't a big enough indie rock crowd to lure in the first place.) So in the absence of kool-thing zeitgeist or some unreasonable facsimile thereof, we're left with Assayas' unsweetened humanism and the rapt even-handedness of his approach to human contacts and contracts. The documentary-like quality emphasized by Éric Gautier's peerlessly fluid hand-held camera combined with fable-like appreciation of high and low cultural totems (from Feuillade and the zap-pow of *The Heroic Trio* [*Dung fong saam hap*] to the collage-like Lettrist-cum-Brakhage abstract experimentalism of the squiggly final sequence) does however suggest an odd, tangential affinity to the once-upon-an-epoch short stories of Donald Barthelme (see *Come Back, Dr. Caligari* and *Sadness*). The segmented, modular way the pieces of *IV* fit together recall on some level the loopy, gallant mood of Barthelme's *fin de* Sixties contraptions, assemble-your-own-meaning constructs of absurdist romanticism, sophisticated Q&A dialogues between friends / lovers / antagonists, and a saturnine yet sanguinary embrace of art, language, and love's comic-tragic dissolution.

In any event, Assayas wasn't interested in turning himself into a tightly defined stylistic brand, or playing to any particular subculture: the fleet-footed techniques he used in *Irma Vep* were all tied to the locality of the milieu and the most efficient way to express it. Assayas didn't really make another film with the same kind of kinetic fortitude and immersive syntax until *Carlos*. (Not to suggest that a charismatic terrorist cult leader and his minions resemble a neurotic filmmaker and his crew, though the idea may have crossed a couple of minds – you know who you are.) *Irma Vep* has artistic "personality" to burn, but Assayas thankfully lacks the killer ego of the hardcore *auteur*, the whip-hand imposing a rigid set of aesthetic dictates on his material. As he's moved between disparate types of projects, each film a different set of problems and challenges to tackle, Assayas has maintained a steadfast openness to trying different gambits, attitudes, even ways of seeing.

The informal first-hand intimacy of *Irma Vep* is a long way from the boxed-up mothball worlds of *demonlover* and *Les Destinées sentimentales*, which are predicated on cultural constructs or literary conceits, and never get beyond that point. But maybe the process of art – the work of art and not necessarily the finished artworks themselves – has a more practical-empirical attraction / application for Assayas. Those films might be exercises in filmic architecture and creative problem-solving, but even

Fiction: Alex Descas and Maggie Cheung as Maggie Cheung in *Irma Vep* (above)

Non-Fiction: Maggie Cheung, dressed as Irma Vep, and Jean-Pierre Léaud on the set

if they leave us (or at least me) cold, they still could have been invaluable to him as vital learning experiences, as ways of working through certain feelings about the techno-sex-thriller or the proverbial overstuffed period drama from the inside. In the light of these kinds of potentially salutary dead ends, the point might be: all the world's a film school and we're merely students learning what we can and cannot achieve with the medium. And we only learn by trial and error – hands-on practice, failure, realization (if we're good and/or lucky enough).

(This raises two questions: are there films that help the filmmaker come to a deeper personal understanding of the cinema or himself, without being able to communicate that understanding at all? I don't mean movies that are too advanced or complicated, but that are in some fundamental and irreversible way too *routine* – that don't have any special ambitions or demands or claims on our attention, but where the director discovers the truth of his own or even the medium's limits? And is Assayas, in such experiments or exercises, a kind of more complex, less clinically self-regarding *doppelgänger* to Steven Soderbergh?)

Irma Vep is a far cry from a dead-end. Every shot hums with sympathetic concentration, so many beautifully composed little odes to disheveled life. As Pauline Kael said of *Jonas qui aura 25 ans en l'an 2000*, it "stays suspended in the air, a marvelous toy, weightless, yet precise and controlled." Call it the poetry of spectrum analysis, the spectrum in question being the human condition as it relates to the production of movies. The storyline is standard but highly functional: Jean-Pierre Léaud plays a burnt-out director who is remaking *Les Vampires* – a black-and-white and silent remake at that – and in his desire to inject some novelty or freshness or plain old sacrilege into this curious conceit, decides to cast the Hong Kong actress Maggie Cheung as one of French cinema's most iconic figures, the anarchist goddess Irma Vep.

From the first frames, the movie dives sideways into the circular swarm of this fictional but eminently believable production, camera sliding through the helter-skelter of activity like a ballerina on roller-skates, soaking up the cluttered atmosphere with insouciant glances. Cheung is almost immediately dropped into the midst of it like an astronaut plunked down on another green world, albeit one whose molehill greenery is obscured by clouds of cigarette smoke and anxious waves of human traffic – a more or less benign Planet of the Apes where she's regarded with a mixture of slightly condescending amazement and erotic fascination.

Maggie Cheung, costume fitting

Assayas has said he was inspired to make the film by her remarkable presence off-screen, not her Hong Kong movie roles, and it comes through in sturdy, intriguing hues. Playing "herself," Cheung projects a terrific down-to-earth modesty and a genuine, unforced quality of mystery. (The quality of mystery is not strained, to rather freely paraphrase the Mekons.) Directors are always trying to get you to fall in love with a certain actress (or perchance falling in love with her themselves in order to make the movie itself more seductive – a way of psyching themselves into the state of desire they want to instigate). Assayas accomplished something much harder and more valuable here. He caught on camera, as if in a home movie operated at the level of Godard or Renoir or Vigo, both the object of his ardor and a sense of her own knockabout subjectivity, and in doing so gave us a unique take on the interrelationship between Eros – with all its heavy-duty intimations of the ur-mythic and the Ideal – and the quotidian.

Assayas and Cheung pulled off a remarkable feat: letting us see this Maggie as a fully rounded, at times wholly unreadable person, someone whose gifts (and even limitations) can't be reduced to the mechanics of stardom. (By "pulled off," I'm also thinking in caper terms: it takes a thief to catch a thief, and looking at the over/undertones of her night-prowler sequence, you might have the sensation of Audrey Hepburn momentarily replacing Grace Kelly under Hitchcock's resolute gaze.) Cheung isn't a projection here, though the irony the movie's predicated on is how this Maggie is used by everyone as a human screen upon which they desperately project their needs and wants. Trying to stay afloat in a foreign country, speaking only English and never quite sure if she's making herself understood or fully understanding her interlocutors, pulled every which way by people who want to use her, she performs a delicate balancing act among a cadre of relatively friendly but unbalanced people. If it's any consolation, they're not necessarily trying to exploit her for craven purposes, but for reasons no less intense for being ineffable: they all want some magical collusion of personality, glamour, pliability, and phantasmal access from

her. In particular Nathalie Richard's costumer, who has a fiercely shy crush on the young woman she outfits in the body-hugging catsuit, and who pursues her with a wonderful mix of arrogance and diffidence. In the layers of sublimely offhand give-and-take between Richard and Cheung, there's a subliminal vibe whose saneness is vaguely clouded by an apprehensive instability. As if the line between screwball comedy and *Persona*-type crisis might secretly be as thin as that latex second skin.

One of the most likable, unexpected things about *Irma Vep* is how gracefully female-centric it is. Despite its concern with the traditionally masculine preserve of film-making, women have the primary voices here, and all the best scenes. If men still hold court and power, it's with the tenuous grip of shabby babies, toddler burn-outs. Male auteur/authority figures Jean-Pierre Léaud and Lou Castel are falling apart (they're each at different stages of disintegration, but while Castel's José Murano replaces Léaud's René Vidal at the helm, I'd be hard pressed to say which is the greater or lesser wreck). They're a couple of slobbery mammals flailing miserably at the ends of their worn-out tethers: Vidal seems to have a heart and integrity under his rumpled clothes, but Murano is a walking (s)crap-heap with an oil-can personality to match. The only reason he's interested in taking over the movie is because "Things are slow" and his unemployment eligibility is about to run out (he doesn't look as if he's been more than fifty feet from his sofa in years).

Cheung, Richard's Zoé, and Bulle Ogier are the motors of the picture; Ogier's magnificent stint as bourgeois bulldozer radiating maternal charm and concern is a high point of *Irma Vep*, but it's something of question mark too. Who is this woman who comes on like Zoé's mother, with all the automatic intimacy and fond exasperation and bossy push-pull crosstalk that implies? Nowhere is she identified as such. I leapt to that conclusion simply because of the byplay between the two women: they *feel* like mother and daughter, but this may be a case of making the same kind of incorrect assumption that Maggie makes when she takes Zoé for straight – when this daunting mother-figure informs her Zoé's got a crush on her, she giggles with schoolgirl embarrassment and giddy displacement, Alice in Wonderamaland.

"Where's Maïté?" someone inquires of the line producer played by Dominique Faysse. "Scouting the sewers." Women's work is never done, but nothing on the movie would go forward without their exasperated tenacity, and that of the P.A.s, stuntwomen, assistants, or René's unseen and apparently long-suffering wife. Zoé is a bundle of neurotic neurons, gesticulating with a cigarette that's a wand-like extra digit. Fitting Maggie for her costume in an upscale sex shop ("I want latex from head to foot"), she's a sensualist dynamo – you can feel the tingle in her fingers, the twitch of her nose reveling in the smell of sweat on Latex. Riffing later on the aesthetic bankruptcy of American films or fighting with Maïté ("I'll murder that bitch," the producer snarls as she's pulled away to a neutral corner), she has an anxious halo that bespeaks a reservoir of tremendous instability barely held in check: the specter of drug problems, emotional difficulties, dangerous liaisons. Richard brings a fascinating bifurcated quality to this woman, impish yet cynical and almost terrifyingly vulnerable once you get past her seen-it-all façade: in her fierce not-quite-androgyny, she seems to bring other scarred worlds to bear on the movie, to anchor its lightness in underground passions, perils, ambiguity. She isn't quite like anyone else in the movie, or the movies themselves – Richard's so much *quicker* than a Jean Seberg or Anna Karina, as if channeling Martina Navratilova's reflexes through memories of the heroines of half a dozen Big Star songs.

Story is secondary to incidents and exchanges – what happens to Vidal after his crack-up, the outcome of his odious replacement, not to mention what becomes of the movie itself, is beside

Setting up the interview scene

the point. Everything hinges on the conversations, motorbike rides at night set to a gentle Ali Farka Touré beat, transcendently awkward partings, the way Ogier maneuvers Cheung around her kitchen with a solicitous matchmaker determination (what is French for "Mama Grizzly"?): "Do you like girls? Have you sex with girls?" There is a phenomenal sense of rootedness in the everyday convergences of things/people/ideas coming together and apart at the same time and in the same tight, beautifully defined spaces. In Assayas' films, we see people thinking, sometimes out loud, sometimes covering up their thoughts with words or gestures; he never lets you feel like you can read their minds and motives like an open book. *Irma Vep* has a particularized air of contingency, of human beings having many unevenly partitioned aspects that can't be telescoped into a tidy, compact idea of character. Zoé has a very winning personality with Maggie, but she's volatile with others in ways that set off little alarm bells. Maïté denigrates her as an unreliable junkie, which sounds like sour grapes, but there's an edge to Zoé that makes you wonder. The passage where Maggie goes with Zoé to a rave and then gets cold feet is one of the most quietly devastating rejection scenes ever because it isn't dramatized in big semaphore movie terms but in very tiny, uncomfortable movements, quicksilver hesitancies, hopeless pleadings. "Why don't you go ahead? I kind of don't feel like it, y'know." "Why not, it's very fun, it's a good rave..." "I don't know, just..." "Five minutes?"

It's hard to quantify why the shot of Maggie driving off in a taxi is so poignant and piquant, illuminated by the interior light, compartmentalized, girlishly waving goodbye, hovering through the Parisian night like a self-sustained organism. Maybe the moment Zoé loses her chance with her is the moment she falls in love with her, but the jellyfish image is more elusive than that, a sliver of something that vanishes into oblivion before it can be named. And then Zoé is a dervish tearing apart her purse looking for a hit of Ecstasy, her face a haggard, strobe-lit mask of fear, nausea, and resignation. You meet someone who seems a little manic but sweet and full of life, but it could all be the façade of someone biding her time until her next relapse; Zoé's a thorough professional who in her own fragile way is like Irma Vep, too, in that she's walking her own private precipice and might fall off the ledge with one good push. Her battles with Maïté are contests of will, trivial and petty yet life-and-death – there's a hidden history there that could open up into a whole other movie.

The seamless way *Irma Vep* transitions from passage to passage is like a flâneur playing hopscotch on a flow chart. From the two "Fuck that bitch" antagonists going at it, it slides a *Nashville* panel and now a journalist (Antoine Basler) is setting up to do an interview with Maggie. This Altmanesque conceit of the grinning bozo who hassles her with his fanboy attitude and lip-smacking pronouncements about the triumph of Schwarzenegger-ism over the effete cinema of René Vidal and France itself is the most blatant routine in the film. This goon is the direct descendant of Geraldine Chaplin's prattling Opal, if she'd sired a son with a soccer hooligan. But Assayas doesn't give the clod any special weight or significance – he isn't made to seem the villain of the piece, any more than Murano is when he's planning to oust Maggie and replace her with her stunt-double, or than Maïté when she's scheming to catch Zoé dealing or lying. It's all part of cinema's mulch-rich pageant, the knaves and the fools vying with the genii and geniuses for screen time. And in the case of Castel's Murano, in his orange jacket looking more like a senile crossing guard than a proper film director, he might just be all of the above.

"René's a pain in the ass" someone announces after he's gone missing and that much is clear, though in Léaud's rich, whispery ennui, enervation is itself a kind of artistry. His loss of faith in his project, himself, and probably cinema as well – he doesn't need some gloating dimwit to tell him he's washed up, his super-ego's already beaten his critics to the punch – is visible in the hangdog way he slumps in an armchair. (He and Castel compete for the most atrocious posture, slouching toward Babylon.) But even if he's a drowning man grasping at straws, the clips of *The Heroic Trio* and *Les Vampires* that pop up in *Irma Vep* like karmic flashbacks feel like sudden immersions in alternate universes. They represent the persistent possibility of the sublime – Feuillade's serial still captivating the people living in a future no one could have quite dreamed, the HK flick Vidal says he caught (like an Interzone virus) in a cheap cinema in Marrakech. And the other clips woven through the film, more Musidora and the '68 *cinéma-militant* viewed on video at the dinner party for the crew, take on a life of their own – Assayas deploys these clips almost like characters, entities that haunt and comment on and motivate the work everyone is attempting to do with their remake. The people who made the agit-prop are embarrassed by its radical naivety ("It's great stuff," chimes Zoé, "Don't repudiate it now"), with its Fidel posters and chalkboard slogans ("CINEMA IS NOT MAGIC. IT IS TECHNIQUE AND SCIENCE"). This crude mock-newsreel has its own beauty, as its soundtrack swells like some Phil Spector production of Marx: a Cubano or Chilean yé-yé singer's idea of "He's a Rebel."

The party is one of loveliest sustained pieces of bourgeois-bohemian sociability ever filmed, Buñuel inverted (even he might be disarmed by these suburban artist-technicians). It has a warm vivacity personified by the bony, gawky Jessica Doyle (the actual costume designer on *Irma Vep*), who momentarily steals the picture when she turns on the stereo and dances kind of Twyla Tharp-ily to Luna's version of "Bonnie and Clyde." Here is the crux of the film's equanimity, in the way it aligns itself with ordinary experience rather than allegory. Jonathan Rosenbaum wrote that the film is about how we live now. (Even if now has become then, it's pretty applicable to the going rates on the international market in social stasis and atrophy.) But he saw that life by the light of the capitalist "sinister": "evil in an everyday environment is no longer represented by Irma Vep and her gang but by the film crew's thwarted energies and desires and their effects, creeping inexorably into one social situation after another." And: "Pervading the shoot is the poisonous atmosphere of alienated labor." To me, this seems as much of an ideological stretch, projection-wise, as any of the thwarted sexual fan-

tasies Maggie is subjected to. Assayas didn't make a sociopolitical-psychosexual para-babble, he made a film about the places where movies and reality intersect.

Hence Jessica Doyle in the background of a scene, having her 15 seconds of immortality, leaving an indelible impression that is as important to the overall gestalt of the film as any other element. (Even if you could blink and miss it.) I don't know if *Irma Vep* is "about" the way people become part of something larger than themselves; it shows rather than tells how the artists and artisans work through the collective insanity that is filmmaking and by hook or crook or roll of the dice manage to make something that lives in memory – a kind of living, breathing permanent history, for better or worse. Tossing and turning and pacing the 6×9 room in her skintight costume, Cheung emerges from the blast-furnace embrace of Sonic Youth into the hallway. Creeping through her hotel, she nervously steps into the world of Hitchcock as if it too were a second (third?) skin. A whole delicious, complex web of associations arises as she sneaks into another guest's room behind the maid: the woman in the room is played by Atom Egoyan's main squeeze / muse Arsinée Khanjian, who is naked

This and the following pages:
frames from the film's ending (René Vidal's footage)

and conducting a frantic phone call like some fleshy apparition of both Isabella Rossellini and Ingrid Bergman. It's as though there could be a different movie going on behind every door in the hotel and Cheung in her beautiful, ridiculous disguise is free to wander into any reality she might find there – there's the feeling that the real is inherently unstable, open to transformation. Yet the scene never loses the sense of being rooted in the moment, in the hotel's routines (the maid moving in a naturally formal way, doing the same thing every night, every hour), the lulling rhythms of the mundane opening into the empire of the fantastic and the phantasmagorical. After Maggie sneaks into the woman's room, she grabs her ornate necklace and darts away down the corridors oscillating between jewel thief and scared kid, suddenly running up the stairs out on the rooftop in a downpour. The movie's circled back to the nocturnal blue lights of *The Heroic Trio* as she breathes in her own crazy, impulsive audacity, fondling the necklace amid the rain, the steam, and the bright lights, as if all rooftop Paris of 1996 *and* 1915 belonged to her.

Then she lets the necklace fall out of her fingers, tumbling in exquisitely corny slow motion (probably the most purely "cinematic" moment in the film) into the street below. In this gesture, she's joined hands and become one with Musidora's Irma. The same is true of the film's ending, where René Vidal's reedited footage is screened for Murano and company. Consisting of our Irma inscribed with scratchy lines, black-out bars, squiggles, circles, beams coming out of her eyes – Rosenbaum and Gavin Smith traced its lineage to Lettrist Isidore Isou's *Traité de bave et d'éternité*, though its rhythmic qualities also align it somewhat with Bruce Conner – it leaps out of the movie to dissolve it instead of resolve it.

As a stand-alone work within a work that also cuts off the film itself in mid-stride, it indicates how much the whole movie thrives on the freedom to not have to tie up every plot point or relationship, a dangling logic à la Irma-Maggie high above the city in the rain, leaning over the roof and dropping the jewels the way a person might drop coins into the fountain and make a wish. "She's no flesh, no blood, she's just an idea," moans Vidal when he's hit bottom. "How can I be interested in an idea?" *Irma Vep* made images and ideas as solid and as uncanny as flesh and blood, transmitting a matrix of experiences and sensations that are nothing so much as a picture of lived life and dream life sharing a common catsuited body.

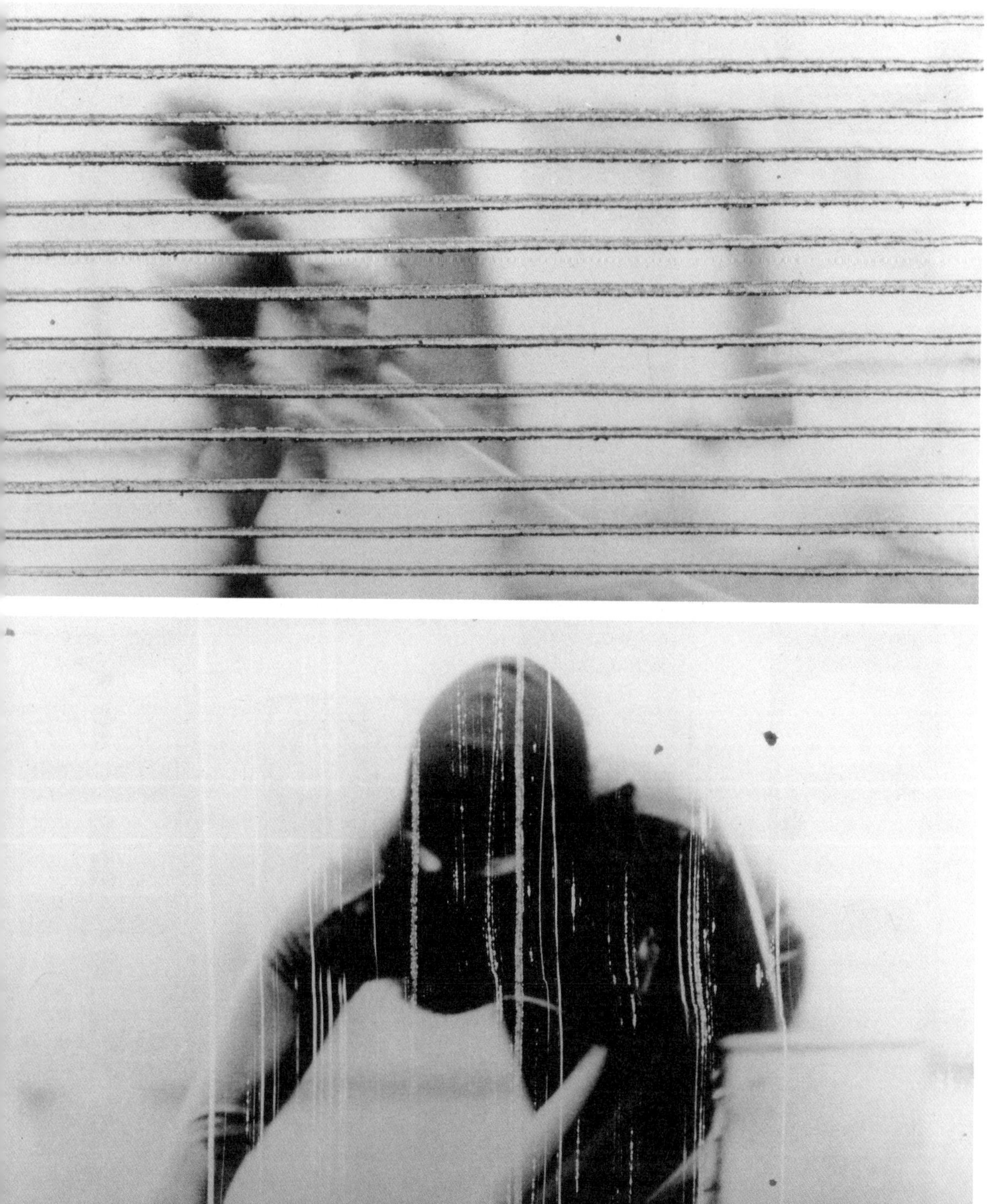

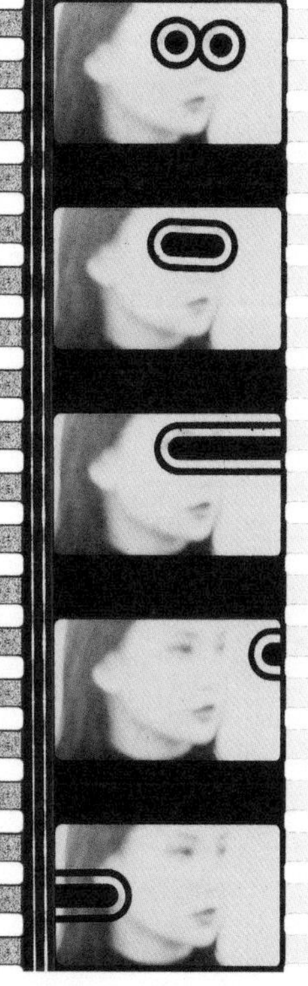

Larry Gross

After Art Cinema

HHH – Portrait de Hou Hsiao-hsien, Olivier Assayas' documentary study of Hou Hsiao-hsien for French TV's *Cinéma, de notre temps* series, is a charmingly casual-seeming work. Assayas accompanies Hou to the Southern Taiwanese city of Fengshan where he grew up, to the principal locations for many of his greatest films, including *A City of Sadness* (*Bei qing cheng shi*), *The Puppetmaster* (*Xi meng ren sheng*) and *Goodbye South Goodbye* (*Nan guo zai jian, nan guo*), as well as to the coffee shops in Taipei where Hou and his screenwriting colleagues plan and design his films and the karaoke bars where he and some of his favorite actors hang out. The film ends with a reasonably liquored up Hou belting out some of the old-style Taiwanese pop ballads he says he prefers to contemporary ones. "You sing best when you're in love," he advises Assayas. Just because it's obvious doesn't mean it isn't true.

The man who emerges from this portrait is gruff, talkative, nostalgic, anything but an intellectual or an aesthete. He is driven by emotions, the tenderness of his memories and feelings for particular people, places, moods and meals. Food and drink are a quite remarkable component of the film, as they should be in any depiction of life influenced by Chinese culture. Many conversations in the film take place during lengthy meals or over tea-breaks. One extended highpoint comes when the wandering camera, expertly manned by Éric Gautier, surveys a meticulous serving of charcoal-cooked Oolong tea in a tiny regional teahouse. That it be prepared in the correct manner is something that interests Hou deeply.

Hou visits the streets where he was a minor street criminal before going into the army and, as it were, getting his head on straight. He tells us how his serious film career took as its point of departure the freedom from martial law and government control of culture that began in Taiwan in the mid-eighties, and which enabled and perhaps compelled the Taiwanese film community to speak about events in the nation's recent history that had never been discussed or represented in public. The moment when government restrictions were lifted and most censorship relaxed coincided with the return from abroad of a group of young filmmakers, among them the great Edward Yang, with excited descriptions of European art cinema. Hou, an already experienced professional craftsman, interacted with these filmmakers and critics and discovered for himself that films could be more than just entertainment. He speaks specifically of Yang showing him Pasolini's *Edipo re*, and suddenly grasping the philosoph-

Hou Hsiao-hsien

ical possibilities of an "objective" perspective as disclosed in the wide angle master shot. (One detail in Assayas' film has gained in poignance since it was shot in 1996: one of the most articulate commentators on Hou is Wu Nien-jen, who co-wrote many of Hou's films and who most of us probably recognize today as the star of Edward Yang's last masterpiece *Yi Yi*, released just two years before Yang's death.)

What do we learn about Olivier Assayas from his picture of Hou Hsiao-hsien? We obviously discover his meticulously detailed love of Hou's work – he subtly reconstructs some of the imagery of *A Time to Live and a Time to Die* (*Tong nien wang shi*), *A City of Sadness* and *Goodbye South, Goodbye* when he visits the places where they were shot. We feel a strong anthropological fascination with everyday life in a booming Asian society, which Hou's life and habits exemplify, thus foreshadowing the underrated *Boarding Gate* and, of course, Assayas' creative and personal liaison with Maggie Cheung. But that being said, the answer to the question of exactly why Assayas felt compelled to make this film is not so immediately obvious.

There is no one theme that unifies Assayas' career in quite the way that the question of Taiwanese historical identity dominates and organizes the productions of Hou Hsiao-hsien. Assayas has worked happily in many disreputable genres (*demonlover* – sci fi, *Boarding Gate* – the international drug thriller) as well as a number of reputable ones (*Carlos* – the biopic, *Les Destinées sentimentales* – the period literary adaptation). His interests in erotic and political intrigue turn up in many but not all of the films. There is a strong autobiographical resonance in some but not in others.

If there is one emotional condition that could be said to permeate all of Assayas' work, it is the "restlessness and uncertainty" that Hou speaks of with cool dispassion more than once in the first hour of *HHH*. Hou uses the phrase as he speaks of feeling like a displaced person in Taiwan as a child, never knowing for sure if it would be possible to go back to the mainland where he was born, as the Chang Kai-shek government relentlessly promised the Taiwanese people they one day would. Taiwan existed from 1895 to 1945 as a colony of Japan, then as a fierce economic competitor with Hong Kong, today as a pawn in the geopolitical chess game between the US and China. Hou makes reference to all of these. This is globalized "restlessness and uncertainty" with a vengeance. Meanwhile, as A.O. Scott suggested in a fine profile written for The New York Times around the time of the release of *Carlos*, Assayas himself (at least since *Irma Vep*) is certainly one of the great contemporary film artists of globalization, and that suggests another affinity with Hou.

There are two occasions on which Assayas has successfully pushed his narrative procedures furthest in unconventional directions. I'm referring to *Fin août, début septembre* and *L'Heure d'été*. Both are films about groups of characters full of ambivalent esteem for a single authority figure (François Cluzet's novelist in *Fin août*, Edith Scob's matriarch in the later film) who is in turn conflicted about this power they have over others. In both narratives, this dominating figure abruptly dies just past the middle of the film, and their respective constellations of friends, children and lovers must tentatively grope toward a new self-definition.

These are the two films that most clearly display the convergence in sensibilities of Hou Hsiao-hsien and Olivier Assayas, if not Hou's explicit influence. They are, like Hou's films, fascinatingly devoid of the kind of emphatic melodramatic expression that their plot situations might readily promote (and which incidentally, Assayas has not shied away from depicting in other films), and they are curiously agnostic in tone, hovering between comedy and pathos but detached in a way that refuses to instruct the audience in how to feel about the characters' uncertain outcomes. Like a number of Hou's films, they follow the characters over a period of at least a couple of years, long enough for us to discover a "development" we would not necessarily have assumed or been able to predict. Ellipsis, a strategy Assayas himself employs in many of his films, becomes elevated in these instances to a defining organizing principle, as it does in the strongest of Hou's films. Long takes and intricate movement within the frame produce a deliberately slow, uninflected rhythm. No matter what you can show about people, they remain enigmatic, and we will always feel that there is more to them that we will never know. "The ancient Chinese aesthetic concept of *liu-pai* – allowing what's visible within the frame to open in the mind of the viewer onto the world extending beyond its parameters – is expanded in [Hou's late films], where space feels like it could unfurl in any direction." Kent Jones is describing Hou's late '90s films, but he could just as easily be describing the sense of space in *Fin août, début septembre* and *L'Heure d'été*.

Let me conclude these brief remarks with an even briefer bit of film-historical speculation. Cinema and especially European cinema from the end of World War II to the late '70s experienced an extraordinary artistic renaissance, giving birth to what we sometimes call Art Cinema. It has far too many characteristics to be enumerated here, but as most students of the period would agree, its greatest productions from Italian Neo-Realism through the Nouvelle Vague, not to exclude the greatest movies of Bergman, Buñuel and Antonioni, involved a radical reconsideration of the norms of commercial narrative cinema represented by Hollywood, often inspired by the previous five decades of artistic and cultural practice we call Modernism. From the eighties on, political and economic forces, especially the expanded hegemony of Hollywood and its all-powerful distribution procedures, destroyed Art Cinema.

What is characteristic of Assayas and the other major filmmakers of his generation (in France I refer to Claire Denis and Arnaud Desplechin, in America to Todd Haynes and Gus Van Sant, in Asia to the aforementioned Taiwanese masters as well as Tsai Ming-liang, Hong Sang-soo and Wong Kar-wai, and there are of course others, feel free to make your own list…) is that they remain interested in exploring unconventional narrative structures that avoid Hollywood commercial norms, but not under the rubric of the totalizing transformational aspirations held by an earlier Art Cinema generation.

Existing in a time that is exhausted with if not bored by cultural-historical warfare, Assayas for all his aesthetic hipness is nonetheless disenchanted with the myth of the modernist breakthrough. He doesn't believe that experimenting with forms is going to result in some revolutionary transvaluation of all values. If you couldn't buy as your guide or authoritative justification (however much you may have admired them) Bresson's radical spirituality or Godard's militant theorization of film and political history or Resnais' aestheticism, where would you look for a pragmatic, disenchanted but capable artistic adventurousness that is thrillingly uncorrupted by the codes of Hollywood, practiced by an artist who restores your faith that something authentically vital and fresh is still possible? It seems to me that Assayas, and perhaps others, may have found a working model for such a practice, and reason for such faith, in the work of Hou Hsiao-hsien.

Kristin M. Jones

The Soul in Times of Danger

"Can stories describe the world?" It's a question the thirty-something editor and aspiring writer Gabriel (Mathieu Amalric) asks a television producer in Olivier Assayas' *Fin août, début septembre* (1998). The producer, with all the crassness often associated with his profession, has bluntly asserted that the best way into a novelist's vision is by way of narrative. The film doesn't completely reject his assertion, though. Unfolding over the course of one momentous year, it tells a story with a large theme – how the dead endure through their work and the memories of those who've survived them – by means of an elegantly elliptical narrative in which quotidian moments yield nearly invisible transformations and revelations. It's a film in which language, especially as related to the possibilities of storytelling and the supple rhythms of dialogue, is essential, but that also stirringly evokes the elusive lightness and energy of visual art.

After the exhilarating imaginative acrobatics of *Irma Vep* (1996), Assayas wanted to make something simpler, based on real-life experiences and closer to the bare-bones naturalism of *L'Eau froide* (1994), with its achingly pure emotion. He turned to a script he had begun in the early 1990s, which was partly inspired by the deaths of several of his friends from AIDS. Whereas his wistfully sun-dappled, Bonnard-esque *L'Heure d'été* (2008), another return to intimate personal themes, recalls the terrible break with the past that the loss of a parent can signify, *Fin août, début septembre* deals with a more unnatural trauma, following a group of friends who form a surrogate family as they grapple with their grief and confusion surrounding the terminal illness of a vibrant adult in early middle age.

Gabriel's mentor and closest friend is the handsome, cerebral, and reserved 40-year-old novelist Adrien Willers (François Cluzet). When they learn of Adrien's disease at the beginning of the story, his friends don't yet grasp its seriousness. His quiet disappearance two-thirds of the way through the film is for them an incomprehensible shock, a "vast silent explosion," as Vladimir Nabokov described death in one of his short stories. And yet *Fin août, début septembre* is also filled with the hum of relationships, creative work, and efforts to survive and find one's place in the world. Assayas has said that in the process of making it he discovered that it was not about death, but about life.

Like a slim novella, *Fin août, début septembre* is divided into six chapters, reflecting the importance art and literature hold for many of the characters, especially Adrien and Gabriel, both of

whom are intimately concerned with storytelling and questions of its place in the world. The chapter divisions, and the fades to black that function like paragraph breaks within those chapters, also mark ellipses in which certain crucial events – the sale of an apartment, the news of Adrien's death, the beginnings of new jobs and relationships and the sputtering demise of others – are unseen but felt, like a heartbeat. Fragments produce a whole that lives and breathes, much like the character at its center. Although Adrien's presence persists even after he's gone, he is ultimately a radiant enigma, viewed through a different lens by each person who loves him.

The numerous couples in the film also affirm this pervasive subjectivity, their conversations rife with contradictory perspectives. As the film begins, Gabriel is ending an eight-year relationship with Jenny (Jeanne Balibar), who still loves him. She claims that they were both happier when they were together; he is convinced otherwise, believes she is idealizing the past, and is eager to move on. He has begun an affair with Anne (Virginie Ledoyen), a mercurial, risk-taking fashion designer who believes that she ruins everything, while he is clearly repeating his own self-destructive patterns. Adrien is secretly seeing the Ecstasy-popping teenager Véra (Mia

Hansen-Løve), who provides him with tender, lighthearted affection. Meanwhile, his former longtime lover, Lucie (Arsinée Khanjian), knows a different side of Adrien, refusing to visit him in the hospital and telling Jenny, who imagines that they were a great couple, that he was brutal and manipulative.

In the second chapter, Adrien travels to his hometown with Gabriel to be filmed for a television program in which they will discuss his early influences. In two extended, subtly filmed scenes on a train and in the station, Adrien suddenly begins to open up about his career disappointments and frustrations, saying, "I never got through to the public – that's what counts." When Gabriel protests ("Being respected counts"), Adrien responds that he missed out on "tangible things, material things." Gabriel presses him further and Adrien ruefully explains that he's really talking about money and the freedom it might have brought him. After they leave the train, Gabriel admits that he is moved by his friend's confessions, but also expresses a fear that he is speaking so openly because he is sick. Adrien scoffs that the conversation is getting too heavy. It's a riveting sequence – Cluzet and Amalric delicately evoke their characters' mutual affection, the unfamiliar territory the conversation represents, and their shared awareness of impending danger – but Adrien's financial struggles are also mirrored by those of the other characters, many of whom are involved in creative work. His worries, loves, and regrets, intensified by his illness, suggest a distillation of their experiences.

Awkwardness, misunderstanding, anxiety, and regret are ever-present and acquire mysterious weight: Anne has a threesome with two men and frets afterward about her foundering relationship with Gabriel; Gabriel and Jenny argue, break up and then begin to make out. The actors' physical movements as well as their dialogue suggest emotions and relationships in constant flux, with Denis Lenoir's fluid, delicately restless camerawork following them into trains, stairwells, hallways, and taxis; other scenes unfold in rooms that are borrowed or in the process of being emptied or renovated. Despite all this instability, the story seems to have been painted with a few sure brushstrokes, each messy interaction flowing seamlessly into the next. The grainy Super-16mm visuals evoke a limpid watercolor sketch, while the bittersweet guitar themes by the Malian musician Ali Farka Touré, recurring at interstitial moments, summon a sense of lightness and intimacy. When Adrien dies, as his death is not depicted, he seems as much to vanish into brightness, into the warm and luminous lives that remain, as into a dark ellipsis.

In Assayas' films artworks have frequently offered external correlatives to his characters' memories, yearnings, and ideals. In *Irma Vep,* of course, it's the cinema of Louis Feuillade and Hong Kong action films; in *Les Destinées sentimentales* (2000), services of fine porcelain; and in *L'Heure d'été,* a collection of exquisite decorative objects and paintings. In *Fin août, début septembre* it's one talismanic artwork, a graceful wash drawing of a stag by the great German artist Joseph Beuys, which Adrien purchased with his first royalty check. Of the stag, which carried powerful symbolism in his work, Beuys said it "appears in times of distress and danger. It introduces a particular element: the warm, positive element of life. At the same time it is endowed with spiritual powers and insight and is the accompanier of the soul." In the context of the film the drawing *is* the essence of art, which Adrien has spent his life pursuing. It's also an emblem of innocence and purity, like the gentle, ethereal Véra and the bouquet of yellow flowers she brings him just before he enters the hospital for an operation.

The penultimate chapter, "The Joseph Beuys Drawing," begins abruptly, with Gabriel sobbing in a bathroom. Adrien has died. At the funeral, his friends are stricken. They comfort each other but each seems alone with his or her own painful memories, from his publisher (Jean-Baptiste Malartre), who recounts Adrien's dissatisfaction with his last book and his own shock at attending the funeral, to Lucie, who despite an acrimonious breakup confesses that she always believed that one day Adrien would be back in her life. Later, as a few friends are clearing the apartment, Jérémie (Alex Descas) reveals that Adrien wanted to leave the treasured Beuys drawing to Véra. "But she's just a kid," Jenny protests, proposing that she be given a gold signet ring as a keepsake. In a brief subsequent scene, we see Véra fingering the ring and then taking the drawing from her bag and turning it over. We glimpse the golden-brown stag, looking as if it is about to leap off the screen, before a swift fade to black.

In *L'Heure d'été,* Charles Berling's Frédéric is the Assayas character perhaps most analogous to Gabriel in *Fin août, début septembre:* much as Gabriel chooses to believe that Adrien had his best work in front of him – as he tells a talented, baby-faced writer who idealizes Adrien after having read his unfinished novel – Frédéric cares deeply about the dispersal of his mother's cultural legacy and finds it painfully difficult to move on. On a visit to the Musée d'Orsay, where items from her estate have found a new home, he insists to his wife that a group of vases immured in a vitrine "mean something with flowers, in a living room, in natural light. Otherwise, they're disenchanted, inanimate." The Beuys drawing in *Fin août, début septembre,* which passes like a flame from Adrien to Véra, remains enchanted, mysterious, alive, loved. When Véra reappears in the film's final chapter, titled "Adrien's Presence," two months have passed since Adrien's death. Gabriel, who knows Véra's face only from a photograph, spots her outside a café, apparently in love with a boy her own age. It's a hopeful vision for Gabriel as he is starting on his own path – as Adrien wanted him to – having found the courage to rekindle his romance with Anne and launch his own writing career.

The choice of Beuys is significant: Assayas has remarked that he admires the artist's work, and the way it is "poised between weight and lightness." A similar equilibrium fuels the magic of *Fin août, début septembre.* In Beuys' multivalent work it stems from his emphasis on the power of human emotion and intuition to release energy and creativity from a seemingly obdurate material world. Beuys, as the curator Theodora Vischer has written in an essay on the artist's work in relation to Romanticism, "is able to dissolve the Romantic polarity; he no longer understands mankind as related exclu-

sively to the spiritual and to the afterworld, but also related to matter, time, and reality. Thus his conviction about mankind's capacity for action, which he expressed superbly in his art." *Fin août, début septembre* also emphasizes that capacity. Is Adrien a brilliant novelist? Assayas leaves this question unanswered, and in the end, it doesn't matter.

Although the nature of Adrien's illness is unspecified and plays no role in the narrative, *Fin août, début septembre* also recalls a time when so many vibrant people still in youth or middle age vanished, slipping away in incomprehensible numbers and leaving stunned friends searching for a way to move on. Among them was Serge Daney, who edited Assayas' writing at *Cahiers du cinéma* and was one of the models for Adrien. Like *L'Eau froide* and *L'Heure d'été, Fin août, début septembre* is at once an anxious reflection of its times and a profound affirmation of the beauty of human emotion in cinema. No other Assayas film captures the power of love and art to shepherd us through difficult times with more purity and grace. The Fluxus artist Robert Filliou famously said, "Art is what makes life more interesting than art." In celebrating art, *Fin août, début septembre* privileges life, with all its uncertainties and possibilities of rebirth.

Richard Suchenski

"How Futile Work Is"

The unusual tone of Olivier Assayas' *Les Destinées sentimentales* (2000) is established by its first four shots. Linked by dissolves, they proceed from a distant view of the rural landscape to a closer shot showing a carriage passing through a field behind barbed wire, a high-angle shot of a funeral procession, and finally a shot of the procession from inside the field (once again obstructed by the barbed wire) [Images 1–4]*. With this series, Assayas shows the field from every relevant angle and puts his film in dialogue with the conventions of 1930s cinematic realism as well as nineteenth century French painting – if the first shot suggests the stark desolation of Jean-François Millet's *Paysage d'hiver avec des corneilles* (1866), what follows evokes the Courbet of *Un enterrement à Ornans* (1849). Accompanied only by sounds rooted in this locale (wind, bird calls, the slow undulation of carriage wheels), each shot is held just long enough to establish its own immanent rhythm before the dissolves reorient the eye around a new camera position, creating a paradoxical impression of both immersion and remove. This sensation is reinforced by the crane-like movement of the camera in the third shot, which will recur at other points in the film and seems simultaneously to draw the viewer into the narrative space and to remind them of its constructed nature, emphasizing the century-long gap separating the time of the film's release from the "Winter 1900" moment announced by the first card after the credits. What Pauline Pommerel (Emmanuelle Béart) says later in the film about Barbazac, the fictional town around which both Jacques Chardonne's source novel and Assayas' film adaptation orbit, applies equally to the vantage point of both filmmaker and viewer: "It's like a distant thing, yet close too. It's like the past."

The most chronologically expansive film of Assayas' career, *Les Destinées sentimentales* was also his first experiment with cinematic duration, pointing the way ahead to the five and a half hour *Carlos* (2010). Yet *Carlos* is by design a diffuse film, centered on a self-absorbed personality who, for all his charisma and verve, is unable to grasp the byzantine networks of international power during the Cold War. By contrast, *Les Destinées sentimentales* is a fully

* For all images referred to in the text, see pp. 132–133

Left page:
"Valorizing craft" – "Recovering the dimension of time." Workers at the porcelain factory and factory manager/owner Jean Barnery.

1
2
3
4
5
6
7
8
9
10
11

12

13

14

inhabited epic, closer in spirit to the oneiric enchantment of *Fanny och Alexander* (*Fanny and Alexander*, 1983, Ingmar Bergman) or the sublime reveries of Luchino Visconti's *Ludwig* (1972), a work that shares with Assayas' film the pathos of aesthetic cultivation laid waste by history. As a critic, Assayas championed both films and he pays tribute to Visconti in the moving and revealing detail of an aging Philippe Pommerel (Olivier Perrier) stepping outside the line of dancers early in the first part of *Les Destinées sentimentales* [Images 5–6].[1] Where Don Fabrizio's withdrawal from the ball is the structural and emotional hinge of *Il gattopardo* (Luchino Visconti, 1963), a moment of extended introspection that anticipates the passing of an entire way of life, the single shot of Philippe Pommerel struggling to regain his composure is precisely that, a privileged moment pulled out of a stream that continues to pass, wholly unaffected by his predicament.

Assayas has described his recent work as moving in the direction of heightened brushstrokes.[2] In contemporary thrillers like *demonlover* (2002) and *Boarding Gate* (2007), this takes the forms of visual abstraction through a style of cutting that transforms recognizable urban spaces into delocalized environments, blurring the boundaries between figure and ground to

1) See, for example, Olivier Assayas and Stig Björkman, *Conversation avec Bergman* (Paris: Cahiers du cinéma, 1990), pp. 100–104, and Olivier Assayas, "Autoportrait du cinéaste en despote d'un autre siècle," *Cahiers du cinéma*, no. 350 (August 1983), pp. 4–8

2) Conversation with the author at Yale University in January 2008

the point where characters appear to be floating through ambient surroundings [Image 7]. In his films of the 1990s, "brushwork" was evidenced above all through the gestural movements of the camera and a dynamic control of contingent elements, a kind of calibrated spontaneity that owes as much to the tactics of the Abstract Expressionists and the early Stan Brakhage as it does to the French New Wave. With *Les Destinées sentimentales*, Assayas bridged these two, never entirely discrete, modes, combining stately Cinemascope compositions with handheld camerawork and using crisp editing to create both narrative compression and a constantly shifting rhythm. Whether the camera is passing gracefully through the aisles of a church or mapping out the movement of figures in multiple planes of space, the mise-en-scène is expressive throughout. Nowhere is the fusion of all of these elements more evident than in the continuous shot in which Jean Barnery (Charles Berling) tells Pauline Pommerel that he is going to return to the Limoges porcelain factory, destroying their Swiss idyll: the camera initially follows both characters, struggling to keep them in the frame, and then begins zooming in on Jean, signaling Pauline's shock through a quick jerk over in her direction and back again, before finally moving over to her face as she rises [Images 8–9]. Perfectly synchronized to the emotional arc of the scene, the choreographed camera movement also encapsulates the complex geometry of obligations, desires and relational ties that shapes the "sentimental destinies" of these characters, suggesting both profound intimacy and desperate confinement.

While the staging of Assayas' film frequently has an Ophüls-like elegance, the cutting is subtly elliptical, its evocative power deepened by its understatement. There is, for example, a simple fade to black after Jean and Pauline meet during a brief reprieve in the midst of World War I; the narrative resumes with a shot of Jean in a car, his awkward reacclimation to civilian life economically articulated through two quick lap dissolves and a cut to the site of his new factory. Cuts mark gaps of often indeterminate length after Jean's return, making narrative time more fluid and imbuing the many close-ups of hands, tools, and porcelain pieces with mnemonic resonance [Images 10–11]. Complementing the intensified focus on the manner in which objects are created, transmitted, and used in this section of the film is a more explicit depiction of the shifting economic structures underpinning those creations and transforming a region that had remained relatively stable for centuries.

In making *Les Destinées sentimentales*, Assayas claimed that he wanted to recover "the dimension of time that is now telescoped by technology," and he found a perfect subject in Chardonne's quasi-autobiographical novel.[3] *Les Destinées sentimentales* was originally serialized, like *Madame Bovary*, in *La Revue de Paris*, during the mid-30s period when Chardonne's reputation was at its zenith.[4] Now remembered primarily as one of the more prominent intellectual collaborators during the Occupation, Chardonne was a leading figure of the literary right whose accomodationist stance was motivated more by an obsessive desire to preserve his region's way of life and by what historian Julian Jackson has called "conservative solipsism" than by genuine sympathy with fascist ideology.[5] Although Chardonne spent time in prison for his pro-Vichy writings and activities, *Les Destinées sentimentales* was republished in single volume form three years after the Liberation by Éditions Bernard Grasset and it remains one of his signature works.[6] A reinflection rather than an inversion of the novel, Assayas' film version retains both the distinctive language and the period detail of Chardonne, but the overall effect is markedly different, not least because almost everything depicted in the film has now passed into history.[7]

3) Anne Gayet, "À propos du film d'Olivier Assayas, *Les Destinées sentimentales*, Entretien avec le réalisateur," *Autres Temps: Cahiers d'éthique sociale et politique*, vol. 69, no. 1 (2001), p. 121. Chardonne, born in 1884, came from a Protestant family in the Charente region that, like the fictional Barnerys, was associated with Limoges porcelain (his maternal grandfather started the major American importer Haviland and Company).

4) The serialization began in December 1933 (*La Revue de Paris*, vol. 40, no. 24, pp. 734–765) and ended in January/February 1936 (*La Revue de Paris*, vol. 42, no. 1, 48–71). The three parts were also published as individual books: *La femme de Jean Barnery* (Paris: Éditions Bernard Grasset, 1934), *Pauline* (Paris: Éditions Bernard Grasset, 1934), and *Porcelaine de Limoges* (Paris: Éditions Bernard Grasset, 1936). Chardonne's sense of his literary heritage is embedded in the title of the three-part book, which evokes an idea of sentimentality rooted in the eighteenth century and invites comparison with Flaubert's last completed novel, *L'Éducation sentimentale*.

5) Julian Jackson, *France: The Dark Years, 1940–1944* (Oxford: Oxford University Press, 2001), p. 208

6) In addition to writing a notorious 1940 piece called "L'Été à la Maurie" (originally published in the December 1940 edition of *La Nouvelle Revue Française*, the first issue edited by the openly fascist Drieu La Rochelle, and then reprinted in the book *Chronique privée de l'an 1940*, Paris: Stock, 1941), Chardonne was one of only three authors to participate in both of the two publicity junkets Joseph Goebbels arranged for "European Writers" in Weimar, first in October 1941 and then again in autumn 1942. Chardonne's colleague Georges Blond explained that they went as "guests of Goethe" (Frederick Spotts, *The Shameful Peace*, New Haven: Yale University Press, 2008, p. 47).

7) In his interview with Anne Gayet, Assayas claimed that he wanted to "work as a historian, in order to reconstruct the past without anachronism or tricks that could invade memory" (Gayet, p. 121).

Pauline is willing to risk both deception and economic disaster to see Jean's vision of a new, beautifully crafted dinner service for a transatlantic ocean liner realized, but as the audience knows (and Chardonne could not), these voyages would soon be brought to a halt by the onset of another, even more catastrophic, World War.[8]

Over the course of *Les Destinées sentimentales*, it becomes clear that the mysterious "hope that lies at the center of all things" Jean speaks about is perceptible only from a point of relative isolation, through a temporary withdrawal from the world of public action. Appropriately, both the novel and the film conclude with an act of reading, an experience that evokes the sort of interiority presumed, by Chardonne, to be vanishing in the age of radio, rapid telecommunications, and cinema. While the dialogue in the film's final scene is virtually identical to that in the novel, it is here that Assayas reinterprets his source material most powerfully. Chardonne has Jean tell Pauline that the passage being read is a text by Paul Valéry "from an old issue of *Revue de Paris*:"

"An Italian gardener scrapes the ground with a sleepy rake. Suddenly, he speaks in his dialect. His words ring out in the midday silence and blend with the distinctive sound of his rake turning the gravel. He seems to say: 'How futile work is!'"[9]

Chardonne does not, however, explain that he is selectively paraphrasing a letter from Valéry to Valery Larbaud that includes charged allusions to "stray torpedo boats" and "dead islands" just after the "sleepy rake."[10] By explicitly citing Valéry while excising the Symbolist evocation of wartime trauma from his quotation, Chardonne is able to connect his practice as a realist novelist to the literary tradition embodied, for him as for Jean, by his illustrious predecessor. In the film version of *Les Destinées sentimentales*, Valéry's name is referenced only through a brief shot of the journal in which his

8) The irony is deepened if the unnamed transatlantic vessel for which the service is commissioned is meant to be the SS Normandie, a new deluxe liner filled with Art Deco furnishings that was launched in 1932 and made its first voyage in 1935 (shortly before Chardonne published the third part of *Les Destinées sentimentales*). The flagship of the CGT line and the most prestigious French ship of the era, it was seized by the Americans after the Fall of France (who renamed it the USS Lafayette) and was decommissioned after catching fire at the New York Passenger Terminal.

9) Jacques Chardonne, *Les Destinées sentimentales* (Paris: Éditions Bernard Grasset, 1947), p. 510

10) Valery Larbaud, "Paul Valéry," *La Revue de Paris*, vol. 36, no. 5 (March 1, 1929), p. 60. Larbaud describes the passage as an excerpt from a letter sent by Valéry to the author several years earlier from a "small town on the French Riviera."

letter was published, visible through the sort of attentiveness that contemporary cinema so often works against, and the quotation evokes a now-broken cultural chain, deepening the underlying implications of the poet's words [Image 12].[11]

In this context, it is difficult not to see Jean as a surrogate for a film director, managing the labor of dozens of staff in a variety of related fields and using industrial means to create an aesthetic object whose refinement extends the achievements of previous generations. The valorization of craft in *Les Destinées sentimentales* – evidenced by the many shots of employees working ardently to give their products the right balance of functionality and sensibility and in the delicacy with which the resulting objects are treated throughout – is given added meaning by the fact that the film was released at a moment when digital filmmaking and distribution were rapidly gaining traction, making celluloid seem as fragile as porcelain. Assayas and cinematographer Éric Gautier arranged nearly every shot to emphasize the particularities of natural light at different times of day, and its reflection off the surface of porcelain baths functions as both a metaphor for photographic development and a mirror for the projected light that gives life to these fragmented images [Image 13]. What gives them perceptual coherence is the Bressonian use of precise and distinct sounds to connect domestic spaces to exteriors that are created largely in the viewer's imagination. Assayas reflexively demonstrates this process in the final scene, representing Jean's interior point of view through a sudden cut, just before he asks Pauline to read to him, to a shot of a gardener raking stones [Image 14]. While the position of the camera makes it clear that the gardener could not possibly be seen by Jean at that moment, the uninterrupted sound covers the disjuncture, linking the ceaseless momentum of time to the hermetic spaces of memory.

11) Although the words used are identical to those found on the final page of Chardonne's novel and the journal "read" by Pauline in the film is indeed *La Revue de Paris*, it appears to be a slightly different issue, as the title of the article is visible as "Carnets" by Paul Valéry rather than "Paul Valéry" by Valery Larbaud. Assayas' decision to use this issue makes Valéry's name more visible and also expands the reference by implicitly associating the words in the film with the poet's famous notebooks, an extraordinarily lucid account of his intellectual activity that he worked on daily until his death in 1945.

B. Kite

STOP STOP START AGAIN

I liked *demonlover* a great deal when it came out, though "like" now seems a strange term to use in relation to a movie of such determined nastiness. But in fact the nastiness was part of the appeal, one felt tough-minded for liking it, for being willing to follow its cycle of torture down to the bottom basement (though the bottom basement turned out to be illusory – the one we reached seemed to have been grown in a culture). And the movie was and is seductive in a certain sense, even queasily sexy in a pasty way, like porn under fluorescent tubing. Perhaps sexiest of all was its aura of standing alone at the hard edge of the now. Together with the lengthy, impassioned interview Mark Peranson conducted with Assayas after the film's Cannes premiere, *demonlover* seemed both diagnosis of the moment and herald of bleak tomorrows. Aligning oneself with it felt brave. The air was cold but we were seeing clearly.

I no longer feel I'm standing with *demonlover*, but then I don't really feel I'm standing anywhere, so I could be standing in it for all I know. At any rate, this will be an exercise in ambivalence and less an essay than an excavation, an attempt to dig out fragments of the piece I would have written 8 years ago, to see if I can dwell again for a while in those attitudes, and then a brief measurement of distance from that point to this.

A CARTOON HISTORY OF CINEMA

In the beginning was the shot, and the shot was sufficient. The first filmmakers placed their camera alongside the stream of the world, a flow of action that neither began nor terminated within the frame, as if aspiring to the humility of a window. The cut emerged under cover of darkness, a magician's secret incision within the static frame which allowed covert incursions – the removal or substitution of a body or object, fantastic changes in scale. The effectiveness of these tricks largely depended on the audience's willingness to believe that movies were less a recorded event than a parallel world that opened briefly, lived a mayfly moment, then vanished. One was offered glimpses of a continuum, but the continuum itself was presumably sacrosanct, or at least resistant to alteration.

Query: Is it significant that it's at this point, in these films, and through these hidden entrances that demons emerge into cinema, scampering out of boxes, springing to now hardened edges of the frame, planting smoke, doubles, absence in their wake? And if so, does that make edits the original evil in this telling?

Response: Possibly but not necessarily. This may be a gnostic gospel. E.g.:

Within the shot, incident formed, first singly, then in short, discrete chains that gradually

knotted into clumps: a rumpus of incident that carried the seed of story. And as the shot absorbed the seed, it conceived another shot as mirror to itself, and then yet a third, as extension, and then a fourth, as token of endless propagation. And the offspring cried with a single voice, and this wordless cry voiced through implication the two eternal questions of cinema: First, How to link one space with another? And then, How to move inside a single space and, so doing, position figures in the frame that they might shade into depth and assume agency?

Query: I just realized: This isn't much of a cartoon.

Response: No, I decided to make it a myth of origin, sorry. Maybe it's sort of a bible cartoon? Well I'll try something else.

Spaces stacked next to spaces, fixed blocks of space connected only by a thin trajectory of action. Then twinned actions causing the blocks to alternate, overthrowing the continuum of world-time in favor of other continua shaped by the machine. Breaking into the blocks to bring forth individual faces, gestures, rudiments of psychology. Using the figures in turn as points of identification through which to carve additional paths through and between spaces. This is a very tidy telling.

THE EYE BEHIND THE EYE

Fritz Lang's contributions to these evolving strategies (to individuate characters, to transmit information, to navigate space) are as significant as those of any of the names I failed to mention in the previous section. He cinched the techniques together into a coherent, flexible network of narration – one that doubled and expanded the communication technologies of his time and forecasted those of ours. He pieced together an elegant operating system and then made it paranoid by introducing a virus, codenamed Mabuse.

But who or what is Mabuse? The title of the first Mabuse film, a fairly close adaptation of a novel by Norbert Jacques, tells us that he is a *Spieler* – a gambler, actor, player, gamer. And the first shot of the film blends all these meanings: a handful of photos arrayed as playing cards. Each card depicts the same face under a different disguise, each disguise denoting a profession and a particular niche in the class hierarchy. Mabuse, who holds the cards, stands outside of all these. His power springs from a practical realization of the irrational underpinnings of every organizational structure. He's able to game the system because he understands the arbitrariness of the rules.

The sequence that follows, which has no counterpart in the novel, puts its counters in place before calling them into action. What links Mabuse in his study, the interior of a train compartment, a briefcase, a car idling on a dirt road, a telephone lineman perched on a pole? The round face of a pocketwatch. Mabuse stares at his as though it were a portal allowing free passage into any point in space, enabling him to see every operational step of the action-mechanism he has devised and set running. And rhymed with an iris, the watch face becomes a portal for the viewer as well, and an emblem for the editing principles of abstract connection that Lang introduced here. Every thriller from then to now carries Mabuse in its DNA.

[FOOTNOTE: The communication systems of modernity may have guided film form from the very beginning, since some of the first parallel edits, e.g. in Griffith's *The Lonely Villa* (1909), were either justified by or created in response to the still fairly new invention of the telephone, which for the first time allowed people to speak to one another in utter ignorance of their interlocutor's surroundings, effectively creating a nebulous interim zone for bodiless communication. That worrying little crack in consciousness, this new notion of a plastic and pliable space, found its reflection in film, which was able to bridge the divide with a splice. Movies could scratch a metaphysical itch by showing each speaker's environment but in doing so they created a precedent for linking incongruent spaces of all kinds, with or without the crutch of the telephone. I've often wondered how human consciousness shifted through exposure to these new ways of perceiving. For example, if one were able to study the entire history of human dreaming in some akashic library, would the turn of the 20th century mark a revolution in the dream vocabulary? Or, alternately, might the modes of editing themselves have emerged in shadowed response to some freedom of movement that has always been ours in sleep?]

The opening sequence of *Mabuse* is built around the theft of a document, a commercial treaty, and given the importance such documents, objects, clues, secrets have in Lang's oeuvre, it's worth briefly noting how this one differs from Hitchcock's definition of the "Macguffin" as an object of no importance in itself which nonetheless drives the plot forward. It's true that the treaty's contents are of only secondary interest to Mabuse, but nonetheless the document is crucial to his plan to game the stock market due to the place it holds in its system. It's a packet of information traveling an expected route within the financial network. Its removal from the network creates a vacuum, which in turn causes investor panic and a sharp price drop, so Mabuse buys. It is later restored, apparently inviolate, leading to a rise in prices and an opportunity for Mabuse to ditch the stock and make a hefty profit.

Hitchcock learned a great deal from Lang, but the apparent proximity and actual distance of the treaty from the Macguffin illustrates a central divergence in their interests. Hitchcock was, among other things, devoted to finding new modes of subjectivity in cinema, to creating new psychologies of looking, so the Macguffin assumes practical significance primarily as plot motor, for the effect it has on the characters and the situations it leads them into (this is a little oversimplified, since it also takes on metaphysical resonance as "the container of the secret"). In his German films, Lang by contrast is less interested in individuals than systems.

BIG FACE, BLANK ROOM

Lang, in later years, told Lotte Eisner of a different opening for *Dr. Mabuse, der Spieler*, a prologue to the prologue:

a brief, breathless montage of scenes from the Spartacus uprising, the murder of Rathenau, the Kapp putsch and other violent moments of recent history. Lang maintains that when it first opened this sequence was intact. [...] Originally, Lang recalls, the opening montage was linked to [the extant opening] by two titles: the first:

'WHO IS BEHIND ALL THIS?'

The second title, a single word that rushed toward the spectator, growing and growing until it filled the entire screen:

'I'

Tom Gunning, whose book on Lang is the source of this quotation, doubts this scene ever existed, noting that Rathenau was assassinated two months after the first part of *Spieler* opened. But let's pretend for a moment that the sequence *does* exist. What exactly does it do? For one thing, it offers a tidy encapsulation of the primary hermeneutic behind every thriller, the question they ask and the answer they typically give. You could tell it this way, as a fairy tale:

At the center of the maze of the world, in a blank grey room, there hangs a face that is the source of mystery. If the maze can be navigated, the room broached, and the face recognized and restored to its body, webs of malign power shrink to a point, and that point can be conquered.

Or you could tell it this way, as Assayas does in the Peranson interview, speaking of mid-90s thrillers such as *Enemy of the State* and *Conspiracy Theory*:

Dr. Mabuse, der Spieler (1922)

"A lot of Hollywood genre films, action films, start off very ambitious, like something that involves the whole universe, something metaphysical, and they end up with two people having a fist-fight in a warehouse."

Lang's description of the sequence is indicative of the extra-fictional impulse just under the surface of these films, the urge to create a fiction that would explain or perhaps embody the hidden order of the world. This urge finds only slightly tamer expression in *Spieler* as it stands, notably in that prologue, which makes Mabuse the hidden mover behind the drunken swings the German stock market was already enduring and which seems to predict the more precarious swings that would follow. The first half of *Spieler* is subtitled "A Portrait of the Times," and Lang seems during this period to have been sufficiently weird / silly / inspired to believe this, to imagine his films as the channel for some literal zeitgeist.

But for the Mabuse-thoughtform to fully emerge, the Mabuse-figure had to recede, could no longer be located in Klein-Rogge's stocky torso and frenzied bulldog jowls. Lang makes a stride toward such abstraction in *Spione*, where the face that answers the question is itself disguised, but only fully achieves it in *Das Testament des Dr. Mabuse*. There the primary hermeneutic sprawls into a baroque, sparking network of messages lost in transit and spiraling in closed circuit until they can be delivered (too late), of questions asked under mistaken auspices and hidden answers, or lies, or answers that only become apparent in retrospect and through a shift of focus. It's the first instance of what I've elsewhere called the machine-film, in which the movie itself seems a sort of artificial intelligence that's been set up to process a certain set of data, of images and sounds, and grinds away to some terminal point of stillness and futility.

Lang's last film, *Die 1000 Augen des Dr. Mabuse*, solidifies a pattern already nascent in *Testament*, a split level of operation which allows it to achieve some form of conventional closure while still projecting its metaphors beyond the bounds of the reel, the screen, and the time of its making. Basically it boils down to a split between the Mabuse system, which is protean, and the Mabuse placeholder, who is bound to a face. The latter can be caught but the former is uncatchable, unkillable, and continues to evolve outside the frame in relation to new technologies and new social paradigms. But the system itself carries out a curious double movement: Each stage in its progressive abstraction is effected by means of technologies which extend its reach further into our shared reality. The thousand eyes of *1000 Augen* are of course video cameras, which literalize the omniscience already suggested by the opening sequence of *Spieler* way back in 1922. But the *Spieler*-Mabuse was something of a supervillain, with powers of persuasion and mental infiltration that verged on the occult. Such abilities are no longer required of those who later take up temporary residence in the role. Mabuse steps between centuries by virtue of a paradox: the ghostlier he becomes, the more real he is.

But one hanging question remains –

WHAT DOES MABUSE WANT?

It isn't easy to answer. The films offer a variety of suggestions, but Mabuse always seems to slither somewhere beyond them. Many of his machinations in *Spieler* are geared toward rigging the market, but that game has already begun to pall. As he later tells Countess Told, "There is only one thing that is interesting anymore. Playing with people and the destinies of people." In his next outing, his stated (transmitted) goal is to "spread terror" in the service of inaugurating a new regime: "When chaos has become supreme law, then the time will have come for the empire of crime." The notion of subverting order in the service of instituting a new order of disorder seems itself paradoxical, especially since crime, practically speaking, only stands as a distinct category in relation to law.

It's perhaps equivalent to the curious passage in *From Caligari to Hitler* in which Siegfried Kracauer, writing on *Das Cabinet des Dr. Caligari*, asserts that the circle, which one might imagine to be the sign of harmony and containment, is in fact the emblem of chaos. Mabuse travels on the axis between chaos and tyranny, an archetype of control and un-freedom that lands as a parasite then spreads as a virus, first feeding undetected on the body politic then gradually overtaking its operations. As such, Klein-Rogge in *Spieler* might be better regarded as patient zero rather than prime mover, an idea reinforced by his barely-carnate appearance in *Testament*, a bony transcription apparatus tuned to the beyond.

HE BECOMES THE WORLD

The name Mabuse is never spoken in *demonlover*. It wouldn't surprise me if Lang's films played no part in Assayas' thinking during its making. But I set up this laborious scaffold because *demonlover* alone seems to me to extend the systems Lang set in motion and to carry them to what seems for the moment like a terminal point.

It implicitly proposes the basic question of every thriller – Who is responsible for all this? – but there's no longer a face to be found at the center of the maze, not even a placeholder. Maybe not even a maze, since the relations between camera and world seem here to have undergone a mirror reversal from the Edenic moment hypothesized in the Cartoon History. Spaces glow and narrow to a plane, a window smear, as if flickering on the verge of the virtual. Mabuse has ceased to be a parasite, he is now the dominant system itself and no more to be named or questioned than we would question the air. The Empire of Crime has arrived and it's indistinguishable from what the shills at *BusinessWeek* used to call "the New Economy." In a climate without love or loyalty, every one can take their turn as the doctor in the pursuit of power, and indeed must do to fuel the machine that feeds indiscriminately on their triumphs and tragedies. In *demonlover*, the machine spits out spectacle. The Mabuse of the *Spieler* prologue was an orchestrator of spectacle across time and space and the telling of the movie molded itself to his omniscience (not for nothing is the figure frequently identified with a film director). *demonlover* saves its nearest candidate for a Mabuse placeholder for the end: it's any-kid-with-a-credit-card. The Blank Room is now explicitly the place of torture, and it can be located anywhere so long as it maintains its Web address.

demonlover begins, like *Spieler*, like a thousand movies and TV shows since, with the theft of a briefcase, a commercial contract. The head of the violated company later says that it isn't the loss of the files themselves that's important, they have backup, but the message the theft sends, a message that must boil down to "We have seen the inside of your operations, you are vulnerable." Karen, the carrier of the briefcase, who was drugged and locked in a car trunk for three days, compares the experience to rape. Perhaps it is so in a corporate sense as well. Because *demonlover*'s central players are corporations, those placeless entities, accountable to no one save their shareholders, which have been granted the legal status of "person" in much of the Western world. For the first half of the movie, we're offered an assortment of grunt's-eye views in the titanic battle between Mangatronics, Volf, and demonlover.com but they're revealed to be three faces of the same beast as the film centers itself on Diane, a double agent who operates unknowing in a nest of double agents. By the end, she's become the equivalent of Kent in *Testament*, a former minion looking for a way out of the blank room. But there's no longer any outside, her escape becomes part of the spectacle and her return loops the action, a cycle of pain and degradation with no exit or off-switch.

[FOOTNOTE: I've heard people complain that the movie falls apart at the end but that criticism has never made sense to me. Nothing happens in the last 20 minutes that couldn't be explained within the terms of the preceding 90, it's just that the film has jettisoned exposition, become a sort of clip reel of highlights, chases, explosions, like the combustive in-flight entertainment we glimpse at the beginning, running unseen over sleeping passengers. It sometimes seems that ambitious thrillers (loosely defined as those that don't end with a fist-fight in a warehouse) can end in one of two ways: eternal return or abrupt termination. *demonlover* opts for the second while implying the first.]

A portrait of the times, yes. *demonlover* feels like a caffeine headache. When the image isn't hanging back in security-cam remove to survey cityscapes or hotel lobbies it's scuttering in that handheld agitation that a decade or more of TV and movie thrillers have entrenched as the signifier of artificed immediacy, always almost too late to capture the decisive action. It's most at home under artificial light, or else light too cold to be comfortable (I've never seen a film with a better handle on the too-bright, too-soon light of airplane dawn. But in general Assayas is great with air travel, his plane scenes revealing by contrast what a weird and phony set of representations we've come to accept in other films for this fairly common experience. Assayas' cabins are never really comfortable, you feel their chill dead air). And *demonlover* is a rarity in that it seems to aspire to video flatness, a tidy corollary to the movie's notion of a world deleting its density in order to push everything to surface: the pixillation of cities behind rain-spotted glass, ghosts of interiority still haunting reflected faces.

For all the sex conducted, bartered, consumed, aborted in the course of the film, alienation from the body is the starting condition for its characters. They wear their bodies as they wear their faces – rigidly, as armour – since, in this world, to open oneself emotionally is to risk losing control of one's own avatar, expose it to the potential infiltration of alien others. The irony here, which is the film's principal motor, is that the spreading surface-world is obsessed with the interior and is forever restaging that fundamental paradox of pornography: the wish to be inside another while remaining forever locked out, which accounts for the strange rituals of porn, in which coitus can never be completed and male performers have to pull out in order to offer their climax to the camera. Unlike *Testament*, which shuffles its images and sequences into discrete data packets, *demonlover* isn't a machine film, it's a film of (jagged, frustrated) flow, that liquid Internet time of distracted attentions that gave rise to the metaphor of surfing the Web. If the notion of screening *demonlover* through Lang is at all useful to anyone, the question arises as to where Mabuse could possibly go from here. And I have no idea.

END DIG, BEGIN WAFFLE

That's basically the piece I would have written eight years ago. I was at the time I first saw *demonlover* undergoing one of my periodic bouts of Mabuse-obsession, but I still find that that framework encompasses a lot of what I find interesting about the film. But I'm much less excited by it than I was then (in fact, to be honest, I approached the task of rewatching the movie with a fair amount of dread). So what's changed?

I do still enjoy thinking about Mabuse from time to time but those movies are able to roll cleanly through my mind, as idea-structures, in a way *demonlover* can't and won't. Some of that is because Lang's plots in the Mabuse movies are sufficiently pulpy and his characters sufficiently thin that the notions of control that run through them carry little emotional affect.

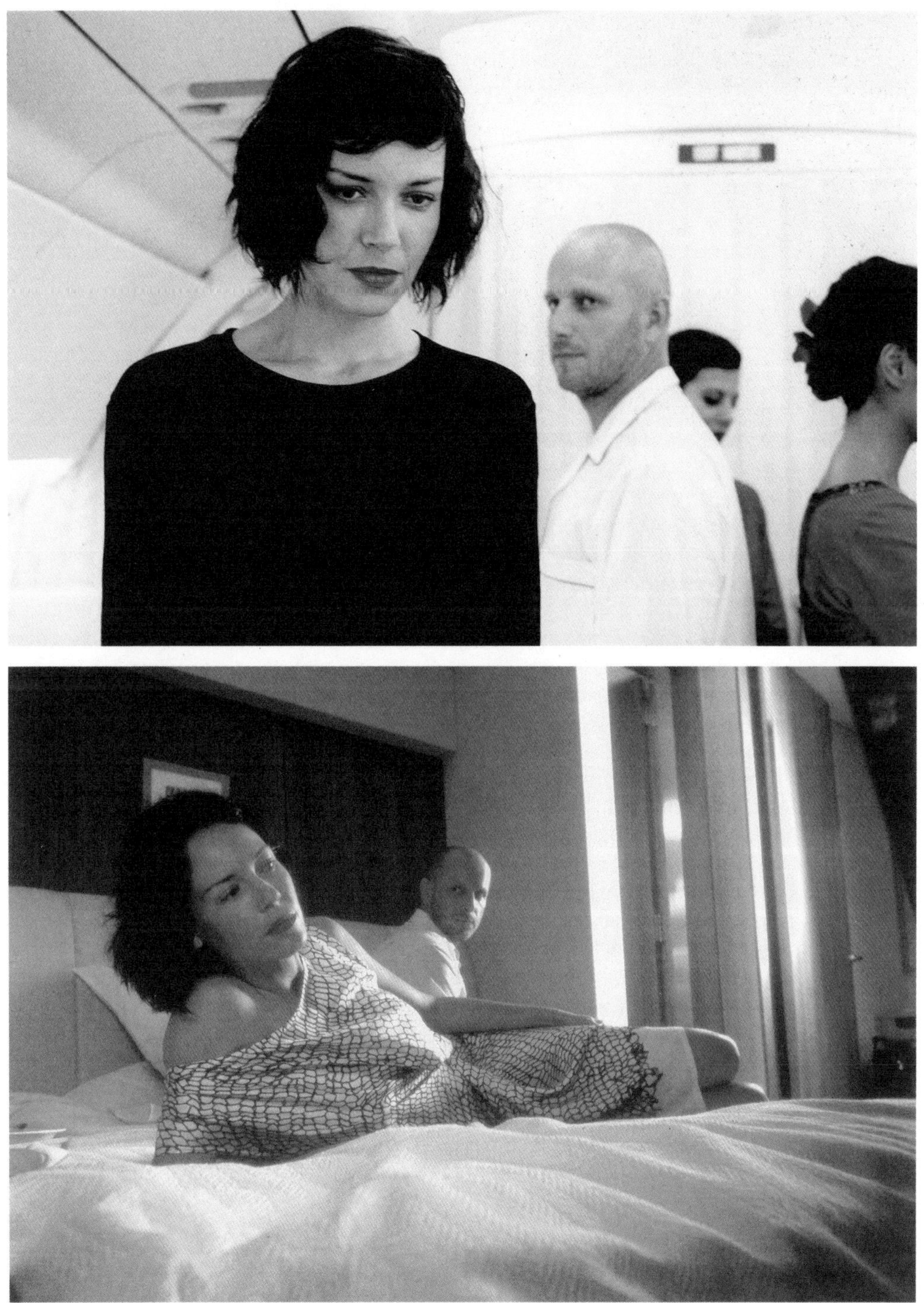

demonlover contains a fair amount of pulp as well, but at least one character, Diane, does begin to assume some depth. But only as she's broken, because in the world of the film sensation is always available but feeling is well buried, and to feel at all is to feel pain.

The Mabuse paradigm was always predicated on pain and violence, and it might be a failing in Lang's films that they remain so diagramatic. The attentive reader will note that I've avoided the equation of Mabuse and the Nazis. It's a connection that makes me uncomfortable because to take it literally renders the films flimsy and silly, so great is their distance from actual horror, while to take it metaphorically, as I'm inclined, makes the Nazis seem one stage in the evolution of the Mabuse system, an idea it would be something worse than silly to argue. My very debatable instinct is that the Lang of this early German period was brilliantly intuitive but not very self-conscious or reflective. I think he sensed a current of the time – his own demon lover – and gave it form through the materials of his imagination, which happened to contain rather a lot of snakes and trap doors.

Assayas says in one of the *demonlover* DVD extras that he considers it "more a poetic film than a theoretical film." If that's the case it seems to me he rhymes in theses, since the movie never touches those uncanny undercurrents one finds for example in Lang or Lynch and indeed seems smart and self-aware to a nearly programmatic extent in its basic take on its larger themes. This may be me imposing a predetermined and too-rigid understanding on top of it, though. Certainly the film has the courage of its unpleasantness, trailing its tropes to their darkest root. I guess part of what bugs me about it now is a sense that the movie grooves on its own callousness. Of course I base this in large part on my own memory of grooving to what I perceived as its callousness on my initial viewings.

There's something sour, almost *Funny Games*-esque, in the notion of a movie that offers thriller come-ons and pays them off with "real" (big quotes) torture. But *demonlover* doesn't feel sour and Assayas is much savvier than Haneke in this respect. Haneke said the people who walked out of *Funny Games* "didn't need it," implying it was a necessary medicinal corrective for those who stayed, but the only fans of the movie I've encountered are youngish males who pride themselves on their ability to tolerate extreme depictions of violence. It's an appetite they speak of as a trial, as if watching hard-core torture porn were a new rite of passage on the hard road to manhood. They're basically the kid at the end of *demonlover*, but if any of them felt at all "implicated" by that scene they kept it to themselves – most of them loved *demonlover* too.

Taking Haneke at his word makes *Funny Games* look pretty stupid. *demonlover* isn't stupid, Assayas knows his audience better than Haneke knows his, but there's something that makes me queasy in that knowingness. The movie is aware that any attempt to "subvert" the cultural relish for the spectacle of torture will only feed back into it, knows that the harder-edged it appears in its critique the more titillating it will become in certain subcultures, but it still includes that last scene as a prophylactic, or a way of keeping some rhetorical distance from the very rhetoric it's engaged for the last 90 minutes (and I don't even want to touch that genetics book and DNA model, which sure look like a way for the movie to hedge even its own late-blooming moralism by ascribing the blame to...what, the human animal?) Well it worked on me. I walked out of *Funny Games* (guess I didn't need it) but saw *demonlover* three times before it found an American distributor (so I guess I needed something).

Pasolini famously described *Salò* as his attempt to create an "indigestible" movie. It has since been digested, but I'd still credit that movie with a kind of coherence that I feel *demonlover* lacks, in its apparent desire to be at once indigestible and seductive. Yet I keep saying the movie is smart and I think it largely is (even its incoherences seem knowing), but maybe its area of inside knowledge is a bit narrower than it appeared. At least I now find myself drawing distinctions between subjects the film seems to know well (porn, blockbusters) and subjects it seems to only posture at knowing (anime, video games, maybe aspects of the Internet).

Query: You admit that Lang and Assayas employ some of the same starting materials, and that perhaps Assayas may be serving them more accurately by making them if not indigestible at least harder to swallow?

Answer: Yes, that's certainly possible, just as it's possible that my viewing may be more in line with the film's intent now that I kind of can't stand it. Honestly, I think it's a really interesting movie, which I'll probably never watch again.

Nick Pinkerton

Better to Fade Away

Time and again, Olivier Assayas has brought his camera to a party. There is the travelling hash-pipe moving to the rhythm of "Knockin' On Heaven's Door" in *L'Eau froide*, the dinner gathering that centerpieces *Irma Vep*, the wheeling tracking shots trying to keep up with the teenagers' estate-house blowout in *L'Heure d'été*, beautiful evocations of the experience of being part of (or, in the case of *Irma Vep*, apart from) the party-organism.

Clean is not a party movie. It's a morning-after movie, a movie about what happens when everyone's gone and you have to start picking up, alone. The film opens with musician Lee Hauser (James Johnston) and his wife, Emily (Maggie Cheung), arriving in Hamilton, Canada, where Lee is booked the following night. There is no sense of being young and hungry on tour, getting in the van for the first time, seeing new cities with wide eyes, meeting new friends and new girls, happy just to be crashing on floors. Lee is a road-worn rocker, punching the clock, and he's on heroin. Emily is a scag-hag, with a reputation in the music press akin to Courtney Love's in 1994. They are driving a sedan that's at least fifteen years old, and Lee, at forty-two, is doing a stopover show *in Hamilton*.

Lee and Emily do some glad-handing at the club, where the band Metric play their jaundiced tour-diary anthem "Dead Disco" ("Overnight to London / Touch down, look around / Everyone's the same"), an acerbic commentary on the cosmopolitan hipster trade-routes which *Clean*, shot in Canada, London, Paris, and San Francisco, follows. Emily fights with Vernon (Don McKellar), with whom she contentiously shares the duties of managing Lee – although it's not clear if Emily actually does anything other than score them dope. Lee and Emily bring the argument over the state of his career back to their motel room, a scene detail-perfect down to the bathroom-sink beers (Johnston is a former member of Nick Cave and the Bad Seeds, and carries the weight of a life-on-tour in his slouch.) He insists he's capable of doing better work. She jumps on him for implying that she's holding him back – almost certainly true, judging from this harridan performance – before storming out to shoot up by herself on the banks of Lake Ontario.

We may think we know where this movie goes from here. The troubled artist confronts his demons, claws his way back from the brink of the abyss, triumphs over adversity against all expectation, and comes away from the journey with an album's worth of great songs of experience – see for reference 2009's *Crazy Heart* (which also has a missing-child panic scene). But

when Emily gets back to the hotel the next morning, she finds her husband, her meal ticket, the cornerstone of her identity, and our potential tortured-artist hero, OD'd and dead. Avoidance of the expected is, in this film, to be expected.

Regarding where *Clean* goes next, a line from John Waters' *Cecil B. Demented* comes to mind: "Before I started doing drugs, I had so many problems. Now I only have one. Drugs. I have a focus now." Emily has lost that focus when she returns to the world after six months in prison for possession, a stay entirely elided by the movie. She gets out to find no-one waiting for her. Then she remembers that she has a little boy, Jay (James Dennis), who's staying with Lee's parents, Albrecht and Rosemary (Nick Nolte and Martha Henry), in Vancouver. Her addict's monomania now replaced by a welter of everyday complications, Emily begins re-orienting her energies toward a role that she's never really played: mother. Albrecht provides the emotional carrot-on-a-stick for Emily's rehab; he has her kid, and doesn't intend to let her see the boy until she gets it together. When Albrecht and Jay come to London with Rosemary so that she can undergo cancer treatment, Emily, trying to begin again in Paris, starts petitioning to be in Jay's life.

Assayas elides a lot of elements which would be emotional paydirt for most directors, histrionic buffets for actors. Depicting actual drug-usage, *Clean* is as discreet as *Requiem for a Dream* is gruesome (there is one scene in which Emily and some friends discover a dead junkie and set about cleaning out his apartment, a ritual more somber and funerary than sensational.) When Lee's parents receive news of his death, shorthand images of their reactions convey the whole: Nolte stunned in his study, Henry wandering in a daze across the yard in overhead long-shot with Nolte behind her, as though she might make the news untrue if she could escape its bearer. Assayas' cinema is a tissue of fleeting impressions from moving vantage points, giving us passing glimpses of characters – Jay trundling out of his hotel room alone to buy comics from a London newsstand, a wild spat between a lesbian couple – and then allowing us to infer the whole picture on our own. DP Éric Gautier's seemingly incidental, whisking camerawork lends Emily's decision to tear up her methadone prescription no more compositional significance than the moment when she swipes her bus pass. When Emily admits to her son what she's denied to everyone else – that she bought the drugs that killed her husband – the moment is given no build-up, is

so casual you could almost miss it. Which is not to say that the movie lacks gravitas. "Change," a word that keeps cropping up in *Clean*, doesn't just happen; it's an ongoing scrabble of backslides and humiliations, little moments which the film endows with a visceral impact. When, in one precisely-edited scene, spaced-out Emily face-plants during a waitressing shift, you jolt as though she'd just been stabbed.

"People change," Albrecht says, "If they need to, they change." Would Emily's sense of maternal responsibility have been awakened without the spur of tragedy? Is she a "good person deep down," or just obeying necessity? Such value judgments are left to the viewer. Assayas, more pragmatist than moralist, is interested in watching *how* she gets by, and the process by which lines of communication open – between Emily and Albrecht, the father of the man in whose death she was complicit, who is now facing his wife's illness and sees in Emily someone who has lost her own mate; between Emily and Jay, the son she barely knows. Nolte, who stepped in late to replace an ailing Alan Bates, gives a discreet, tender performance, his words carefully negotiating the creaking instrument of his voice, mindful not to kick around too much gravel (in contrast to many filmmakers in the last decade-plus, Assayas casts Nolte for his

abashed nobility, not for his picturesque dilapidation). Cheung embodies, through every step of her character's rehabilitation, an obliterated woman piecing her life and her personality back together from salvaged fragments, as if starting over after a house fire. She is almost forty in the film and allowed to look it, until she tidies up her nest of hair, and a new alertness creeps in behind the methadone blur.

This straight-ahead character study seems traditional when compared to its immediate predecessor in Assayas' filmography, the cold, corporate-park nightmare of *demonlover*, but these two continent-hopping films have more in common than a quick glance might suggest, both being concerned with entertainment production and distribution mechanisms: Manga porn in *demonlover*, rock music in *Clean*. Assayas loves music – his next project was a documentary of the Festival Art Rock in Saint-Brieuc – even as he acknowledges the grinding economic facts of the business. With *Clean*, Assayas looks at pop as both a manufactured commodity and an art medium, as he looked at cinema in *Irma Vep* (the attraction/repulsion dialectic in those films is not present in *demonlover*, hence that film's gelid quality).

Music is an industry in *Clean*, but it's also the movie's heartbeat, essential to Emily's destruction and to her recovery. The film uses, sparingly, music by Brian Eno – most prominently "An Ending (Ascent)," "Spider & I," "Stars," and "Taking Tiger Mountain" – and when it immerses the soundtrack, it feels like warm, healing liquid rushing in through a sluice. Emily has also recorded her own music, shopping around a demo made during her time in prison. One character, hearing the songs on which Emily hopes to launch her new career, gives an honest appraisal – "Not good, not bad. Like a lot of other stuff." This isn't inaccurate, but the idea here isn't to show the budding of genius. Making music is, for Emily, a way to reconstruct a sense of self that still allows her to stand outside of straight life – a tough and true representation of the role that art can play in shoring up a breached identity.

Beyond playing as a kick-the-habit drama – though it is that, and a rare, stoic example of its type – *Clean* has elements of marketplace tragedy, a kind-of rock biz *New Grub Street* (I almost wrote "21st century rock biz," but there is much here that already seems antique, like the dickering over CD reissues.) The business-end of things is frequently spoken of and seen to here: We deal with the settling of Lee's debts through property sales, Emily's hustling for jobs back in Paris, the repackaging of Lee's

discography after the funeral ("[He's] worth a lot more dead than alive," notes Vernon, breaking down Lee's post-mortem upswing to Emily, "It was on the cover of *Mojo*"). And though Assayas either breaks up or ignores potentially big scenes, he always pauses to count his character's change. Transaction is the movie's hidden-on-the-surface theme, the camera, as in *demonlover*, watching the movement of Canadian dollars, Euros, and pounds with the assiduous attention Robert Bresson brought to the circulation of money in *L'Argent*.

No filmmaker working today is as acutely aware of the daunting gulfs of generational difference as Assayas. "Kids intimidate me," Albrecht notes to his wife, "Because they understand everything." It might better reflect Assayas' view to say that they understand different things; when I spoke to the director in 2008 during his press tour for *Boarding Gate*, he noted that "Every single time I have to discuss meaning or the dramatic logic of my films, it's always with older viewers. Younger audiences are accustomed to a completely different logic in terms of moving inside images and films, and I think they move using more poetic connections. And the disturbing factor is, I'm not sure if this is good or bad." A similar ambivalence toward the changes in cultural perception, the gains and losses that occur in the passing between generations, is at the heart of heritage films like *Les Destinées sentimentales* and *L'Heure d'été*; the business of rock is *Clean*'s business, and the movie shows a great understanding of pop history's sedimentary layers.

Premiering at Cannes, 2004, where Cheung won a deserved Best Actress prize, it was a couple of years before *Clean* received a cursory release in the States. Considering the vintage of its musical guest-stars, you might think it had been shot in 1997. Tricky, here appearing as a friend of Lee's who Emily petitions for help in her efforts to regain custody of Jay, is several years past his NME Album of the Year heyday. Emily gets a response to her demos from a producer, David Roback of Mazzy Star, who last charted in the mid-90s (a character in the film has to think a bit before saying, "I remember Mazzy Star"). These points of reference place Lee and Emily within an older generation – for pop is always a young man's game – several paces behind the perpetual new class of Next Big Things. It emerges in the course of the film that Emily once had a bit of niche celebrity herself, when she hosted an MTV-time clip show, for which she's periodically recognized. Sandrine (Laetitia Spigarelli), the twentyish personal assistant of Jeanne Balibar's television exec, is impressed as though meeting an elder stateswoman; later, Emily interviews with a schlubby department store manager with a bad comb-over who recalls watching her program: "It was my generation," he remembers, before elevator doors shut on them like a closing coffin.

A 2010 retrospective of Assayas' films at the Brooklyn Academy of Music was titled "Post-Punk Auteur." This indicates Assayas' own era of pop-cultural identification – he was born in 1955 – and his hip musicophilia, but it also hints at something deeper about his art. For as much as the post-punk period had to find a future beyond The Sex Pistols' "No Future," Assayas confronted a post-New Wave French film culture that frequently resembled a cul-de-sac of despair – the 1994 suicide of Guy Debord, the suicide-fixated oeuvre of Philippe Garrel, Bresson's deathtrip *Le Diable probablement*, Jean Eustache's cautionary-tale life and death. Assayas absorbed it all without becoming immured in it, searching out his own path, which included looking abroad, particularly to Taiwanese cinema of the '80s, for new ways of registering contemporary experience.

Emily's voyage toward change doesn't end in a safe harbor of resolution, but with the sighting of another vista: the rarest of shots in Assayas' quick, close, present-tense cinema. At a recording session which she finally manages to wrangle, Emily steps out to catch a smoke, and looks out over San Francisco Bay. It's a landscape intended to contrast with the images that opened *Clean* – night skies poisoned by Hamilton's noxious industry – but now clogged night has been replaced by a fresh, cool day. It's an expansive moment in a movie that's kept so consistently and intimately on top of its subject, a deep breath of clean air that is Assayas' final defiance of rock cliché, of burning out and fading away, an image in defiance of death itself.

Chris Chang

The Doctor Is In

Auteur theory, as everyone knows, is an exact science. Consider – from a cine-empirical perspective – the phenomenon of noise. Review its scientific meaning, particularly definition 5, in the *Shorter Oxford English Dictionary*: "Fluctuations or disturbances (usually random or irregular) which are not part of a signal (whether audible or not), or which interfere with or obscure a signal." *Noise*, the 2006 documentary by Olivier Assayas is, at the very least, a fluctuation in the director's signal. It is a distinct exception to the so-called rule (oeuvre). Attending to noise is often diagnostic: we listen to sputtery engines, wheezy lungs, and beating hearts for signs of health and/or its compromise. In some examples of auteur theory secondary objects in a body of work – I hesitate to call them less healthy – can be seen to contain insights into things masked by the greater precision of their more robust or fully realized counterparts. Can, for example *Les Anges du péché* shed light on *Le Journal d'un curé de campagne*? If the answer is yes an operative metaphor has been established.

~

Saint-Brieuc – a three-hour TGV jaunt west of Paris – is the sleepy capital of Côtes d'Armor, one of the five administrative divisions of Brittany. Once a year, in late spring, the town rouses itself for the self-explanatory Festival ARTrock. For the 2005 edition, Assayas accepted an invitation to guest-curate. He was apparently granted carte blanche, but in light of his well-known musical tastes, there must have been a point where rock & roll dreams ran into a massive reality check. (Not unlike a bouncer.) Suffice to say that neither Brian Eno, Bob Dylan, the remains of Roxy Music, nor even the Feelies took the stage. On a more positive yet ultimately frustrating note Sonic Youth were the headliners. While all members are seen in various solo-projects, the band itself does not appear on screen. Lee Ranaldo: "I'm not exactly sure what led us to not be in the final film. Contractual obligations?" It was a time near the conclusion of the band's working relationship with Geffen Records – so corporate interference (with the proverbial signal) would be no surprise.

With a five-person camera crew that included Assayas, Éric Gautier, and Michael Almereyda, the director proceeded to film and edit together a relatively straightforward document of the concert – albeit one without the ostensible main event. Visual elements (abstract, ambient, and otherwise) consisting of pre-existing and specifically prepared films and footage, were contributed by Assayas, his collaborators and, notably, the avant-polymath/

Jeanne Balibar

Kim Gordon

SY-consort, Jim O'Rourke. Some of the material was projected live during the sets; some was added to the film in post.

Excerpts from *Door*, a potent short by O'Rourke, were chosen by Assayas to bookend the film. *Door* is the kind of work that would make Michael Snow proud. It's a single, fixed-position, 18-minute tight shot of an old, closed door, seen from the inside of an apartment. A bright light, rhythmically waved off-screen, casts queasy pulsating shadows. The soundtrack consists of exquisite ear-splitting feedback. Tension mounts. The door opens. There's no one there.

~

Anything designated ambient can walk a fine line between the universal and the innocuous. Case in point: imagery of rippling light dancing on water, super-imposed over footage of the duo White Tahina, could have probably been added elsewhere in *Noise*, without any real stylistic consequence. You could call the effect gratuitous – but that would be a bit like disparaging the liquid-light shows at a Velvet Underground gig.

White Tahina is endowed with an irresistible archetype – and Assayas is by no means alone in his fascination with it-slash-her. She is, of course, The Dangerously Alluring Femme and, in this particular case, her name is Joana Preiss. Preiss is not only a singer and actress but also an occasional runway model (which is to by no means undersell the talents of her musical partner, the laptop-tweaking, noise-wreaking, multi-media artist Vincent Epplay). To date, Preiss has had supporting roles in three Assayas films, but is perhaps best remembered for the carnal enthusiasm she brought to Christophe Honoré's 2004 Bataille adaptation, *Ma mère*.

Within the context of *Noise*, Preiss is part of another significant trend: she, along with her dangerously alluring co-performers Jeanne Balibar, Kim Gordon, and Emily Haines – the latter the singer and keyboardist for the energetic Canadian band Metric – have all acted in Assayas films. In fact, it's not too difficult to imagine the director organizing his own (unapproved) Lilith Fair. Musing along these admittedly suspect lines one notices a few glaring omissions: Asia Argento, who has collaborated with the composer Hector Zazou, among others, is absent from the ARTrock stage; and Assayas' former wife Maggie Cheung, seen working the microphone at the conclusion of *Clean*, is also missing. Mention could also be made of Virginie Ledoyen, based in part upon her remarkable performance in the non-Assayas AIDS musical *Jeanne et le garçon formidable*, if not

Joana Preiss

for the fact that her singing in that film was, much to this writer's chagrin, dubbed.

~

The all-male lineup of Text of Light, a performance collective including Ranaldo (guitar, electronics), Alan Licht (guitar, electronics), Ulrich Krieger (tenor saxophone, electronics), Steve Shelley (drums), and Tim Barnes (drums), provided the film's most complex noise. For connoisseurs of a well-wrought sonic maelstrom, this was the ticket. The ensemble is comprised of a revolving membership that pivots around Licht and Ranaldo (ARTrock, as it happens, was the first time Shelley participated). The band, active since 2001, takes its name from the seminal Brakhage work. Their performances always rely on film(s), typically by Brakhage, but in the past Harry Smith, Hollis Frampton, Pierre Clémenti, and Ron Rice have made appearances. Text of Light adamantly reject the "live soundtrack" designation. Rather, they treat the projected image as a fellow band member – i.e., an entity that can act on its own and, just like a real musician, do so unpredictably. Licht: "Part of Text of Light's modus operandi is to choose films we're unfamiliar with and only to look at them very occasionally – letting the correspondences between the music and what's happening on screen be aleatory, rather than trying to continually react to what's going on in the film, or plotting out a score ahead of time."

Another pattern emerges from *Noise*: both Sonic Youth and the films of Stan Brakhage were integral parts of Festival ARTrock – but neither appear in the Assayas film. Text of Light has dealt with this sort of situation from its inception. Ranaldo: "Through discussions with the Brakhage estate we were given approval for our project. Many purists object to the notion of using his films in a context with music – but Brakhage himself accepted that it might happen, and had no objections as long as, in such a context, it was not presented as 'a screening of

Brakhage films.' We'd never be able to release any sort of DVD, as that would mean using the [Brakhage] footage. And that was simply not possible." What was possible, however, was to sit down with Assayas and figure out a way to shoot their way around the situation.

For the Text of Light scenes Assayas filled the gap, so to speak, by integrating his own visuals. These included imagery of a rainy Canadian motorway, nocturnal aerial footage, and vaguely ominous views of an oil refinery. Some shots are clearly reminiscent of locations from *Clean*, a film made two years before (we can assume these were outtakes). In *Noise*, a particularly resonant moment occurs in conjunction with a massive saxophone squall courtesy of Ulrich Krieger. Assayas uses an image of a flaming smokestack similar to the one in the scene from *Clean* in which Emily (Maggie Cheung) shoots up in her car. In *Noise*, the flame is super-imposed upon Krieger's wailing horn.

(Free-associative anecdote: we learn from Krieger's CV that he has transcribed Lou Reed's "Metal Machine Music." *For classical instruments*. A psychiatrist – name withheld – once explained to me that "free association" does not exist. "All association is guided," he snapped. The same could be said, I suppose, of free jazz.)

~

The first performance in *Noise* features Alla, aka Abdellaziz Abdellah, an Algerian-born musician. The last is by Mirror/Dash, aka Kim Gordon and Thurston Moore. Taken together the two acts form what could be, if not the beginning and end of a narrative arc, then its sonic counterpart. Alla provides perhaps the cleanest "signal" of the festival. His set-up is a model of simplicity: a rug, three oversized pillows, and an oud (an 11-stringed fretless member of the lute family). He plays barefoot, seated on the floor, cradling the large pear-shaped instrument in his lap. The microphones placed near him feel unnecessary, intrusive, and a bit sacrilegious.

Gordon and Moore revel in distortion. While Alla prefers no special effects; Mirror/Dash seem to subsist on almost nothing but (yes, they still use guitars). Even when Gordon sings, she has two microphones, one feeding through some sort of processor. Prima facie, the sensibilities of Alla and Mirror/Dash seem as divergent as the two worlds they come from, i.e., that of Arab traditionalism versus that of a postmodern – or at least post-punk – West. Does this particular dichotomy remind the reader of something pertinent to a discussion of Assayas' films? (Hold that thought.)

Both Alla and Mirror/Dash, like all musicians, share a Beckett-like imperative to fill space with sound. It's a self-imposed mandate you can see in the expressions on their faces. Equally important, but much more poignant, is the fact that both performances contain a palpable sense of mourning and loss. You don't need to understand Alla's language to feel the sentiment. With Mirror/Dash, particularly with Gordon's vocals, you can turn to a few of the words themselves: "He is just a boy… I will never know him…" Is she singing about Kurt Cobain? Or are the lyrics addressed directly to her husband, i.e., the man standing on stage next to her? Whatever the case may be, it's near impossible to watch this sequence now, seven years after the fact, without thinking of the end of one of rock & roll's most iconic relationships. It almost sounds like the scenario for an Assayas film…

~

Cinema's most obvious medical metaphor is surgical, i.e., the cut or edit. Assayas, in an interview conducted during the post-production of *Carlos*, turned the trope into something even more visceral. Discussing his methods for choosing music, he mentioned trying out different tracks with various scenes to determine "which will take" – as if he were performing organ transplants. Throughout his filmography there have been numerous moments in which ears have pricked – triggered by soundtrack decisions simultaneously ingenious yet glaringly conspicuous. In *L'Eau froide* we see a restless teenage boy (Cyprien Fouquet) twist the dial of his transistor radio and "randomly" tune in Roxy Music's "Virginia Plain." It's an electrifying moment that feels anachronistic – but it's not at all *out of time*. It's an *out-of-place* psychological state that the character, at that point in the narrative, struggles with. He's magnetically drawn to the music and it seems to respond – as good songs can – by telling him he needs to – and will – escape.

At the very end of *Boarding Gate*, after Asia Argento has survived truly bizarre (and kinky) ordeals, the image goes out of focus as she dejectedly ascends an escalator and exits the film. The credits roll to Sparks' truly bizarre (and kinky) "#1 Song in Heaven." Similar to the use of "Virginia Plain," the effect is highly charged, and very Brechtian. The song's implicit irony (God is Giorgio Moroder!) transforms the film's conclusion, and thereby the entire narrative, into a meta-cinematic exercise – albeit one with inescapably real emotion. *Boarding Gate* could have easily ended with a murder: in the final scene Sandra (Argento) flicks open a switchblade that she is clearly ready to use. The victim has his back turned. But she has a change of heart and withdraws. And then Assayas, with a little help from Sparks, opts for a truly peculiar closure: a blurry image wedded to the upbeat sound of a disco afterlife. WTF?

Which brings us to *Carlos* and the aforementioned Arab / post-punk pseudo-schism (re: *Noise*, cf. Alla / Mirror / Dash). Assayas wanted to use the Feelies throughout, but the band, apparently fearing what they perceived would be an uneasy association between their music and an infamous terrorist, declined. A rare case, as it were, of an organ rejecting the body. Enter Wire: whatever the British band's 1986 song "Ahead" may actually be about – "Lips growing for service / Eyes steady for peeling / Bring on the special guest / A monkey caught stealing" – it is now, at least in some cinephilic circles, a theme that will forever be associated with a Venezuelan-born, pro-Palestinian revolutionary. (Additional Wire songs appear on the soundtrack, particularly "Dot Dash," but they function more as transition music.)

Culturally appropriate or not, "Ahead" feels all but anthemic during the motorcade sequence in which Carlos, acting as if he were a triumphant head of state, acknowledges the paparazzi. The wedding of sound and image is both discordant and indelible. To emphasize the point, one need only take note of The Dead Boys' "Sonic Reducer" later in the same film. It's a much more jarring song used to much less disjunctive effect during the Swiss-border-shootout sequence. Assayas knows how to hide the seams between sound and image when he wants to. Sometimes he just doesn't want to. And sometimes, as in the case of a documentary such as *Noise*, he can further complicate matters by inverting the "organ transplant" idea, i.e., by suturing new imagery upon existing music.

~

Noise, of course, is a Frankenstein monster. And the monster is at heart a gentle creature. The auteurist signal, if you will, may be at its most diffuse in this film, but that's pretty much as it should be. Assayas set up the key associations and then set the whole thing free. (Not unlike jazz.) That sort of liberating temperament has attracted like-minded artists throughout his career. Ranaldo: "The recording of the soundtrack for *demonlover* was perhaps the most perfect and pleasurable experience we've had composing music for film." Strong words from a soft-spoken fellow traveler. And then came Tricky: "I meet a lot of directors. And I don't meet a lot of directors with no ego. To be a director and be shy … That's wicked! That impresses me." As it should.

Kim Gordon

Afel Bocoum (above)
Marie Modiano (left)

Gina Telaroli

Anywhere and Everywhere

When you are traveling and you go to some place in the world, you get to an airport, and from the airport you take a cab, and that taxi takes you to a hotel and at your hotel you sit in your room and turn on the TV. Someone then comes and picks you up, because you have an appointment with someone in an office somewhere. You've been there two days and you never see anything remotely connected to what the country is about, what the country has been about. You have been traveling but you stay in just one place. But the reality is that most of the reality there is gone. Whatever was real there has been neutralized. Whatever is happening is what has been happening on your drive from the airport to the hotel. It's not that you've been missing reality. You've been at the core of reality and it's horrible.

Olivier Assayas

The modern world is defined by technology: the screens looked at, the modes of transportation used, the way money is exchanged, the artificial products consumed and the multitude of means by which people communicate. It's also a world defined by "the world." Borders mean less and less as we become more and more adept at crossing them, whether literally or figuratively. Experience comes in fast, short bursts; from one moment to the next, one place to the next with a click or a ding or a push of a button.

Windows are looked out of and into – yet another screen. Terrence Malick movies and websites like http://mapcrunch.com provide adventure and access to natural landscapes. Cars are driven to the grocery store or, maybe, a farmer's market and produce is marveled at without any real knowledge of where it came from. More hikers need to be rescued from deep in the woods than ever before. Instead of bringing a map or a compass for their journey they bring an iPhone to guide them, ignorant of the fact that a few sacred places without any reception whatsoever still exist.

As a filmmaker, Olivier Assayas is extremely attuned to the modern technologically blanketed world and his 2007 film *Boarding Gate* takes special notice of it. His film lays out a world of businessmen (and not the brightest ones), their women and the generalizations that come out of their mouths. Fluorescent-lit offices, dreary warehouses, fast car rides and cardboard cutout hotel rooms make for a reality that is, as Assayas asserts, pretty horrible. Thankfully he transmits the particulars of this world in the form and spirit of a stripped-down, rough and tumble B-movie, pairing the banal with the thrilling.

Boarding Gate opens in a haze that eventually settles on the clear, telling image of a gun bar-

rel. Two businessmen, Miles (Michael Madsen) and Andrew (Alex Descas), are on a shooting range in an unidentified European country (we eventually learn they're in France). They finish shooting, head to their car and get in. Through the car windows we hear them talking. Nothing they discuss – money, deals, leaving the company behind – is specific:

MILES: Listen, I gotta talk to you about something. I've been meaning to tell you for a while now. I'm going to quit, I'm going to get out. I'm going to sell my shares and start from scratch. Besides, I don't think you even need me right now, I think you'll be alright.

ANDREW: It's not the best time.

MILES: Well listen, I've thought it over quite a bit and there's nothing else I can do. I'm so far in debt with these people, it's what I have to do.

ANDREW: Have you found a buyer?

MILES: Yeah, it's a company called Golden Eagle out of Singapore. I've borrowed a lot of money from these people and this is the best way for me to pay back my debt. You're still going to be running things, I've worked that part of the deal out.

ANDREW: I know Golden Eagle, they aren't that reputable.

Characters confront each other not with carefully crafted words but with a bare minimum of language – their interactions are primarily physical. The majority of the cast speaks English as a second language but the real reason behind the lack of pungent or articulate dialogue is that Assayas is less interested in what people say than in how they say it and where they're going after they shut up. References to Russia, China, Singapore, Lebanon, and the United States are scattered throughout conversations. Companies have symbolically empty names like Golden Eagle and Abacus Import. The details are all interchangeable.

When Miles and Andrew return to the office, Sandra (Asia Argento), an old girlfriend of Miles, is there. The former couple circles around the room, the camera covering their movements from multiple angles and locations, as they reminisce about their relationship, which was anything but simple. At Miles' bidding, Sandra would sleep with other men for money, to get him off *and* to gather info on his clients – she was both mistress and employee. We know very little about these two but the scene is incredibly and immediately intimate.

Film history is densely populated with women who trade sex for money, and more often than not they're sympathetic figures – good women caught in bad circumstances. They are confronted with the sudden, brutal reality of their bodies as commodities, worth only as much as men are willing to pay.

Godard's Nana, Naruse's Mama, Ophüls' Lola Montes, and William Wellman's Gilda Carlson (in the 1931 film *Safe in Hell*) aren't much different from Sandra. What sets Sandra apart is the woman who portays her, Asia Argento. Argento's father, her personal history (and its overexposure in the media), and her body covered with tattoos all conspire to blur the line between her actual self and the characters she has played. The first shot of Sandra in *Boarding Gate* is of the back of her neck, where the number 23 is inked. The tattoo in this case is Argento's, but it's also Sandra's, they own it equally. Yet, despite the exoticism shared by Argento and Sandra, despite the shocking nature of her actions (both enacted and re-told), and her unusual level of comfort with her sexuality, she's a fairly average player in the cinematic game of women for sale.

However, the world she growls and claws her way through is different. It lacks the romance of 1960s Paris or 1980s Los Angeles, for that matter. In 20 years it might have some nostalgic currency (a depressing thought) but for now it stands as an accurate depiction of an all too recognizable present. A present that no doubt rubs off on Sandra and how she is perceived.

In the cinematic sisterhood of women of the night, Sandra has a kindred spirit in Hanna Schygulla's Maria Braun. *Boarding Gate* is the third in an unofficial trilogy of Assayas films, with *demonlover* and *Clean,* that focus on the lives of non-traditional women who live their lives outside of socially prescribed gender roles. They live those lives in environments defined by capital and the greater world through which it flows.

Die Ehe der Maria Braun is also a part of trilogy, Fassbinder's BRD trilogy from the late 1970s and early '80s, followed by *Lola* and *Veronika Voss*. Assayas, like Fassbinder, has chosen to focus on a female protagonist who wields her sexuality as a weapon in order to explore the economic, aesthetic and political issues of his time. While they are not connected in any

direct way, certain elements in the trilogies mirror each other: the aura of sexual decadence in *Lola*'s brothel scenes is transmitted via computer screen and commodified in *demonlover*, issues of drug dependence and its effect on family and career are central to *Veronika Voss* and *Clean* and Maria Braun's use of sex as a tool that enables her to provide for her husband and her own economic independence finds a powerful echo in Sandra's situation.

For both Maria and Sandra, sex is never a means to an end only. Sex is something both women need. Maria satisifies herself (while earning needed money) while her husband is at war and then in prison. Sandra does what her partner requires in order to turn him on and get herself off while earning the neccesary capital to survive. Both ladies spend a fair amount of time parading around in their undergarments but spend very little either fully naked or having sex. Sandra does engage in S&M play and, as many of the film's publicity stills are happy to remind us, sits on a desk in an office surrounded by glass windows as she fingers herself. Her wide-open sexuality is very much of its time, and it is also rooted in the context of her conversations and relationships.

In that first scene together, as the two begin to discuss the finer details of their relationship, Sandra moves away from Miles and toward the camera. She's shot in close-up. Miles is behind her in a blur of flourescent light. We can see her face, he can not:

SANDRA: I would have done anything for you.
MILES: And you did.
SANDRA: Because I believed in our relationship, you were just taking advantage of me.
MILES: Taking advantage of you? I could have picked up a two dollar hooker off the street to do the same fucking thing.
SANDRA: You wouldn't have got such good info.
MILES: I didn't give a damn about the info. You think some sweaty drunken half-hearted businessman is going to tell you anything important at 3 in the morning. Sure I thought maybe once in a while there'd be a small piece of information that would give me an edge in a business deal.
SANDRA: So, it was all a game for you?
MILES: If that's what you want to call it.

The language is blunt and her face drops as she recalls her past demons in this new light. Miles can't see her, and her reaction must be judged as an honest one. She then strolls over to his desk and begins to touch herself. It's sexual and overt, something women just don't do. (If they must, they do it under a blanket in a dark room.) But Sandra's masturbation is less relevant than the fact that she does it *after* her former lover has embarrassed her. She knows that in this situation her power is in her body and she wields that power when she has to.

After she leaves Miles' office, we learn that Sandra has a new job. She works in a warehouse for Lester (Carl Ng) and Sue (Kelly Lin), a married Asian couple who import expensive furniture and the drugs concealed within. Sandra checks in the furniture and steals some of the drugs for herself. What comes next jolts us away from the relatively becalmed nature of the movie thus far. When Sandra's drug deal goes awry Assayas quickly moves into sparse B-movie mode with a series of action sequences that hurtle everything forward.

There's no indication that something is about to go wrong when Sandra attempts to sell off the drugs she has stolen from her employers. Thus far this is the story of a businessman attempting to leave his business, and the re-emergence of an ex-girlfriend. After a matter-of-fact exchange in the warehouse, there is a sudden burst of violence. Adrenaline surges and it's almost impossible to get one's bearings. This drug deal shoot-out, bathed in ugly fluorescent light under a dingy green night sky, is shot largely in close-ups and with a chaotic handheld camera amidst extremely fast and seemingly haphazard cutting. It is a scene of carefully crafted chaos, not unlike the moment in Assayas' *Irma Vep* when the music starts to surge after the director of the film within the film, Jean-Pierre Léaud's René Vidal, has had a breakdown. As Sonic Youth takes over the soundtrack, Maggie Cheung wanders around her hotel room in her latex catsuit costume, presumably getting into character. Soon though, she is exploring the staircases and hidden corners of her hotel and as jewels are stolen and the lights start to turn a not-so-subtle shade of blue, the line between fact and fiction blurs. With two sweeping set pieces, Assayas charts new courses for both his characters and his audience.

The unexpected action high in *Boarding Gate* is immediately followed by a scene of Sandra and Lester making love. The couple are shot in natural colors and blanketed (again like *Irma Vep* – when Cheung is on the roof in the rain) with grainy, cool, blue evening light. The camerawork is gentle, the close-ups masked in shadow, the continuity more fluid, and the quiet hum of the city blends with the couple's gentle moans. The movie settles down and for a brief moment everything is grounded. Assayas' elliptical structure and the economy of action suggest, without quite demonstrating, that Sandra and Lester are very much in love.

The next sequence is even more powerful, a 22-minute tête-à-tête / S&M session between Miles and Sandra that slowly and inexorably builds to Miles' murder at Sandra's hand. The sequence is patterned after their first conversation, and in both scenes windows and doorways frame the space. Reflections abound and the immediate geography is as difficult to sort out as knowing who is being honest and who isn't (with each other *and* with themselves). The content of their conversation is ridden with clichés. But, as in the earlier conversation, words are not important. It's the exchanged glances, gestures and shared knowledge of each other's bodies that count.

Boarding Gate was inspired by the true story of Édouard Stern and Cécile Brossard. Stern was a 50-year-old French banker who was found dead in Geneva in a latex suit riddled with bullet holes. Brossard, Stern's mistress, was suspected of the crime and fled to Australia before returning to confess to her crime. What Assayas does so brilliantly is take that very real story and build it around the character who is neither the obvious victim nor the heroine.

Despite everything – the chain of events, the prowling camera work and the time we've spent with Sandra – Assayas' centerpiece keeps uncertainty about motive in the air until the subject of Sandra's rape is brought up. Among many other things, Sandra is a casualty of a male-dominated world in which men imagine that women want, indeed ask, to be sexually assaulted and degraded.

The rape story comes up right before Sandra attempts to leave the apartment. Miles won't let her go, and in forcing her to do something against her will, once again, he has signed his own death sentence. Sandra re-enters his apartment and she knows she has no choice but to kill him. It's an emotionally loaded moment. She reaches deep, pulls the trigger and then works to steady herself. As she stumbles, so does the camera. Her body hits the floor and the camera moves up and down and back toward her. She begins to get herself together and stumbles haphazardly around the house, and the impact and intensity of murder are felt in the movement of the camera as it continually shifts perspective. Sandra collapses for a moment and Assayas cuts between her sprawled body and Miles' corpse. The physical toll slowly reveals itself as the camera pulls away and Sandra regains control of herself, gets up and frantically attempts to wipe away her crime.

After the murder Sandra is rushed by Lester, who we now understand as the apparent instigator of the murder, through a club and onto an airplane headed for Hong Kong. Despite the

fact that she's surrounded by passengers, this is the first time we've seen her alone. As opposed to *demonlover*'s opening plane scene, which thrusts us into a closed world in which every character appears to be enacting a pre-defined role, here we are left alone with a character we are coming to know very well, and who is momentarily able to shed her role. The camera is steady and Brian Eno's "2/2" from "Music For Airports" drifts around the action (or the momentary lull), wrapping Sandra and the audience in an enveloping warmth.

At one point she emerges from the bathroom into darkness. She walks by rows of sleeping passengers and over to a window, opening its shade to reveal a startling burst of natural light. It's exhilarating, disorienting and in many ways the defining moment of the film – the darkness of all that has come before suddenly making itself felt in the contrast. Any concrete concept of where, when and why is nowhere to be found, perhaps because it never existed to begin with.

As the film continues, action (warehouse shootout in Hong Kong) again gives way to a brief passage of solitude (a ferry ride), followed by a zig-zagging journey through anonymous food courts, nameless streets, in which bursts of light and gunfire continue. Chaotic cutting raises heartbeats, juxtaposed with passages in

From Olivier Assayas' photographic production diary (second row, third from left: Sylvie Barthet)

which the soundscapes of Brian Eno, longer takes and cooler color palates provide respite. And during each moment of respite, each break from over-stimulated reality, Sandra is all that remains.

In Hong Kong, she meets with the jealous and duplicitous Sue and a shady business-woman played by Sonic Youth's Kim Gordon. Sue drugs her at a Karaoke bar and then ships her off to Gordon, who gives her money and tells her to go to China. In these sequences, in which multiple plot strands are tied up, the movie's momentum is frankly disrupted, yet they have a quality reminiscent of the in-between time when you wake up from an accidental nap – the annoying drowsy period eventually fades and consciousness returns.

In the final scene, a bastard child of *Romeo and Juliet*, a very different pair of lovers is caught in a terrifying world in which the intentions of others, and even one's own, are destined to remain forever ambiguous. On her way to yet another airport, Sandra spots Lester. She follows him as he meets with Andrew and accepts payment for Miles' murder. The scene harkens back to the first conversation at the very beginning of the film, a reminder that business is always business and that, in a world of never-ending transaction, business is all there is. As she watches Lester taking money from Andrew, Sandra realizes that her new love isn't much better than her old. Of course Lester and the audience know that he does love her and will be meeting her in 6 months time when they will both be financially and emotionally free. All Sandra knows, however, is that she's been dragged through the mud, used and discarded yet again. She follows him and readies her knife blade.

She stares at Lester from behind as he waits for a car to pick him up. The camera cuts to a close-up of the nape of his neck, echoing that earlier image of her own tattooed neck. Her face changes. Anger morphs into a mixture of love and sadness. It's an extremely intimate moment, and the tone is set by that image of Lester's sweaty skin. She stares longingly, closes the knife blade and the camera loses its focus.

As Sandra goes up the escalator in a blur, Sparks' hypnotic and strangely uplifting "#1 Song in Heaven, Part 2" slowly fades up and the world keeps on turning.

Where will Sandra end up? Who will she end up with? Nowhere and everywhere, everyone and no-one? As the song builds it doesn't matter much because she, like the audience, needs to move on to her next destination.

Asia
ARGENTO
小心登革熱
齊來把蚊滅
Beware of dengue fever
ACT NOW!
2868 0000
Please call 2868 0000 to report mosquito problem
機電安全
Walch
Boarding Gate
Production Truck
Boarding Gate
French Crew Van A

Kent Jones

Cosmic Pulses

In Lou Reed and John Cale's *Songs for Drella*, a 1990 tribute to Andy Warhol in the form of a song suite, there is a song appropriately titled "Work." "Every Sunday when he went to Church," sings Reed, "he'd kneel in his pew and say, 'It's just work / All that matters is work.'" Warhol had a work ethic to be sure, but one not dictated or governed by outside forces; rather, it originated with him alone and answered to nothing but his own inner voice. In other words, work as life itself, merged with thought, energy, desire, perception, ambition, and spiritual awareness. To live is to work, to work is to create, to create is to walk one's own path in the world.

For Olivier Assayas, Warhol is a giant of cinema and painting and the philosophy of art, but he is also an exemplary and inspiring figure because of his endless drive. Assayas himself never stops working, and for him the communal creative energy of Warhol's factory is reimagined and reinvigorated over and over again one film shoot at a time. In *Irma Vep*, albeit from a semi-parodistic angle, he looked directly into the chaos and agitated forward motion of a low budget production. In the 2008 documentary *Eldorado*, filmed for Arte, he explored another set of altogether different factory conditions. The French choreographer Angelin Preljocaj – friendly, articulate, wide awake, *engaged* – could easily be a character in one of Assayas' fiction films, breathlessly shifting ground from rehearsal studio to millinery shop, from the role of interpreter of rhythmic and sonic space to artistic court of last resort, from collaborator to impresario to creator and back again, and always in motion. The film is a little rhapsody of creatively generated movements of all shapes and sizes, from Preljocaj and his dancers torquing and stretching and rolling their bodies to the fingers of seamstresses cutting lengths of piping and gluing sunburst patterns on the costumes. And, there is also the movement of thought, of Preljocaj and that of his company as they work out the dance and, most touchingly, of the composer as he discusses the extremely complex piece in question with the choreographer.

Eldorado continually shifts back and forth between the rehearsals and preparations of Preljocaj's piece and his discussions with Karlheinz Stockhausen. This is the last filmed interview with Stockhausen, who would be dead within the year. At 78, he had come to resemble his former teacher Olivier Messiaen – a little portly, more than a little owlish behind silver-rimmed glasses, benign and gracious yet intensely fixed on questions of rhythm as it relates to the life of the body and the movements

of the universe, on the ambition of harmonizing art with the complexity of nature and the acknowledgment of its impossibility, on music as science and life as preparation for another higher spiritual order. The film's most touching moment comes when Preljocaj asks Stockhausen if he incorporates the mistakes made by the machines he programs into his pieces, as an acknowledgment of nature's vast and incomprehensible workings. There is a lengthy silence as the composer quietly ponders this grand and piercing question, which he finally answers in the negative. A beautiful paradox: the artist who has devoted his life to moving with the rhythmic flux of nature edits mistakes out of the process because they would disturb the evocation of a higher, incomprehensible order. There's something sharp, dizzying and uplifting about this little film and its shuttling motion between an old visionary among his machines and the young men and women complementing his ferocious and genuinely awesome music (the piece in question is "Sonntags-Abschied") with such supple motion, and its contrasts between the joys of group creation and the tough, angular purity and density of the music. Dancing to Stockhausen is like passing through a piece of quartz crystal, and it's appropriate, not to mention stirring, that the film ends on one dancer, waiting in the wings in the dark, taking a breath, readying himself for the passage.

Geoffrey O'Brien

The Secret Life of Objects

We enter the movie – it feels almost like an intrusion – in the middle of movement. Children are hunting for hidden treasure, under the guidance of an adolescent just at the age (it's discernible at a glance, in the midst of all the running around) of distancing herself from their games. We don't know where we are but it isn't difficult to simply dive into what is offered: the ideal summer afternoon, in which in a few shots the adventurous geography of childhood is laid out – its spiraling paths and dizzying hillsides, every point in space an opening into the unknown – not with an exaggerated sense of wonder but simply there to be looked at, inhaled, with voluptuous appreciation.

But these moments are already disappearing. A relentless forward motion is always taking us into the next thing, a different thing. We are being taken into the kitchen, among the adults. A roast is being put into the oven with a careful and loving deliberation that is the portrait of a lifetime. The camera keeps winding ahead: a man is twisting open a bottle of champagne as he emerges into the outdoors, spraying a cascade of liquid into the intimate midst of a family gathering. Within a few seconds we seem to know everything. (The exposition is unobtrusive but absolutely thorough, as minimally exact as one of Ibsen's opening scenes.)

It's a 75th birthday celebration for the woman, Hélène Berthier (Edith Scob), whose three far-flung children are gathered around her with their spouses and offspring, a woman whose lifelong mission has to been preserve and celebrate the work of her uncle, the painter Paul Berthier, whose upcoming retrospective in San Francisco has been commemorated in a just-published book that the celebrants are now examining and critiquing. The scene is neither frantic nor contemplative. It simply moves quietly but relentlessly forward as things do, always going just a little faster than anyone is ready for. An old photograph, reproduced in the art book, shows the same garden with a different set of people enjoying it in the same fashion. Even as the static image is being held up for comparison with the present moment, that moment is already spinning into something different.

By the end of the first long scene there is a sense of completion, as if everything were all over before it had properly begun. The mother has announced that she will die; the eldest son Frédéric (Charles Berling) has steadfastly resisted that knowledge. There is an immense question, posed at the outset, about what will happen to the beautiful house and the beautiful artworks it contains. Whatever follows has an air of the inevitable; almost everything that happens to these people could have been foreseen. The events with which the film will concern itself might from a certain angle seem a succession of banalities, unrelieved by the slightest melodramatic twist to turn the story on its head; they are simply the sort of things that tend to happen in such cases. Lives unfold, moving toward maturity or moving toward death. (Of course, the specifics of the case are not everyone's idea of ordinariness. The disposition of an inherited art collection worthy of the Musée d'Orsay is not everyone's problem; but it is ordinary to these individuals, because it happens to be their life.)

In the event this succession of banalities is a succession of profound and unsettling surprises. The film is surprising because its characters are constantly surprised: astonished, as people generally are, that the inevitable in fact comes to pass. It is a shock that people should age; a shock that they should die; a shock for parents to appreciate that their children have lives of their own; a shock for children to appreciate, perhaps much later on, that their parents had lives of their own.

In relation to the rest of the film the first scene is the lost treasure: an entirely separate and closed-off film, a portrait of a world whose end is announced by the solitary shot of Hélène sitting alone in the dark after everyone has gone, meditating in silence on her own death. It is the only moment that approaches a fixed and permanent state. She is preparing to enter the realm of the unchanging. The extraordinary compression of what has come before can be gauged by the extent to which we seem to know her. The radiant force of Edith Scob is like nothing else in the film. She is a sort of living ideogram inscribing a meaning that can never quite be reconstituted. She has not merely registered a visual presence whose memory persists spectre-like, but, with every darting and delicate gesture and glance, she has described a way of life, an emotional narrative, a system of implied values and relations.

She is already a creature of the past, complete in a way that no one else is. The survivor of a world that no longer exists, we have watched her executing a dignified retreat from what surrounds her, not least from the condescension of her own children to which she responds with her own form of rarefied condescension, as if gazing at them from the plateau of a superior understanding. The rest are all struggling to define themselves, to get a handle on where they stand in relation to things; she is already an achieved definition. She has become

On the set,
with Éric Gautier

a kind of reclusive prophet whose prophecies are sealed up and undeliverable.

By the next scene she has already died, and enough time has passed that the initial grief has subsided. The shock of that reaction is not the film's subject. A slower and more muted process is at work. Her death is not yet completed, and will not be until the very end of the film. The long death of Hélène Berthier encompasses not only her physical disappearance but the disposition of the objects in which she sought to preserve what she loved – objects that to her were not objects at all but extensions of life. Another invisible film lurks behind this one, the story of the ghostly figure of the artist Paul Berthier, Hélène's idol and love object, a figure who has already entered a world of myth that might make the successor state inhabited by his descendants seem washed-out and soulless by comparison. Nothing of him (aside from the faintest and most unreliable of memories) remains but these objects, those he created and those that accrued to him in the flow of a vibrant creative life. But to those who survive they have become problems, enigmas, fetish objects: or, simply, for one of the heirs, a practical solution to the problem of how to afford housing in Beijing.

Her son Frédéric wants to continue Hélène's self-imposed task of preservation, even if it was a task that may have destroyed her life: "There is the residue. There are the objects." We learn quite a lot about these objects in the course of the film: the pair of Corots, the Redon painting, the Degas sculpture shattered long ago in childhood play, the notebooks of Paul Berthier, the Art Nouveau vases, the valuable pieces of furniture. But we are given only the most fleeting glimpses of them, and are never permitted to contemplate them apart from their context. The film is only peripherally about their qualities as objects. Their magnificence, such as it may be, matters only as it is part of what they mean to all those who find themselves involved with them.

This is not to say that the objects are a pretext. If this were a novel, like *Cousin Pons* or *The Spoils of Poynton*, they might be symbols, counters, plot devices. Here, as physical presences, they assume the weight virtually of characters. We witness how different people look at them, handle them, move in relation to them. No novel could achieve anything like the moment when the housekeeper Eloïse brings flowers into the house after Hélène's death and, declaring that "empty vases were like death to her," puts an old vase in the metal sink to fill it with water. We have already learned that, unknown to her, the vase is a work of great value. To see an object of such worth so casually plunked down, and then to experience a sort of humdrum ecstasy as it fills with water – the most ordinary miracle anyone could ask for – speaks, as they say, volumes. It lasts about a second. *L'Heure d'été* has many of the virtues of a literary work – it is in fact as symmetrically pointed a screenplay as could be imagined, with its important themes sounded discreetly but unmistakably in the dialogue, and with even the most random incident contributing to an overall equipoise – but all that structure and discourse would be for nothing without its expressive soul, which resides in the actors and how they situate themselves in relation to space and time.

The plot of the movie is the fate of the house and the art. Hélène's death is the only catastrophe in a narrative otherwise devoid of deaths, illnesses, or accidents. Frédéric's daughter Sylvie has a brief run-in with the police over a shoplifting incident: that is the sum total of melodramatic incident. The rest, apart from the question of what will become of the inherited artifacts, is a matter of family chitchat: the sister Adrienne is going to get married again and live permanently in New York, the younger brother Jérémie and his wife are going to relocate to Beijing, Frédéric is going to go on trying to come to terms with his evidently not very fulfilling career as an economist and to patch up his relations with the daughter he doesn't seem to spend much time with. Hardly enough plot material for a decent postcard. We go thus far and no farther with these people. We learn the provenance, value, and subsequent destiny of nearly every inherited object but are told just enough about each of these lives to keep at every moment the main thematic line in view. Nonetheless we know them; we see them.

The narrative has clearly imposed limits. The central dilemma about the fate of the art provides the structure of the film itself. It can be taken as a lucidly constructed debate on the meaning and function of art, in which every

character participates by every means available, except for those characters (the lawyer, the cop) for whom art is a matter of indifference (and whose indifference is itself part of the argument). While the characters talk about art, they themselves are part of an analogous artistic structure. In the midst of this, pretty much at every instant, other potential story lines come into view that we are free to imagine. The rigors of the screenplay contrast with a sensation of openness, of life spilling out in different directions at every turn.

The intimacy of the playing is such that very few concrete details are needed to get a sense of what these lives are. The laughter of her siblings at Adrienne's announcement of her remarriage is held just long enough to make her start to get annoyed, and then the annoyance is quickly brushed aside. The brothers flare up in anger at each other at the lawyer's office, then joke together at a coffee shop afterwards as if nothing had happened. Lisa's presumably long-suffering marriage to the discontented Frédéric is conveyed almost wordlessly in every moment of her performance.

As in his other films but here perhaps more than ever before, Assayas is able to track, unemphatically but decisively, the tiny mood changes of a room full of people through a long scene like the family discussion that culminates in the decision to sell the house. Scenes like this, or the meeting at the lawyer's office, or the

On the set

quick casual streetcorner goodbyes that may well be forever, are recorded with an absolute justice of tone, an ordinariness not satirized or commented on but merely observed, with the occasional flare-ups of emotion not given any excessive, that is to say movie-ish, weight.

This justice of tone finds its hovering center in an almost accidental protagonist, Charles Berling's Frédéric. We first encounter him hurtling into the midst of the birthday party, not quite getting it right with the uncorking of the champagne, and his subsequent trajectory is indeed that of a man never able to follow through as intended, a man never quite at ease, somehow unfinished, tangled up in his awkward inability to come to the point, in his painful mix of sincerity, anger, resentment, self-doubt, self-righteousness. He clings to the house and its artifacts as the only things that tie him to a past to which he is devoted but whose full implications he dodges. The revelation that his mother had a passionate affair with her aging uncle is something he cannot acknowledge; that is to say, he has never fully understood what the art meant in the first place; and he has certainly never cared to realize fully who his mother was. His difficulties in talking with his own children are of a piece with that evasion.

Yet after all he is the only one who really cares about the art, and his constantly self-lacerating existence is nevertheless made to seem more richly interesting than the overseas careerism of his siblings. He at least asks the questions for which he is unable to find anything like satisfying answers. Our knowledge of all these people is partial, but theirs, of themselves and each other, is equally so. Hélène, in her one scene, perhaps sees more than any of them, but her wisdom is already that of a past to which she is the only surviving link, well aware that she herself is on the edge of vanishing. In her absence there is no character to whom anyone might turn for an overarching grasp of the situation in which they are engulfed. Each sees his or her part of it, and these separate spheres join up only in the most transient fashion, usually in moments beyond words. Speech here is an attempt to bridge the gaps, and it is Frédéric who most valiantly and unsuccessfully makes that attempt.

The objects, then, are transmitters of something that no one can precisely define or understand. Compared to the durability of physical materials, feeling is fragile and elusive. In the same frame we see the objects that will persist and the people who will disappear. The frame itself is an object, made possible by a machine. So that this story about the transmission of objects and the transmission of memories becomes a kind of science fiction movie. In this process of objects moving from hand to hand and from generation to generation, the living people can be seen in a certain light as mere accessories. When art becomes for once not background or clue or symptom but the central focus of a story, it turns into something eerie and incomprehensible.

The objects are treasured for their association with memories; but the memories will be lost. Most of them will never even reach the point where they can be transmitted. What we see assures us that the private worlds of each of these characters will remain mostly private, not fully expressed even in their lifetimes. What persists, in living minds, is a fragment of a fragment of a fragment. The objects themselves are more or less stable – they can be shattered but they can also be put back together, as we are shown in the visit to the Musée d'Orsay's restoration wing – but what they are changes over time, even to Hélène. They are at best signposts to places no longer there, just as the film itself is a map of disappearances and transmutations. Everything is always dissolving. Along with the dissolution of Hélène's privileged order of intermingled love and art, we are given telegraphic flashes of the dissolution of France into a more flattened-out globalist world represented alike by Jérémie's Chinese career, Adrienne's American marriage and made-in-Japan industrial products, the American-style music at the party. In the end the art will go to strangers anyway, including the museum-going tourist who barely looks at the art because he's making plans by cell phone to see a movie. Maybe he's off to see some hideously debased product of the torture porn era that Assayas predicted in *demonlover*; or maybe he's off to see *L'Heure d'été*.

Greil Marcus

What the Film Wants

"I remember one day we were doing camera tests, and also doing hair tests, and with wardrobe, all the creative departments," the actor Édgar Ramírez says of his leading role in Olivier Assayas' five-and-a-half hour *Carlos* – a political travelogue, an on-the-run biography of the terrorist who, born Ilich Ramírez Sánchez in Venezuela in 1949, now serving life in Clairvaux prison in France, from his murder of French police in Paris in 1975 to his kidnapping of OPEC oil ministers later that year in Vienna, from his hideouts in Syria, Yemen, Hungary to his capture in the Sudan in 1994, was a one-man spectre haunting Europe – "and then we're having lunch: Alexander Scheer," the German actor who plays Carlos' almost obscenely loyal terrorist comrade Weinrich, "and then Nora von Waldstätten," the Austrian actress who plays Magdalena Kopp, Carlos' wife, "Olivier, and myself. And suddenly, Alexander, who's the most spontaneous one, he goes" – and Ramírez adopts a serious, considered, almost abstractly intellectual tone – "'Like, guys, I'm not sure if you feel the same thing, but, really, I have no idea how to play this character.' And then, I froze, and then Nora goes, 'Yes, quite honestly, I have no idea how to play this character.' And then it's me, and I say, 'You know what, I have no idea how I'm going to play Carlos.' And, a pause, and Olivier: 'Actually, I feel very relieved – because I have no idea how I'm going to shoot this movie.' That set the tone for what was going to happen. Everybody just relaxed. We said, 'We're here, it's just like soccer – it's just, score.'"

For all of its blindingly fast action sequences, which capture the confusion and fright of an act of violence from a half-dozen perspectives simultaneously – terrorists firing on an Israeli airplane at the Orly airport and then fleeing police through crowds in a panic belied only by their guns and grenades – for all of its moments of instant murder and summary execution – for dozens of moments during which, not after, the person watching says *What? Did that happen? Is it over? So fast?* – Ramírez' story captures the heart of this movie.

"I had no preconception of Carlos," Assayas says. "I did not want to interpret Carlos. I did not want to try to figure out *motives* ... I always thought the image of Carlos would come out of the accumulation of facts. He would take life in front of us. People would ask me, 'How do you see Carlos?' 'Who is Carlos for you?' I always have a hard time answering, because it's a metaphysical question. When you tell what amounts to the life story of someone, can you assume that an individual is one person, who ultimately

does not change, for the essentials, or that, eventually, we can be different persons at different moments of our lives? I've always believed there are different chapters in lives, that people can be transformed as history is being transformed around them – and also that individuals are defined by the way that they adapt to changing times. In the case of Carlos, it's particularly interesting in that we are talking about an individual who is caught up in history, with a major H. He is within the *fabric* of the history of his times. So I thought, in the end, the facts speak much more precisely of who Carlos is than anything that would have to do with melodrama, with psychology, with some fake human texture. I think in the end, Carlos has a lot of human *believability*. And it's not brought by what I wrote in the screenplay. It's simply brought by the presence of an actor, the physical presence of an actor."

That's one way of describing the openness, the playfulness, of the spirit in which they worked: Assayas, Ramírez, and the actors who revolve around Ramírez, whose presence is so strong it's as if he, as an actor, really is the star and they are planets helpless in the face of his gravity – especially Scheer as the finally apostate Weinrich, von Waldstätten as the inexorably emptying Kopp, Julia Hummer as the bloodthirsty Nada, Katharina Schüttler as the terrorist Brigitte Kuhlmann, who takes more pride following orders than she ever could giving them. That's the deep-focus version. But the same process – the same shared spirit – took countless other forms.

"We didn't rehearse at all," the director says. "We didn't rehearse for the camera, we didn't rehearse for the sound. What I was telling my cameraman was, 'I think he's going to do this, but he may also do that. If he does this do that, if he does this other thing, try this other thing, but in any case try to end up where he does this other thing, and then there's this other guy who will be coming, and he has a grenade, so try to get the grenade when he throws it and it rolls on the ground. And OK, we're shooting.'" You can see this on the screen: it's a lot of the reason the viewer is caught up, suspended in the action on the screen, in the historical moment it defines, with past and future sucked into the immediacy of what's-happening-now.

Visually, perhaps the most striking instance of the shuffling of perspectives inherent in such a process, a process where discovery trumps intent, comes with the transfer of the OPEC oil ministers from their meeting place in Vienna to a bus that will take them to the airport where they're to be flown to an unknown fate. The

viewer knows this happens. The viewer probably knows what happened next – how, for the terrorists, the whole spectacular enterprise, capturing the attention of the world, came to nothing. That is not how it plays. It starts, Assayas explains, with documentary footage of a press conference by the Austrian Chancellor Bruno Kreisky. "We have good 16 mil footage of that conference. There were a lot of journalists, microphones, something we could not have recreated, at least not accurately – and it's a very short scene, so it's a matter of budget. So at one point I said, why not inject our actor, who plays Kreisky, into the 16 mil footage. So we did – and at the end of that scene, which is in black and white, because most of the documentary film is in black and white, we move to the scene of the bus coming to pick up the hostages, and it's in black and white. And we see the bus arriving, and gradually as the bus arrives, it moves back to color, and all of a sudden we realize that this bus, which we thought was historical, and coming from the same material as the Kreisky footage, is not historical – which is confusing to a lot of viewers, because a lot of viewers believe that it's the real Kreisky. It gradually comes back to color, and it comes back to our narration, and we just drag you into the narration again, of Carlos taking the hostages out of the building and pushing them into the bus."

The result is that the modified or corrupted documentary footage dissolves the sense of artifice in the fictionalized film that we're actually watching, and the presence of the actors in the fictionalized film dissolves the in-the-past nature of the documentary footage, so instead of looking at this and saying, once upon a time, this happened, the feeling is, this is happening now – and regardless of what we might know of the historical events, the feeling is that we don't know what is going to happen next.

The result is also a lack of melodrama, across the entire terrain of the film – but along with the absence of building suspense with suspenseful music, or of people saying "If you go out that door, I won't be here when you get back," there is another way in which action-as-history and history-as-action deprives the movie, and whoever might be watching it, of the usual clues that make up our minds for us: a complete lack of introspection on the part of the characters – Carlos, Kopp, Weinrich, and especially the contingent of German women who have such notable roles, whether they are fellow militants, lovers, or both. If that can create a frustration for the viewer, it also captures the craziness of the action as it leaps through the years. When people are asked about their motives, something that happens any number of times in the film, with any number of characters, individuals who in the moment before have been speaking in the most naturalistic manner about whatever concerns them – what they're going to make for dinner, whether there's a cop outside – respond with, "I want to take part in the anti-imperialist struggle," or "I am devoted to the Palestinian cause," or "I'm a militant and I follow orders." They shift directly into a robotic discourse. That can seem bizarre to a person coming to the film cold, now – but to Assayas, and to Ramírez, it is part and parcel of being caught up in history, or attempting to dissolve oneself into it.

"I grew up in the Seventies in France," Assayas says. "You had to be involved politically in what was going on. And your involvement was way beyond your person. You were part of the coming revolution. And the coming revolution was an ongoing debate. Were you a Trotskyist – and what variety of Trotskyist are you, what variety of Maoist are you, what version of anarchist are you? And a lot of your self-reflection was *absorbed* by discussing those nuances, making sense of those nuances, but with the constant notion that you were a tiny part of something bigger. Being concerned with one's self, or

with the complexity of one's psyche, had a *name* at that time: it was called petit-bourgeois individualism. It was despised. It was hated. It's the reason why, for instance, I wrote for a while in *Cahiers du cinéma* – it's a movie magazine, but for a few years, it was caught up in Maoist politics. At that time, possibly one of the most beautiful movies in French history was released, *La Maman et la putain*, by Jean Eustache, and *Cahiers du cinéma* had nothing else to say, in front of this huge masterpiece, but that 'This is petit-bourgeois individualism.' It was not *cool* to talk about your emotions. It was not relevant. It was completely outside the framework of what people were expecting from you. The whole *meaning* of who we are is brought into this meta-language." For Ramírez, it was a question of language: "'I'm an internationalist,' 'I'm a freedom fighter' – they were like mantras that people use for guidance. Like taking out your religious book, and holding on to that. In the case of Carlos, I think that he reached a moment where he became his own ideology. He became his own cause. And all the leftist rhetoric was also used as a way to manipulate the people around him. Whenever someone was going off track, he would throw phrases as lasers, to get people back on track. 'You're not paying attention to me. You are not making love to me. You are making love to other women, and I'm not enough for you' – immediately, he would call up revolutionary theory to put cover on the emotional issues that were coming out in a specific moment. There's one scene where one character says to my character, 'Well, you're sleeping with my girlfriend. She told me she loves you, so I just wanted to know your opinion – she says she loves you and there's nothing I can do, what do you think about it?' And my character says, 'Yes, she was very clear, there's nothing you can do, it's her life, that's it. But I hope – that this situation doesn't affect your commitment to the revolution.'"

In the willingness to let the action take its course, in the refusal to judge the characters, or even to let them judge each other, there is a sense of humility before one's subject – and nothing in *Carlos* more completely fixes Assayas' confidence that the subject is itself a kind of collaborator in the infinitely complex enterprise of filmmaking than the approach he took to scoring the movie, though scoring is not the right word.

From scene to scene – Carlos preening naked in a mirror, the takeover of the OPEC conference, the shooting of a military policeman at a Swiss checkpoint, a weapons delivery, a breakdown in communications – the movie is less scored than invaded by post-punk songs so ro-

Édgar Ramírez, with
Nora von Waldstätten (above),
and on the set

mantic and tough they create empathy for situations even as the film withholds it from its characters. As we hear, almost see, numbers by the Feelies and New Order, or the Dead Boys' "Sonic Reducer," most viscerally Wire's "Dot Dash," a song that seems to terrorize itself – not in any way keyed to the scenes with chronological, soundtrack-of-our-lives banality – the songs raise the question of whether the best and most adventurous music of the late 1970s and early 1980s was itself as animated by international terrorism, by the spectre of a world where at times it could seem that only a few armed gnostics were in control of anything, as by anything else.

But even more interesting is what Assayas didn't use – what didn't work, and why. "I had absolutely no notion when I was making this film of the kind of music I would be using," he says. "I never use scores; I use songs that I like. In the case of *Carlos*, I didn't have a clue. I tried a lot of stuff, and the film did not want it. I thought that this movie needed classic movie music, which is something I never do, I never use, still, maybe, the length of the film, the epic pace, maybe I could use some kind of orchestral movie music. The film laughed in my face when I tried it. It rejected a lot of stuff. At one point I was just desperate – I thought, maybe no music at all – why not? I started trying stuff – I was just shooting in the dark. And then – I had this Feelies track. It was perfect. All of a sudden, it gave me the right note. And then I used a lot of Feelies music – until the last minute, I had eight or nine Feelies tracks on it. And then all of a sudden, I had this e-mail, from the guys who represent the Feelies: 'The Feelies want to see the film, they're extremely uncomfortable with the notion of their music associated with terrorism.' What do you mean, I said – it sounded great, it was perfect! It made complete sense. But there was no way of having a conversation: 'The Feelies are not comfortable having their music associated with anything dark.' They allowed us to use one track, which is important, because it takes you into the film. But then it was much easier – because I knew what the film wanted."

What Assayas is talking about is the imperative, the momentum, of a film itself thinking. If you are open to the world you are attempting to depict and the means by which you might do so, once you begin the enterprise of filmmaking, the thing you are making will tell you what is and what is not possible, what will violate its personality and what will light it up. Over its great length, crisscrossing the map like a tribe lost in the desert, that is what happens in *Carlos*.

Kent Jones

Lost Companions and Fleeing Ghosts

How do you make a film about people who lack self-awareness? Or, to be more precise, people who have learned to cultivate a form of systematic self-censoring that they take to be self-awareness? The answer is precision, about absolutely everything: the language and the way it is spoken, the gestural exchanges between those who speak it, their shared sense of beauty and terror and its exact placement on their horizon-lines.

Après-Mai is a visionary work *so* precise and settled about everything in its field of remembered experience as to be almost unprecedented – nothing in this movie is announced, fussed or labored over, everything simply breathes and exists. Right from the start, we are deposited within a moment in time – or "the times," as Guy Debord puts it in a situationist bulletin read in voiceover by Assayas' autobiographical surrogate Gilles (same name as in *L'Eau froide,* this time played by Clement Metayer): "The times are most certainly revolutionary, and the times know it." The aching poignancy of *Après-Mai*, made 18 years after *L'Eau froide* but from a completely different perspective, is that the times know they are revolutionary, but the people living them do not.

Or, at least they don't know *how* revolutionary, or precisely what kind of revolution they are in the midst of, least of all when they speak the robotic language inculcated by the French Communist Party. There's a great exchange after an outdoor screening of a collective documentary about Laotian insurgents. "Doesn't revolutionary filmmaking call for revolutionary syntax?" asks someone from the friendly audience. "The films have to be made in the simplest syntax because they must be understood by the proletariat," answers a filmmaker, who adds: "And isn't 'revolutionary syntax' nothing more than a petit-bourgeois affectation?" "Our films are made for the people," someone says a little later, "not for aesthetes." It's easy to imagine this entire exchange rendered in a completely different, altogether comic tone by, for instance, the Coen brothers. But what's so magical is the beauty of the people as they utter this dogma, their passionate and guileless conviction that they are speaking "correctly" and justly – the same holds true for the CP filmmaker's admonishment of Gilles when he discovers that he is reading the Belgian Sinologist Simon Leys' *Les Habits neufs du président Mao* – "There is no Simon Leys, it's a CIA plot to undermine the Cultural Revolution...Be careful what you read." Indeed, there is a precisely defined gap throughout this film between the words spoken by the characters and what they express with their movements, their stillnesses, their looks. They tremble with an unspoken sense of something nameless, in the process of *happening*. You feel it acutely in the performance of Felix Armand as Alain, a dead ringer for Humbert Balsan in *Lancelot du lac* (in fact, they are distant cousins), who grows increasingly immobilized and violently perplexed, his every word weighted with uncertainty. You feel it in the presence of India Salvor Menuez's Leslie, the pale, red-haired, clear-eyed beauty Alain pairs off with after she puts a tab of acid between his lips and kisses him on the mouth minutes after they've met. He sees her off to Amsterdam to have an abortion (she wants to do it alone out of "principle," because too many people speak of abortion with contempt), and tells her to see two paintings by Frans Hals while she's there. One of the great joys of Assayas' work is that you never know exactly where the narrative will alight. A few moments later, what we might have taken for an aside is enacted onscreen, and we actually see Leslie looking at the canvases – a sustained shiver of pure being before artworks, their greatness, their luminosity and their mystery intertwined (what is this painting to me and what am I to this painting?), deepened by the fact that she is communicating with her sad boyfriend across a distance and isolation that has grown over the months from mutual embarrassment, after the first plunge into immediate intimacy that you take when you're young. *So* young...

Après-Mai is Assayas' most directly autobiographical film, covering the territory of his high school activist years in post-'68 France, and there are many scenes that dovetail with his memoir *Une adolescence dans l'après-Mai* – graffiti and defacement actions and Molotov cocktail attacks followed by violent encounters with the police and security forces, contentious meetings, the distribution of mimeographed leaflets and on-campus sales of underground newspapers. There are also elements that recall *L'Eau froide* – a fraught relationship between Gilles and his father (this time played by André Marcon), a dazed, diffuse party in a château with a bonfire in the courtyard, a profound attachment to a dark, troubled girl (Carole Combes). But apart from the new film's larger scope (temporally, thematically, experientially), it is also the work of an older man. The darkness and confusion felt by the characters no longer sets the visual tone – *Après-Mai* is sunlit and aerated where *L'Eau froide* is dank and overcast, it is more mindful of the greater world of nature which holds the characters and not so single-mindedly fixed on their torments and frustrations, and

more apt to shift to a wider and more benign perspective.

Where does politics end and love begin, at what point does love give way to art, how does art lead back to life, how does life inform politics and vice versa? These are not questions that the film asks because it knows that they are unanswerable. Neither do the characters ask them – rather, they *embody* them. At the time – and the entire movie is *about* being alive at the time – these were not abstract issues but pressing, immediate, constant concerns, carried in *Après-Mai* in glances, postures and hesitations, and in only the occasional utterance or exclamation.

With each successive film, Assayas has moved a little further beyond the set-piece, the moment which declaims its own significance, and from rhetoric which paves the way for a turning point or a movement toward resolution. With the greatest care, he preserves and enriches our sense of the flow of time, in which the magnitude of an event is neither felt nor fully processed at the moment it occurs, but in the ripples and aftershocks that follow across the years. There are indelible visions great and small – the first sudden explosion of violence in which truncheon blows are rained down on students scurrying every which way; a quick silent graffiti action, a series of deft vertical/horizontal moves in which young bodies move like cats over fences and along ledges to spray-paint slogans and symbols and slap posters on the walls; a girl silhouetted against a sudden inferno, experiencing one final grace note before a leap into oblivion; a mourning ritual in which Gilles lights two candles under a tree in broad daylight and burns one page at a time of Gregory Corso's *Gasoline*, a gift from his lost love. And there are the young characters them-

selves, or rather the young people who play them – Metayer's unruly mop of hair, sweet smile and intelligent serenity, his storm of confusion and doubt a momentary condition of youth that feels to him like forever; Armand's enormous soulful eyes, growing bigger and wider with every scene, under a handsome forehead and receding hairline; Lola Créton as Christine, the most wholesome, least troubled, and most compliant of the kids, with an apple blossom beauty and softness (she's the one seasoned professional of the bunch, but she is just as fresh as the rest of them); Menuez, a freckled American redhead with closely set eyes and a level gaze, warm yet guarded, her character so sophisticated yet so unaware of the degree to which her beauty harmonizes with the Hals paintings; Mathias Renou's fierce, tight-lipped Vincent, two piercing eyes under a mountain of red hair, assuming a militant stiffness at all times; and Combes' dark, willowy, full-lipped beauty, a white apparition behind long black hair, tossed from side to side. Assayas pulls off something miraculous here: he seems to catch them all unawares, over and over again, as they keep making first contact with the moment and with themselves in the moment, like real adolescents. There's a transcendent unity in their quietly hesitant voices, their loose postures, the way they wear their silver rings and scarves and peasant blouses, their wide-eyed stillness in the face of uncertainty.

A clip from Bo Widerberg's *Joe Hill* (a good militant date movie), the passage from the Laotian documentary and a lovely image reminiscent of *Les Deux Anglaises et le continent* aside (a matter of the spirit of the era rather than an homage to Truffaut), *Après-Mai* has interesting relationships with three films, two from the period and one recreation. Bresson's *Le Diable probablement* has long been a key movie for Assayas, which he rejected at the time of its release, a time when he could not hear what Bresson was saying precisely because "it was what I felt deep inside me." There are moments in *Après-Mai* that seem like, and yet completely unlike, Bresson's film, moments in exquisite harmony with its vision yet opening that vision out in ten alternate directions. Similarly, there is real concord between the painting sequences in *Après-Mai* and Bresson's *Quatre nuits d'un rêveur*, a film that remains more difficult to see and which Assayas knows less well – two young men alone in their quiet rooms, painting and drawing with the same feverish obsessiveness and concentration. *Après-Mai* also has an obvious kinship with Philippe Garrel's May '68 film, *Les Amants reguliers*. Age differences aside (Garrel and his friends actually took part in the events, while the younger Assayas and his friends literally came "after May"), and the two films share many similarities in tone and in their respective thematic arcs. But I think *Après-Mai* is even fresher in its approach, less self-conscious about its special relationship with the era, more oxygenated and more satisfying as a whole extended movement.

There is another link as well. In *Après-Mai*, Assayas has his own Nico in Combes' Laure, and she appears in the final images, where the film's multiple threads (art; the simultaneous rejection of consumerism, status quo politics and leftist dogma; love; self-awareness) suddenly and unexpectedly converge. For all its terrible sadness, confusion and loss, *Après-Mai* is not a lament. It is, in a very real way, the celebration of a moment, actually an instant, now long gone, when young people somehow found it more difficult to sell themselves short, when they thought twice before resorting to the paltry ambition of amassing money, when they felt a greater freedom to be unhappy – to simply *be*. There was a lot of cruelty and destruction, of the self and of others, back in those days. But better to die young and free, no matter how confused, than to slowly perish in a lavishly appointed cage, where the fleeting and the evanescent, the spirit of quickly passing beauty which enchants and empowers this movie from start to finish, is nowhere to be seen.

Early and In-Between

COPYRIGHT (1979)

Assayas on *Copyright*, from a *Reverse Shot* interview with Eric Hynes: "To me it's like a student film; it's your first movie and you make all the mistakes. And you feel so bad that you try a little harder to do better afterward. I haven't watched it in a while. I don't think I'd be nostalgic – the problem is that the acting isn't very good. It happened in the time of post-punk, French rock'n'roll, which was very much a scene I was involved with at the time. My friend Elli [Medeiros] was a singer in a French punk band called Stinky Toys, and she was the star of almost all of my short films. Elli's boyfriend, who was the guitar player in the band, did the music for *Copyright*. It was just this little cue on the synthesizer. We produced the soundtrack, and he did four or five versions of that cue and we were happy with it. He found a friend who released it as a record, and all of a sudden, it became a hit. And even now, once in a while, you hear remixes. "L'Rectangle" – people know it, it's famous. They're stupefied that this was the soundtrack to my first short film, which I've been hiding almost since I made it... *Cahiers* [du cinéma] at the time had a festival of short films, documentaries that they championed, and they selected *Copyright*. Afterwards, [Serge Daney and Serge Toubiana] came to me and said that for the past few years they'd been mostly involved in politics, but now times were changing and that they wanted to open up again to cinema. They were looking for younger writers, since it had been the same group writing for the magazine for so many years, and they asked me to write for them."

RECTANGLE – DEUX CHANSONS DE JACNO (1980)

The earliest among the short films Assayas still publicly shows, *Rectangle* is a diptych of Jacno songs/videos – "Anne cherchait l'amour" and "Rectangle." He strips his commissioned backstage promotionals of all embellishments, whether narrative, formal or confessional: both videos seem to play like a rotating system of shots, as if grabbed from a security camera, of the band members at work. Each musician is isolated, methodically pounding his instrument, indeed becoming one himself, in various parts of the city. Made not long after the birth of the music video, both shorts frame their subjects within ("Rectangle") and outside of ("Anne) empty high-rises; the primitiveness of the approach – around three cycling shots each – is just as entrenched in the "primitiveness" of the Cold Wave, post-Krautrock songs as in the postwar, suspiciously post-apocalyptic architecture. The framing of each shot of "Rectangle," a

Rectangle – Deux chansons de Jacno

Laissé inachevé à Tokyo

thrum of perpendicular lines at the junction of doorways, windows, screens, and frontally filmed housing complex facades, makes an endless, crisscrossing motif from planes of space: a cold and appealing aestheticism, buffered by a cellophane blue rain from outside the windows.

David Phelps

LAISSÉ INACHEVÉ À TOKYO (1982)

The MacGuffin of *Laissé inachevé à Tokyo* ("Left unfinished in Tokyo") seems to be both its subject and to provide a model for its mercurial form: a series of "top secret" documents passed among members of an amateur spy ring and improbably enacted as the movie itself in the form of intertitles, video interviews, and a yakuza pastiche. Clad in a kimono and sitting in a garden, László Szabó tells Elli Medeiros that "you asked for records for your novel" as a way of explaining why she's been caught in her unsubstantiated predicament and must escape Japan. But it's never clear if the records are simply her novel or the source or subject of her writing. The writer's life may be the stage for the writer's fiction, or the fiction may be the stage for the life; each character, modeling

Winston Tong en studio

gloves or fedoras as icons refracted across airport stairwells, abandoned docks, or HLM roofs, is a generic figure of a world they have either imagined or reimagined from pop culture.

The credibility of the movie, or the credibility of the spies in their generic disguises, seems less the point than their incredibility once these masks start confronting each other. As living MacGuffins, the characters act not according to private convictions, but the surface concerns of whatever movie-world they're in – being in Tokyo means battling yakuza, being in France means writing a first novel and posing for TV. Chic alienation out of Antonioni is apparent too in the high-contrast black-and-white of *Laissé inachevé* – the patterned dresses against public spaces' gradients of plastic whites; the relegation of the heroine to a compositional fulcrum point at the edges of the screen – but she seems less of an alienated body in a world of appearances than the perfect product of all these images.

In later Assayas, the slow dissolves of *Laissé inachevé* will be replaced by harder cuts in, jolts from one casual, captured moment to another. So all the scrupulous disorientations of *Laissé inachevé*, spun like a roulette wheel between a closed system of spaces, times, and styles, can be seen as Assayas' own way of conjuring up some ghost beneath the surface. Each style becomes a formal parody once the plotline which substantiates it is lost to ellipsis, and finally Szabó, failing as both a Japanese citizen and a spy, slams the confidential documents into the camera, as if bungling the typewritten reports from *Made in USA*. The promise that all the unopened reports will explain what's going on and why is lost. Rather, the reality of this movie can only be gauged by its fantasies. *David Phelps*

WINSTON TONG EN STUDIO (1984)

Winston Tong en studio, shot from a series of fixed camera positions in high-contrast black and white, is less a portrait of the former Tuxedomoon vocalist at work (on tracks for his 1985 album *Theoretically Chinese*) than a muted affirmation of group creativity and resistance to the commercial pressures and enticements of the music business circa 1984. The darkly romantic Tong, clad in shimmering leather, and his more ordinarily attired collaborators are visually and sonically isolated as they lay down their separate tracks – Tong singing and speaking lead vocals,

n Yuk

Hotel Atithi

Niki Mono (in glorious close-up) singing back-up, Tibet on keyboards, producer and former Associates member Alan Rankine on guitar, and Jah Wobble on bass – and their individual vocal and instrumental contributions are carried into and gradually faded out of the mix as Assayas shifts to discussions of the omnivorous industry and the surrounding culture. The tone is quietly mordant and bitterly reflective during the bulk of the discussions, in pointed contrast to the tightly focused and concentrated performances. *K.J.*

MAN YUK (1997)

Man Yuk was one in a series of short pieces commissioned from a variety of filmmakers by the Fondation Cartier. Assayas' contribution is a silent portrait of Maggie Cheung near the beginning of their brief marriage, composed in layers of color and motion. It is a study of Cheung in hand-held close-ups as she laughs, converses with unseen friends and applies and then removes cream from her face, juxtaposed and sometimes visually "mixed" with images of shimmering prismatic light and rushing water. Cheung becomes a creature of a world in restless motion. *K.J.*

HOTEL ATITHI (2005)

Hotel Atithi, a short film co-signed by Assayas and his editor Luc Barnier, is comprised of images assembled for the Mirror / Dash (Kim Gordon and Thurston Moore) section at the 2005 Festival ARTrock de Saint-Brieuc, curated by the filmmaker and commemorated in his 2006 documentary *Noise*. "Kim Gordon asked me to project something during the Mirror / Dash performance. And as I collect images, little bits of things that are abstract and experimental, some of which I shoot off of television, we assembled a 35-minute piece. The result is midway between a light show and experimental cinema."

In fact, *Hotel Atithi* (named for the image of a Mumbai hotel sign which continually floats within the frame) strongly resembles the interstitial video montages of images from old movies and television shows and commercials which one would see spontaneously paired with recorded music before and between sets in rock clubs during the late 70s and very early 80s. Images of a river surrounded by mountains, a figure skater, Mia Hansen-Løve opening and closing her eyes during a late night cab ride somewhere in Asia, cityscapes, a woman in negative, on their own and set within layer upon layer of visual and sonic abstraction, are denatured, deprived of their innocence and impregnated with a looming sense of universal transformation, in the form of transcendence, destruction, or both. For anyone who lived through the era, the film will resonate sweetly. Anyone who knows Assayas' work might also see *Hotel Atithi* as an indefinite extension of the most abstract passages of *demonlover* or *Boarding Gate*, or perhaps as a phantom set of images and sounds that Judith Godrèche's Louise in *Paris s'éveille* might have glimpsed at a club, or that Nathalie Richard's Zoé in *Irma Vep* might have dreamed after a rave. *K.J.*

FOR YOU (2006) / SCHENGEN (2006)

Two music videos shot by Assayas – the first for his old friend, former lead singer of Stinky Toys and star of his earliest short films, Elli Medeiros; the second for French singer/songwriter Raphaël Haroche, aka Raphaël. *K.J.*

QUARTIER DES ENFANTS ROUGES (2006)

Assayas' contribution to the omnibus film *Paris, je t'aime* is about an American actress (Maggie Gyllenhaal) shooting a period film in the 3rd *arrondissement*, first seen sashaying through a party and looking to score some hash. The recommended dealer (Lionel Dray) arrives and the question of power immediately comes into play – he's dark and bearded, she is almost translucently light-skinned; she's a movie star and he's a drug dealer. She asks him to walk with her to the nearest cash machine, he raises his hand behind her – will he mug her? molest her? caress her? The shifting points of view and perceptions (of the audience, the dealer, the actress) are extremely intricate and delicate – this is one of those passages in which Assayas deftly edges his way to the instants between fully comprehended moments, when he catches the currents of pure sensation as an interaction is in the process of playing out and embedding itself in memory.

The bills are too big, they go to a bar to break them. The dealer wants to come and watch her shoot, she gives him her number, she returns to the party and smokes herself into oblivion before getting into her 19th century costume. From her trailer, she calls the dealer. "Do you need me?" She asks for more, and he sends an assistant – "He's making a delivery to an important client." A nice, too neat piece of short fiction whose best features – the ATM exchange, the return to the party, and Gyllenhaal's believably open, unsettled presence – beg for a larger canvas. *K.J.*

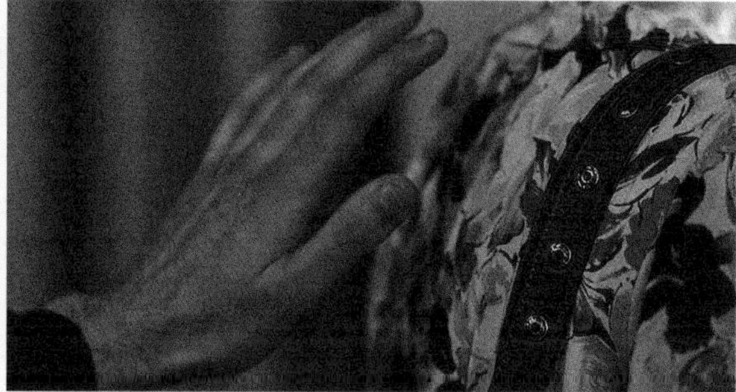

Quartier des enfants rouges

Recrudescence

RECRUDESCENCE (2007)

This 4-minute anecdote was Assayas' contribution to *Chacun son cinéma*, a film comprised of 35 short films by 35 filmmakers from around the world to commemorate the 60th anniversary of the Cannes International Film Festival. A dark bearded man (George Babluani) spots a chicly attired girl walking into a modern multiplex. As we watch the bustle of activity in the lobby, the money exchanged for popcorn and soda, the Debordian aura of the film's title is felt. The girl meets her boyfriend, the man follows them into the cinema, and we suddenly find ourselves in the environment of contemporary big budget movie exhibition – the rows of plush red seats with plastic cup holders, carpeted concrete floors and "pleasingly designed" wall patterns, everything blanketed with 5.1 surround sound, all familiar yet strange when encountered *within* a film. The girl starts making out with her boyfriend and the man sees his opportunity to steal her purse. Sometime later, the man sits in a bar drinking his second beer. The girl calls her cell phone, and he answers. A recrudescence of what? The need, or even the obligation, to connect? *K.J.*

Collaborators

Denis Lenoir, Éric Gautier, Sylvie Barthet, and Luc Barnier in conversation with Kent Jones

DENIS LENOIR
DIRECTOR OF PHOTOGRAPHY

I shot Olivier's second short fiction film, *Laissé inachevé à Tokyo*, which was very interesting, not at all standard master-medium shot-close-up grammar, but at the same time extremely classical. Classical with imagination and talent, but classical nonetheless. When we shot *Désordre* a few years later, it was a shock for me. Suddenly, it was a different way of working, it was new to me and obviously new to him, and it was not a way of shooting he had developed with me or with anyone else. It was just coming from his own head, and it was a conscious choice and desire to take this step forward and away from classical filmmaking. I'd had little experience as a DP and it was extremely stimulating, in the sense that I was running and trying to just keep up with him. He was *way* ahead of me at the time. I guess I was able to catch up, because he asked me to do the following film. On *L'Enfant de l'hiver,* which is a little like the black sheep in his filmography, he tried something new, which was to use the crane during a lot of the shooting. We discovered as we were doing it that this was slowing down the action and it gave him some problems in the editing, so he decided that it was not good for him. But it was on a particular scene in *L'Enfant de l'hiver* where I remember understanding that by covering an actor moving in a room with an 85 mill lens, rather tight, but with a tight eyeline to the actor off-camera, and then doing the reverse and respecting the eyeline – with some variations like starting with one actor and then it becomes a two-shot with a switch to a second actor, to add some complexity – he had the whole scene with total freedom of movement, with every moment of every shot dense and full.

Since I've been living in the States, I've become used to everyone, even the good filmmakers, thinking about giving themselves an infinity of options in the editing room. That's the goal. Olivier is different. He certainly wants to give himself options, but it's less a matter of shots or angles than of pace and acting, which is different. He's really betting his movie on every shot. How he cuts a scene depends on what comes before it and the pace of the whole film, if he wants to accelerate or slow down on a particular scene, so to keep that possibility open he might shoot a few things that he may or may not use later. But unlike with almost *every* other filmmaker, I don't remember ever filming a shot with Olivier where it was like, "Oh well, let's do that, it could always help" – never *ever*.

From my point of view, *L'Eau froide* was a big break. Suddenly he was choreographing the actors and blocking them in such a way... We had scenes involving many characters, and he quickly became a master of designing shots in which the people would move in and out of frame. I would follow one and pass on to another one, and all this was *somewhat* improvised. He always has, every morning, a shot list in his pocket, handwritten, in blue pencil with beautiful handwriting, and it's distributed to some members of the crew, but of course he's able to leave it behind and change his mind and do something else when he wants to. Anyway, on this film, he became masterful at working in this manner. This kind of shot is rather easy to *conceive*, but the difficulty is actually making it happen and getting it to work on the set, and he was fantastic at understanding how to modify the shot so that it could actually *function*. We would do a take, it wouldn't work because one actor had hidden another actor or come too early or too late into the frame, and Olivier would understand that we had to go back two steps to correct the speed or the movement to make it all fit together properly and smoothly. This happened with *L'Eau froide*.

Very early in his career and in mine, I don't remember on which film, I had to operate the camera on an extremely difficult shot where I had to turn around and be on one leg and then move my legs as I was filming, and it was very difficult for the focus puller because there was no depth of field. It was extremely tough for the boom operator as well, and Olivier told me, "Yes, I want the crew to be as focused as the actors." I remember some extremely small locations on *Une nouvelle vie*, working with a central column Panther [dolly] with the smallest footprint possible, and it was extremely challenging, but it was such a joy. There was a joy in knowing that you're part of an important film by a major director. And you're having fun *because* it's difficult and *because* it's tricky, because you know also that you can miss once or twice and it will be okay with everyone, but no more than that. For me, as a lighting cinematographer, it's obviously fun. But even for the focus pullers it's fun. I remember once we were putting tape marks on the ground for the actors and for the dolly moves, and these guys were taking photos of the abstract drawings, the insane spider web these marks were making everywhere in so many different colors. It was difficult, but they were proud of themselves and having fun.

On the first five films, we wanted to de-saturate the colors, and at the time the only way to do it was on the prints themselves. So we used the skip bleach process. The result, artistically speaking, is stronger blacks, stronger contrast, more grain, and de-saturated colors. It's not great for skin, because you're pulling out the pinkness of Caucasian skin tones. It hadn't been done much before, only twice to my knowledge – Roger Deakins did it on *1984* and Bruno de Keyser did it on Tavernier's *Un dimanche à la campagne*. One of the problems with it is that every distributor in every country has to do it, and it's costly. But it was cool, and it was not absurd. In those days, on a small budget, you couldn't control the palette when you were filming in the street, so by de-saturating everything you removed whatever would pull the eye away from where you wanted it to go, and give some kind of unity to the whole thing. We did that through *L'Eau froide*, and then we decided that the process had run its course for us and it was time to go back to something more natural, which is what happened with *Fin août, début septembre*. Then, with *demonlover*, we were able to do our first digital color correct.

I don't know how it is with Éric [Gautier] and Yorick [Le Saux], but Olivier and I almost never talk about the movie we're going to make. So many directors are giving you movies to watch, photos to look at, but Olivier? Never. On *demonlover*, we hadn't been working together for quite a while, and this was the only time he decided that he needed a certain kind of preparation, which he'd never done before and hasn't done since. I was working in Slovakia on a film called *Uprising*, and we had a lot of e-mail exchanges – mostly from him to me, notes that I later copied, with his permission, for the rest of the crew, because I thought they would also be important to the AD, to wardrobe, whatever. He was writing scene by scene about the light, but also about things like the luggage – in one of the first scenes, when they're taking their luggage through the airport, he wanted it to be real luxury luggage, Vuitton or Hermès or whatever, not a copy or something cheap. Via e-mail, we discussed the nature of the image in the corporate world, the nature of the image in the Mexican scenes, all that. It was not a dialogue really. I was allowed to give input, but maybe it was a way for him to gather his thoughts – the need to communicate them to someone else gave him a reason to do it for himself.

On *Carlos*, as you know, there were two DPs and we shot roughly half of it each, and with almost no discussion between either Yorick and I or Olivier and I, and it is seamless – no one can tell who shot what – which conforms to my theory that it's the director who's doing the image of the film, not the DP.

Carlos was a nightmare, because even though there was a large sum of money from Canal+, things didn't go well with the producers. I don't know all the details, thankfully, but it was extremely heavy all the time. We had six months of work, 95 days of shooting spread out over six months and it was just...eating him up. At the same time, he has this ability... Complaining in the car to the set in the morning was also a way for him to warm up, I guess, for the moment that he would be on set and dealing with actual creation. I don't think *Carlos* would have been possible without Sylvie Barthet, the production manager. But also, Olivier is very good on the production side. Then, he's no longer Olivier the artist, but the man with the passion and the hunger and strength to make his films *happen*. I mean, I've been with him so many times where, a few weeks before day one, money was missing, the producers were not ready to go for it, and he was just *forcing* them to keep on working up to the point where there was no turning back and it would have been stupid to stop. I remember...which one was it? *Fin août, début septembre,* I guess. At the last minute, he decided, "Okay, we're doing it in 16." Actually, to move from 35 to 16 is not *so* economical. But it was a way to make the producer believe that this would be such a savings that we could go on, even though we all knew that the difference was not that big. His productions are always so fragile that he cannot afford to wait for more money or for an actor to sign. For Olivier, if the movie is not happening *now*, it will never happen again.

Cinematographer **DENIS LENOIR,** born in 1949, has shot eight feature-length films with Olivier Assayas; their collaboration began with the 1982 short film *Laissé inachevé à Tokyo*. He has also worked with Bertrand Tavernier (*Daddy Nostalgie*), Patrice Leconte (*Monsieur Hire*), Catherine Breillat (*La Belle endormie*), and many others. Since the late 1990s, he has mostly worked in the U.S. He is a member of the AFC (Association Française des directeurs de la photographie Cinématographique), the ASC (American Society of Cinematographers), and the Academy of Motion Picture Arts and Sciences.

ÉRIC GAUTIER
DIRECTOR OF PHOTOGRAPHY

Olivier is a great filmmaker, and he should be more recognized and celebrated than he is in France, but the fact that he *isn't* is not so surprising. It's very French. I remember I was shooting *Intimacy* with Patrice Chéreau in London, and it was the 80th birthday of Pierre Boulez. He was celebrated for one whole month in London. Almost every night at the Barbican Centre, there was a huge program of concerts, not quite free but very cheap. It was all over the papers. But in France? Nothing. Zero. Of course, when he's dead it will be a different story.

Olivier is a great writer, that's first. And then there's his taste and talent for casting, and as Alain Resnais says, "80% of directing is the choice of the cast." Olivier's casting is always perfect, and most of the time it's surprising. He likes to use people where you don't expect them. And with not very well known actors… On *Après-Mai*, where the actors were all adolescents, many of them non-professionals, most of the preparation time was spent on the casting.

Certainly Olivier is the most "American" of the French directors in his way of using bodies, of choreographing. That's very rare in French cinema. He really is a choreographer. And the camera…he used to say that he thinks of me as an actor, and not just when we're shooting hand-held. He works very well with actors, which is also quite rare. There are plenty of French directors who work well with the camera, but with actors? The approach to acting is usually very abstract.

However, on the set, he doesn't talk very much to actors. Most of the time, it's just about rhythm and movement in the room or the space, how fast, how slow. In his films, people are always moving, and then they stop to talk. It's very rare that people walk and talk at the same time. He really loves to have them stop and speak, face to face. And you'll notice that he likes to break a steady situation with a gesture or a movement, which connects to a new feeling – the character might change his mind, or realize something. So it's a question of rhythm.

He starts on the set with an idea of what is happening in the mind of a character, but he never goes to psychological things – never never never. He's like a musician. "Speak louder" or "Not that loud…" "You're very upset, but take it slowly…" He obviously hates it when an actor makes a big show and starts overacting to show how great he is. But it's the same with the lighting and everything. He never tries to show off with the camera. On the last film, with the teenagers, for some reason he did a lot of shots with a crane. He was very worried at the beginning that it would look artificial, but I had an intuition that he was right – it gave him something lighter and more aerial. We used it on *Les Destinées sentimentales*, but that was a more classic story and a different kind of movie. Of course, we used it for the very last shot of *L'Heure d'été*, and in a way it had the very same feeling here, the feeling that life goes on, that things pass from one generation to the next – it's connected to youth. You know, his astrological sign is Verseau (Aquarius), and he's very light, never heavy in the way he speaks and the way he thinks – he's very fast, like a spirit.

When you watch his films, you have the impression that he understands you. But that's the way it is with all great movies or great books. There's a natural freedom in his movies, the feeling that his characters are free to think and to live. We think alike in that sense. We get along very well, and I give him great freedom and it's a pleasure to stay with it because we are always experimenting. Like on *Clean*, it was a great partnership between us and with Maggie – the three of us worked very closely together. I did almost no lighting in this film. What was most important was the choice of locations. The scouting. He wanted to feel the real life of the places, but at the same time he wanted her character to feel very alone. So we shot hand-held with long lenses. It was very complicated technically, working with long lenses and trying to be clear. So it was like jazz – you have the tune and then you improvise. We would go into the restaurant, for instance, figure out the action, I would suggest that she sit here rather than there because there was more depth in the background, then I would prepare a little lighting. I always try to have a very strong style for the film, even when we're working naturally. And those scenes all look simple but they're technically very difficult to achieve – for instance, sometimes you have extras who aren't very good. And the most complicated thing about this way of working is to decide: are we happy or not? Do we have it, or not? If there's a take where I've lost focus but she has the right look, then we keep that – it's so much better than re-doing it ten times before we have perfect focus. It's just a question of making a decision, and that means that we have to trust ourselves, to maintain our confidence and be self-assured when we're shooting. Again, it's like jazz – you might have a small mistake here and there but you use it, it's part of it.

Irma Vep was our first film together and we made it for nothing in four weeks. We allowed each other the freedom to do it by sticking to the idea of making decisions very quickly and decisively at the very last minute. If you decide something too early, it's more conceptual, and then you are a prisoner. You can't get rid of it, even if you say, "Okay, it was the wrong direction, I changed my mind." It's still *there*. So most of the time what I try to do with Olivier is to stay blank and just absorb everything, like a sponge. What's most important for me is to keep reviewing and thinking through the continuity, and to literally map out the structure of the film, like a musical score, in five or six pages, because I need to *see* it. Sometimes Olivier can be so surprising when he shows up on the set, so if I want to be very modest and give him freedom, and build a strong style, I always need to look back at the context and know exactly where I am in the movement of the film. He's just as surprising in his political opinions. They're coherent in a way that is completely different from the kind of coherence you find in the media. But it's the same with Arnaud [Desplechin] and with Alain Resnais. Unpredictable. Most of the time, I know what people will think of something. With these three, never. That's one of the reasons I've made so many films with them, because everything they do and say is surprising. They're all demanding and very experimental. It's hard, but rewarding, to be on the edge between one thing and something else – strong and fragile at the same time.

Cinematographer **ÉRIC GAUTIER**, born in 1961, has shot five features and two documentaries for Olivier Assayas, beginning with *Irma Vep* (1996). He has also shot most of Arnaud Desplechin's films, and worked with such directors as Alain Resnais (*Coeurs*, *Les Herbes folles*, *Vous n'avez encore rien vu*), Patrice Chéreau (*Ceux qui m'aiment prendront le train*, *Intimacy*), Léos Carax (*POLA X*), Walter Salles (*Diarios de motocicleta*, *On the Road*), and Sean Penn (*Into the Wild*).

SYLVIE BARTHET
PRODUCTION MANAGER

I met Olivier through Françoise Guglielmi, the line producer for IMA on the series "Tous les garçons et les filles de leur âge." I also worked on Emilie Deleuze's film *L'Incruste* for that series. I had seen *Désordre* in Paris when it was released; I didn't see *L'Enfant de l'hiver* at the time but I remember running into Olivier when he was shooting near the location of a film I was working on at the time. I did see *Paris s'éveille*, and I remember that *Une nouvelle vie* wasn't quite finished when we met. I was impressed by his films, and for that reason I was intimidated. But we spoke the same language – not that either of us speak a lot, but what I mean is that we understood each other immediately – and during the preparation for *L'Eau froide* we became closer.

Once we started working together, I was deeply impressed by Olivier. I still am. I admire his freedom. He is always inventing, and he always surprises me – for instance, with the way he invents as a choreographer, setting the camera and the actors in motion at the same time. It's now been a long time, we've made many movies together, but I'm still impressed by his precision, his obsessive attention to detail. His moviemaking has changed over the years, because he's more mature now, and his precision has only increased. Actually, I think that *Après-Mai* is his best movie – it's so intimate and autobiographical, so special.

I really don't know where he finds his energy. He can work 14 or 16 hours a day, and he always has the same energy. At the same time, his way of working gives energy to the actors and everyone on the crew. On the set, he's like a maestro with his orchestra. He speaks individually to everyone on the set, he develops personal relationships, he's always trying to get the best out of the crew. With the actors, it's different – he doesn't speak as much, he gives them freedom to improvise, and he gets the best from them. On the set, he's amazingly concentrated, he takes care of everybody and he *respects* everybody, even when something makes him unhappy.

There's always the pressure of money – on *Carlos*, the best example of this problem, we had to work together every single day to find solutions to our difficulties. He knows the cost of absolutely *everything*, which is not true of every filmmaker. I think we share a clear understanding of exactly what he wants on the one hand and exactly what I am able to give to him on the other – there's no ambiguity. But we've never had a shoot *without* the pressure of money. *L'Heure d'été* was a little easier because there were very few locations and relatively few actors. *Après-Mai* was very difficult, because it should have had a higher budget. *demonlover* was a different kind of experience, very bizarre. It was a relatively expensive movie for me. It was written with French actors in mind, then Olivier thought about foreign actors, the production okayed it, we cast Connie Nielsen and Chloë Sevigny, we had a lot of shooting days, everything was okay, but then we had trouble getting enough time in post-production. *Irma Vep* was amazing because we had so much trouble from the beginning. We started the prep, Dacia asked us to stop but we didn't. Around Christmas, we really *had* to, there just wasn't any money. And then, Dacia signed with Canal +, and we went ahead and made it, very quickly. I remember going to Hong Kong and meeting Maggie. We came back, talked it over, and I called her. I said, "Do you agree to do the part?" and she said "Yes – how much are you offering?" I was so ashamed by the low amount, but she agreed. Perhaps *L'Eau froide* was the shoot where we had the most fun, because there's been more pressure with time and money on every production since then, but I always enjoy it with Olivier.

When I read his scripts, I have a clear vision of what he's after. My job is to give him what he wants, to work with the production, the crew, everyone – I'm more involved with his movies than I am with the others. It's become difficult for me to work with other directors. It's just not the same kind of relationship.

SYLVIE BARTHET, born in 1955, has been Olivier Assayas' regular production manager since *L'Eau froide* (1994), and she is a co-producer of *Après-Mai* (2012). She has also served as production manager for such filmmakers as Benoît Jacquot (*La Désenchantée*), Arnaud Desplechin (*La Sentinelle*), Leos Carax (*POLA X*) and Michel Piccoli (*La Plage noire*). She is the line producer of Brian De Palma's upcoming *Passion* (working title).

LUC BARNIER
EDITOR

Apart from certain differences intrinsically linked to their personalities and their respective ideas of cinema, the principal difference between Olivier and Benoît Jacquot, for instance, is essentially one of method. When I'm working with Benoît, I start editing from day one, and he comes to the editing room one day a week throughout the shooting, to see the work and confirm the choices he made and the axis of construction for each scene. By the end of shooting a first assembly exists, and this is the version we work from during the editing.

With Olivier, the work – whether it's the choice of takes, on which we always agree, or the axis of construction per scene – requires very little debate. Curiously, it's been that way ever since we made the first short film together, *Laissé inachevé à Tokyo*. It is as if our collaboration was *always* ordained and organic – he somehow transmits to me the intuition of what he wants on the most intimate level and, consciously or unconsciously, I am given a vision of the entire film in the making. (I must say that in this sense, working with Benoît is very similar.) With Olivier, there is also a real harmony between the fluidity, energy and the nervousness of his mise-en-scène and the way I myself work when I'm editing.

On each film with Olivier, we have a very workable version after three or four weeks, leaving us with precious time to set the rhythm of the film and confirm our choices. But what has evolved over the many years of collaboration is that I feel, perfectly and immediately, his breaking point – the instant when my desire, always on the side of the film, to continue cutting a scene is checked by his refusal to go any further!

Both ways of working bring me a lot of pleasure and excitement because they are each based on mutual trust and complicity, which seems essential to me in the editing, the understanding, or maybe the intuition of the film we are in the process of making.

With *Clean*, it seemed to me that Olivier was coming out of the purely intimate vein he initiated with *Les Destinées sentimentales* and *demonlover*, and I loved this evolution – it was as if his cinema had taken on a larger scope, a new way of looking at the world, a vein that continued with *Boarding Gate* and *Carlos*, between which he was capable of pulling back and returning to an intimate autobiographical scale with *L'Heure d'été*.

I know that the scene in *L'Heure d'été* where they decide to sell the house was a nightmare to shoot, but neither Olivier nor myself had any difficulty cutting it. The only scene that ever posed a difficulty for me was the "meeting of website buyers" in *demonlover*, which was shot with two cameras in constant motion while the characters were sitting, motionless, at a round table. This scene gave me problems because of the choice of axes, the choice of movements; I was trying hard to find the rhythm because of the complexity of the camera movements, and in terms of which actors were in and out of the frame at what point – I…*we* had a hard time finding it, but once we did the scene remained unchanged.

Since the beginning of our collaboration, we have never ended up with a "flat" scene, meaning a scene where we had to go back to zero and do the best we could. This can happen when you realize that a mistake has been made in the structure of the scene – but even on scenes that were very difficult for Olivier to shoot, it hasn't happened. Similarly, we never "fake" the stories of his films, something that has happened to me on other films where I literally had to reinvent the narrative.

I agree with Denis [Lenoir] that *L'Eau froide* was a turning point in Olivier's work. The mise-en-scène of his four previous films gave you a sense of what was to come, but they were staged and shot in a more classical manner – three of them in 1.85, one in Scope, all on 35mm – which we had fun disrupting during the editing. Apart from the natural evolution of Olivier's style, the sense that *L'Eau froide* was a turning point is probably due to the fact that it was his most overtly autobiographical film, and his first feature shot in Super-16mm, handheld, and composed in enormously long *plans-séquences*. Also, apart from Virginie Ledoyen, all the other actors were beginners, which made for a significant level of improvisation in the acting, but not the mise-en-scène, from take to take. With this greater freedom, I think that Oliver was able to assert his style.

LUC BARNIER, born in 1954, has edited all of Olivier Assayas' narrative features, but their collaboration began with the 1982 short *Laissé inachevé à Tokyo*. He is the co-creator, with Assayas, of the experimental short *Hotel Atithi* (2005), and he has edited films by many other directors including Chantal Akerman (*Toute une nuit*), Idrissa Ouedraogo (*Tilaï*), Youssef Chahine (*Adieu Bonaparte*) and several films by Benoît Jacquot including *Sade*, *Tosca*, and *Les Adieux à la reine*.

Olivier Assayas

Ten Films

ZERKALO (MIRROR)
1975, Andrej Tarkovskij

Tarkovskij's heartbreaking masterpiece. For some reason this film is considered obscure, but it is extraordinarily clear to me, as close as cinema can get to dealing with autobiography, childhood memories. Just to think of the evocation of his absent father through his poems makes me shiver. Everything Tarkovskij ever touched, including his masterful essay on cinema – *Sculpting in Time,* which every film student should read – is blessed with a grace that makes him, beyond cinema, one of the greatest artists of the XXth century.

LE DIABLE PROBABLEMENT
1977, Robert Bresson

Bresson had an overwhelming influence on my early approach to movies. I felt that if cinema could reach the heights Bresson had reached, then it was worth it to follow that path and devote one's life to its practice. As it is with all such influences, you have to somehow outgrow it, if only to become yourself. But through the years my awe of Bresson's work has remained intact. This film, which deals with the Seventies, a period when I was a teenager very similar to the one portrayed by Antoine Monnier, has always held a very special place for me.

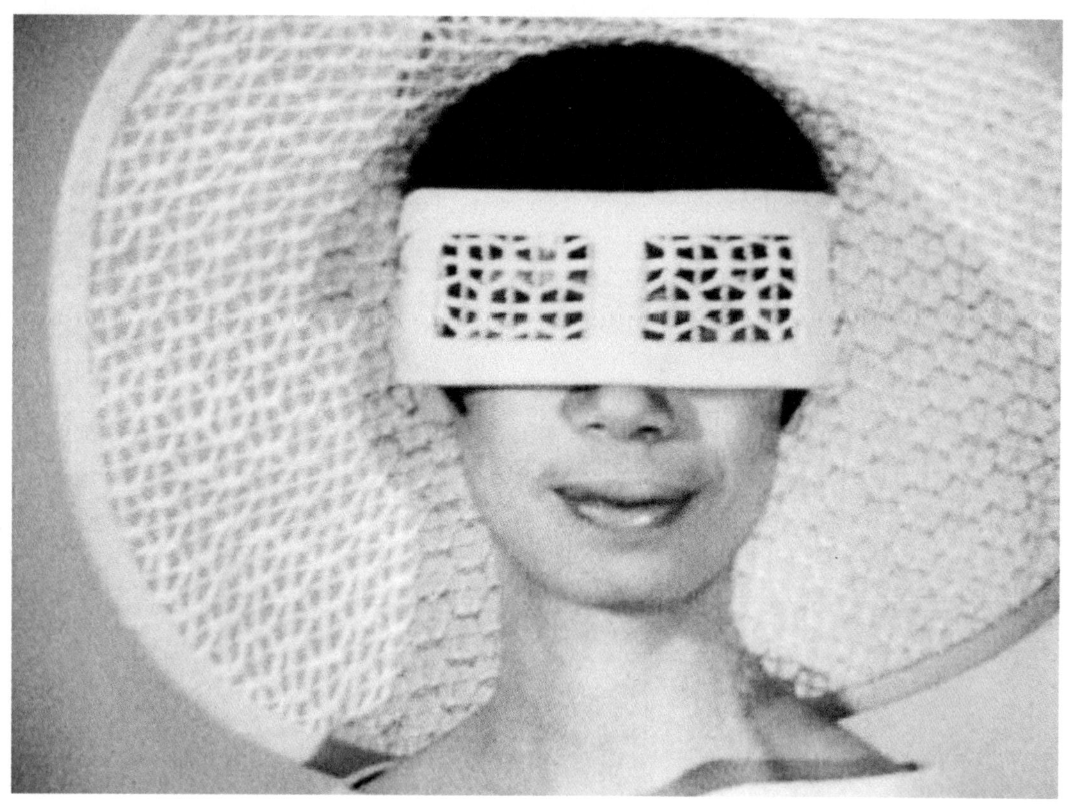

IN GIRUM IMUS NOCTE ET CONSUMIMUR IGNI (WE TURN IN THE NIGHT, CONSUMED BY FIRE)
1978, Guy Debord

I was 25 when I saw this extraordinary film, but I had already read it a few times – its commentary track, a striking essay by Debord, maybe one of his most important, had already been published. It is about youth, about historical opportunities, about time passing too quickly, about the vanity of all things, about the world falling apart and the shrinking possibility of any revolutionary alternative. Any generation can read it, see it, and feel its dark fascination echoing through its own history.

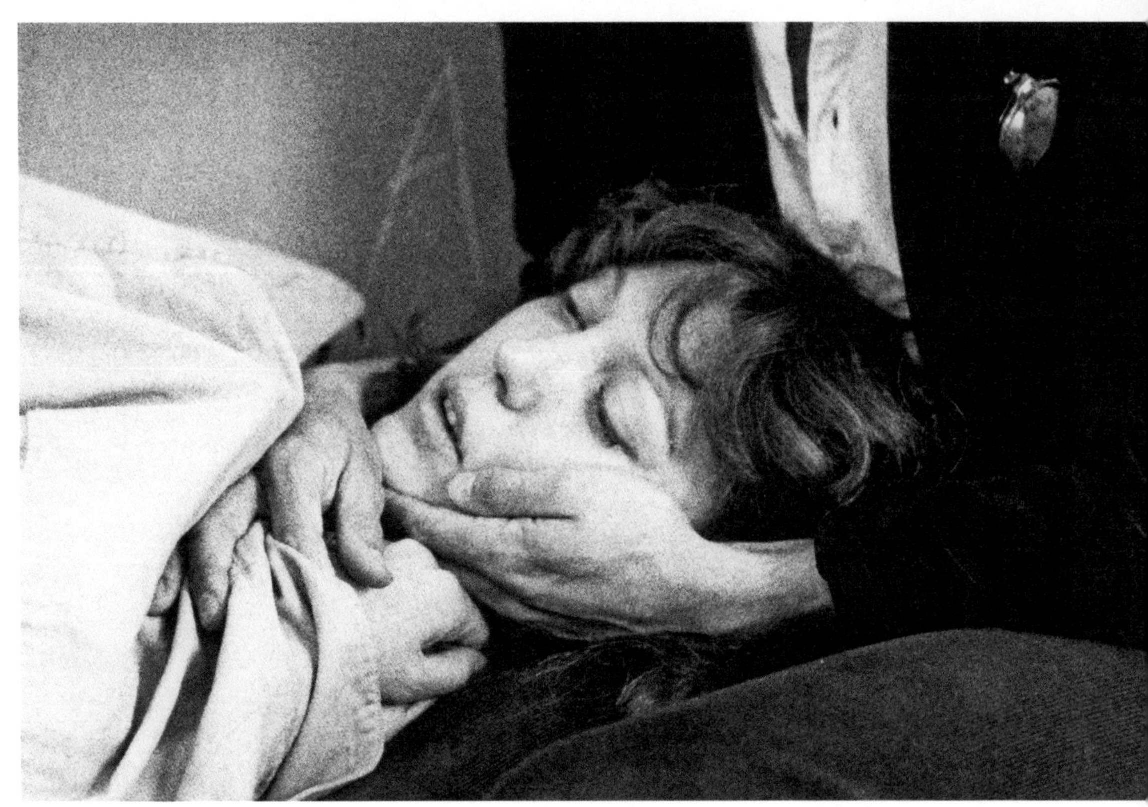

L'ENFANT SECRET
1982, Philippe Garrel

I don't know if this is Philippe Garrel's masterpiece, he has made many great movies. But certainly this is the one that has had the most profound, the most defining influence on me. Shot in the late Seventies, released in 1982, after long years in limbo, this is Garrel's farewell to the abstraction and experiments of his first period. Painfully, and self-destructively, he explores a new territory of raw narration, a poetic autobiography, which reopens for other filmmakers, including myself, the possibility of a modern, radical, figurative cinema.

LUDWIG
1972, Luchino Visconti

These days, Visconti seems largely forgotten, overlooked as some kind of decadent aesthete, a baroque stage director who turned to cinema and made a few flamboyant period pieces in his time. So, maybe it's time to check him out again. Visconti is one of the few geniuses cinema has produced. The scope, the depth, the mad ambition of his greatest achievements are somehow beyond cinema, relating – as the greatest movies of Pasolini also do – to the very history of the XXth century, and the terrifying changes European societies have undergone. Yes, Visconti is a figure out of the XIXth century looking at us, but not as an academician, rather as a daring modernist putting to shame the timid transgressions of contemporary artists. *Ludwig* is his crowning achievement, even if he never saw it finished.

FANNY OCH ALEXANDER
(FANNY AND ALEXANDER)
1983, Ingmar Bergman

No filmmaker has had a greater influence on me than Ingmar Bergman, and I had the privilege of meeting him and publishing a book of our conversations. He has been a model I have been obsessed with all my life. He is an extraordinary writer, possibly the greatest playwright of the XXth century, and one of the great inventors of forms in the history of cinema. He redefined himself many times, creating masterpieces in each of his various periods. He also wrote one of the great artistic memoirs of his time, *Laterna magica*. *Fanny and Alexander*, which he considered his last film even though it predated the sublime *Saraband* by twenty years, is a testament, a summation, and the transcendence of all he had previously achieved. At 5 ½ hours, it is, like *Ludwig*, bigger than cinema.

INVOCATION OF MY DEMON BROTHER
1969, Kenneth Anger

Kenneth Anger is a great filmmaker. Period. He is not an experimentalist, a satanist (not *only*) or a magus, even if that kind of comes closer to describing him. He invented his own cinema, as Andy Warhol did, a rival to Hollywood, a rival to basically everything that has been made in movies since the magical, mysterious silents. He believes that movies deal primarily with the invisible. He may be right.

LA MAISON DES BOIS
1971, Maurice Pialat

The hidden jewel of French cinema. Possibly the greatest film in the history of French cinema. No, I am not overdoing this. Pialat has defined ever since his first feature a raw naturalism that makes most of traditional cinema feel fake, contrived. His films are both angry and tender, dark and elegiac, intense in the way life is and movies rarely are. But there is also another Pialat – happy, luminous, reconciled, possibly, after Renoir, the truest heir of Impressionism – who comes into full bloom with *La Maison des bois*. Shot as a mini-series for French TV, it gives Pialat more time, more space, a consistent budget and none of the pressures associated with the business of cinema. The joy, the light, the very grace of filmmaking radiate in every shot.

LE COMÉDIEN
1948, Sacha Guitry

Guitry is certainly one of the most fascinating figures in the rich history of French cinema. He was already past 50 and an accomplished playwright, actor, and stage director when he started making movies, in the early '30s, at the moment the talkies gave him an opportunity to bring to cinematic life his virtuosity in dialogue, the constant daring of his dramaturgy, his sharp eye for social criticism, his formidable screen presence and his love for actors; most of all actresses, and specifically his wives, each of them defining a distinct period of his work.
Le Comédien is the biography of his father, the great actor Lucien Guitry, who was the single-most important person in Sacha's life.
In this cruelly underrated masterpiece Guitry expresses his admiration, his affection, the conflicts that marred their relationship and most of all his love for the theater, the memories and melancholy of a life spent on the stage. For me it is up there with *French Cancan*.

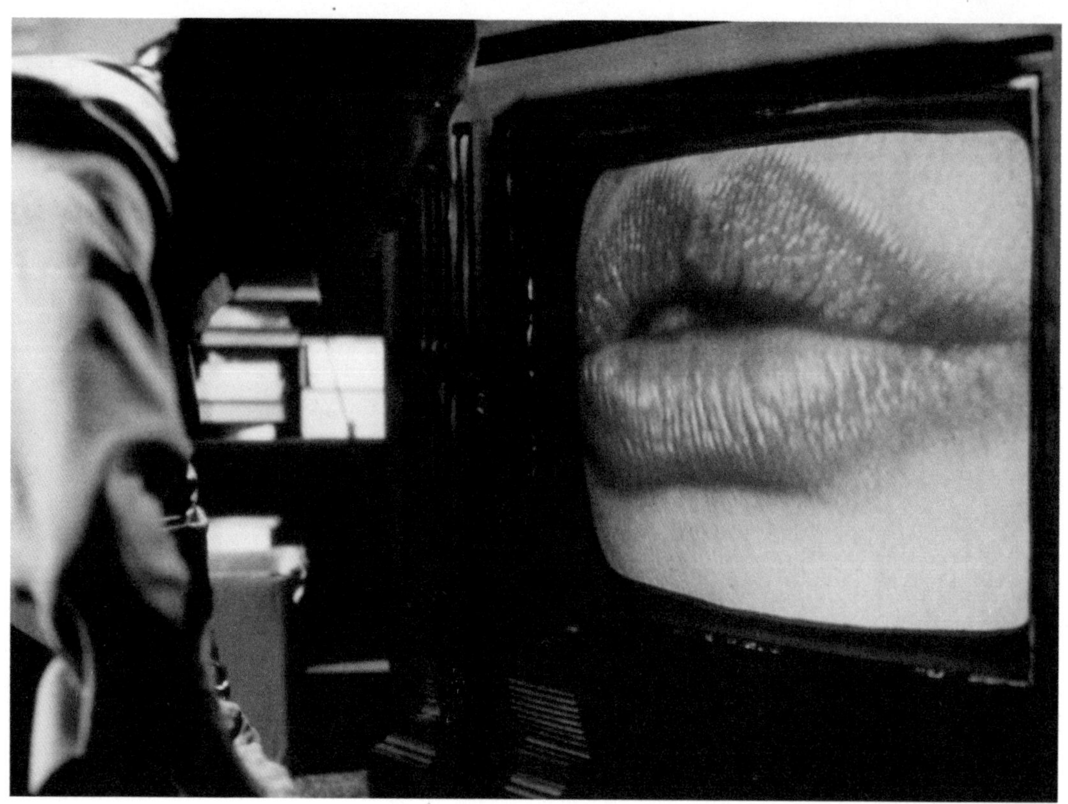

VIDEODROME
1983, David Cronenberg

I have been a fan of David Cronenberg ever since I saw *Rabid* in a suburban multiplex when I was in my early 20s. He started as a genre filmmaker, but for me he was never *genre*, he was a science fiction *auteur* right from the beginning, and he has grown with almost every new film. *Videodrome* is one of his masterpieces, for me the most important. When I saw it, it struck me as the film perhaps in closer touch with the undercurrents of modern society than any other I had ever seen, a visionary work. At the time it didn't even have a French distributor, and I did my best – I was writing for *Cahiers du cinéma* – to lobby for its release. It has stayed with me since, and its daring, abstract, poetic imagery still haunts me.

Appendix

Timeline

JANUARY 25, 1955 born in Paris to Rémy Assayas (aka Jacques Rémy) and Catherine de Károlyi
NOVEMBER 2, 1958 brother Michka Assayas born
1967 Guy Debord's *La Société du spectacle* published
MAY 2, 1968 beginning of "events of May 1968"
MAY 25, 1968 "historic" Accords of Grenelle finalized
SUMMER, 1968 visits London for the first time
1970 begins to paint
1971 sees first rock concert in Dublin: the Nice, Yes, the Bonzo Dog Band; visits India and Nepal with father and aunt
1972 works as apprentice to Jess Franco
1973 Jean Eustache's *La Maman et la putain* released
1975 reissue of *Internationale Situationniste* bulletins published by Champ Libre
1976 works as apprentice on production of *Crossed Swords* in Budapest, meets Laurent Perrin; "Anarchy in the U.K."/"God Save the Queen" single released; Ulrike Meinhof found dead in cell at Stammheim
1977 works as editorial apprentice on production of *Superman;* helps his ailing father with writing scripts for *Maigret* television series; "White Riot"/"1977" single released, sees the Clash at the Palais des glaces; Robert Bresson's *Le Diable probablement* released; Andreas Baader, Jan-Carl Raspe and Gudrun Ensslin found dead in cells at Stammheim
1978 Debord's *In girum imus nocte et consumimur igni* first screened; *Oeuvres cinématographiques complètes* published
1979 makes first short film *Copyright*
1980 makes *Rectangle – Deux chansons de Jacno*; begins writing for *Cahiers du cinéma*
DECEMBER 1, 1981 death of Rémy Assayas, age 70
1982 makes first "real" short film *Laissé inachevé à Tokyo*; "Made in USA" issue of *Cahiers du cinéma* published; Philippe Garrel's *L'Enfant secret* released
1983 Robert Bresson's final film *L'Argent* released
1984 meets Hou Hsiao-hsien, Edward Yang and Wu Nien-jen in Taiwan; "Made in Hong-Kong" issue of *Cahiers du cinéma* published
OCTOBER 1984 makes *Winston Tong en studio* in Brussels
1985 writes last text as working critic and film journalist for *Cahiers du cinéma;* collaborates on screenplays for André Téchiné's *Rendez-vous*, Laurent Perrin's *Passage secret*
1986 first feature *Désordre* released; collaborates on screenplay for Téchiné's *Le Lieu du crime*; death of Andrej Tarkovskij, age 54
1987 death of Andy Warhol, age 58
1989 *L'Enfant de l'hiver* released
1990 *Conversation avec Bergman* published
1991 *Paris s'éveille* released
1993 *Une nouvelle vie* released
MAY 1994 *L'Eau froide* released, shorter version (*La Page blanche*) shown on Arte
NOVEMBER 30, 1994 Guy Debord commits suicide, age 62
1995 writes *Irma Vep* in ten days, meets Maggie Cheung
1996 *Irma Vep* released
1997 *HHH – Portrait de Hou Hsiao-hsien* shown on Arte
1998 marriage to Maggie Cheung (divorced in 2001); *Fin août, début septembre* released, meets Mia Hansen-Løve for first time during casting
1999 *Éloge de Kenneth Anger. Vraie et fausse magie au cinéma* published by Cahiers du cinéma; death of Robert Bresson, age 98
2000 *Les Destinées sentimentales* released
2002 *demonlover* released
2003 death of Maurice Pialat, age 77
2004 *Clean* released
2005 *Une adolescence dans l'après-Mai* published by Cahiers du cinéma; *Guy Debord: Oeuvres cinématographiques complètes* DVD collection released (prepared by Debord's widow Alice Becker-Ho and Assayas)
2006 *Noise* released
OCTOBER 30, 2006 death of Catherine de Károlyi, age 87
JUNE 29, 2007 death of Edward Yang, age 59
2007 *Boarding Gate* released; *Tout est pardonné*, first film directed by Assayas' partner Mia Hansen-Løve, released; death of Ingmar Bergman, age 89
2008 *L'Heure d'été* released; *Eldorado* shown on Arte
2009 *Présences*, a collection of critical writings, published by Gallimard
NOVEMBER 15, 2009 daughter Viki born in Paris
2010 *Carlos* released, shown on Canal+
FEBRUARY 12, 2012 death of Laurent Perrin, age 56
2012 *Après-Mai* released

Filmography

COPYRIGHT

FRANCE 1979

DIRECTOR/WRITER Olivier Assayas **CINEMATOGRAPHER** Dominique Le Rigoleur **EDITOR** Hervé de Luze **PRODUCTION DESIGNER** Yves Prince **COSTUME DESIGNER** Laurence Dupré **SOUND** Patrick Baroz **MUSIC** Jacno **PRODUCTION MANAGER** Nicole Back **PRODUCTION** Les Films de l'Aigle **CAST** Laurent Perrin, Elli Medeiros, Pascal Aubier, Berta Dominguez, Michel Raskine

16MM, COLOR, 35 MINUTES

RECTANGLE – DEUX CHANSONS DE JACNO

FRANCE 1980

DIRECTOR/WRITER Olivier Assayas **CINEMATOGRAPHER** Christian Bachman **EDITOR** Chantal Colomer **SOUND** Patrick Baroz **MUSIC** Jacno **PRODUCER** Jean-Luc Besson **PRODUCTION** Dorian/Le Disque Moderne **CAST** Jacno, Elli Medeiros

16MM, COLOR, 8 MINUTES

LAISSÉ INACHEVÉ À TOKYO

FRANCE 1982

DIRECTOR/WRITER Olivier Assayas **CINEMATOGRAPHER** Denis Lenoir **EDITOR** Luc Barnier **PRODUCTION DESIGNER** Jean-Paul Ginet **COSTUME DESIGNER** Jézabel Carpi **SOUND** Patrick Baroz **PRODUCTION MANAGER** Nicole Back **PRODUCTION** Palo Alto Productions **CAST** Elli Medeiros, Nasaki Takatsuna, László Szabó, Yoshi Mamada, Benoît Ferreux, Hiro Yamashita, Pascal Aubier, Yoshi Iizawa, Katsumi Furukata, Anton Feral, Seriko Nutini, Arielle Dombasle

35MM, B/W, 21 MINUTES

WINSTON TONG EN STUDIO

FRANCE/BELGIUM 1984

DIRECTOR/WRITER Olivier Assayas **CINEMATOGRAPHER** Denis Lenoir **EDITOR** Nicolas Klotz **SOUND** Marc Mallinus **MUSIC** Winston Tong **PRODUCER** Michel Duval **PRODUCTION** Equateur, Les Disques du Crépuscule **WITH** Winston Tong, Jah Wobble, Alan Rankine, Tibet, Niki Mono

16MM, B/W, 11 MINUTES

DÉSORDRE (DISORDER)

FRANCE 1986

DIRECTOR/WRITER Olivier Assayas **CINEMATOGRAPHER** Denis Lenoir **EDITOR** Luc Barnier **PRODUCTION DESIGNER** François-Renaud Labarthe **COSTUME DESIGNER** Françoise Clavel **ASSISTANT DIRECTORS** Michel Béna, Fanny Aubrespin, Claire Devers **SOUND** Philippe Sénéchal, Gérard Lamps **MUSIC** Gabriel Yared **PRODUCTION MANAGER** Baudoin Capet **PRODUCER** Claude-Éric Poiroux **PRODUCTION** Forum Productions International **CAST** Wadeck Stanczak (Yvan), Ann-Gisel Glass (Anne), Lucas Belvaux (Henri), Rémi Martin (Xavier), Corinne Dacla (Cora), Simon de La Brosse (Gabriel), Etienne Chicot (Albertini), Philippe Demarle (Marc), Juliette Mailhé (Cécile), Etienne Daho (Jean-François), Philippe Laudenbach (Gabriel's father), Maxime Leroux, Salem Ludwig, Pierre Romans, Allen Hoist, The Woodentops

35MM, COLOR, 90 MINUTES

L'ENFANT DE L'HIVER (WINTER'S CHILD)

FRANCE 1989

DIRECTOR/WRITER Olivier Assayas **CINEMATOGRAPHER** Denis Lenoir **EDITOR** Luc Barnier **PRODUCTION DESIGNER** François-Renaud Labarthe **COSTUME DESIGNER** Françoise Clavel **ASSISTANT DIRECTOR** Hubert Engammare **SOUND** Olivier Schwob, Joël Rangon **MUSIC** Jorge Arriagada **PRODUCTION MANAGER** Jean-Louis Godfroy **PRODUCERS** Paolo Branco, Jean-Claude Fleury **PRODUCTION** Gemini Films, G.P.F.I. **CAST** Clotilde de Bayser (Sabine), Michel Feller (Stéphane), Marie Matheron (Natalia), Jean-Philippe Ecoffey (Bruno), Gérard Blain (Stéphane's father), Anouk Grinberg (Stéphane's sister), Nathalie Richard (Leni), Vincent Vallier (Jean-Marie), Virginie Thévenet (Maryse), Myriam David (Marie), Pierrick Mescam, Serge Riaboukine, Michel Raskine, Inès de Medeiros, Guy Patrick Sainderichin, Pascal Bonitzer, Marie-Jo Delacour, Gianguido Spinelli

35MM, COLOR, 83 MINUTES

PARIS S'ÉVEILLE (PARIS AWAKENS)

FRANCE/ITALY 1991

DIRECTOR/WRITER Olivier Assayas **CINEMATOGRAPHER** Denis Lenoir **EDITOR** Luc Barnier **PRODUCTION DESIGNER** François-Renaud Labarthe **COSTUME DESIGNER** Françoise Clavel **ASSISTANT DIRECTOR** Etienne Albrecht **SOUND** Jean-Claude Laureux, Gérard Lamps **MUSIC** John Cale **PRODUCTION MANAGER** Baudoin Capet **PRODUCERS** Bruno Pesery, Angelo Rizzoli **PRODUCTION** Arena Films, Christian Bourgois Productions, Films A2, Erre Produzioni **CAST** Judith Godrèche (Louise), Jean-Pierre Léaud (Clément), Thomas Langmann (Adrien), Martin Lamotte (Zablonski), Ounie Lecomte (Agathe), Antoine Basler (Victor), Michèle Foucher (Louise's mother), Éric Daviron, Edouard Montoute, Samba Illa Ndiayae, Laurent Jacquet, Patrick Sabourin, Sasha Boselli, Thierry Guerrier, Elli Medeiros, Daniel Langlet

35MM, COLOR, 95 MINUTES

UNE NOUVELLE VIE (A NEW LIFE)

FRANCE 1993

DIRECTOR/WRITER Olivier Assayas **CINEMATOGRAPHER** Denis Lenoir **EDITOR** Luc Barnier **PRODUCTION DESIGNER** François-Renaud Labarthe **COSTUME DESIGNER** Françoise Clavel **ASSISTANT DIRECTOR** Pascal Chaumeil **SOUND** François Musy **PRODUCTION MANAGER** Baudoin Capet **PRODUCER** Bruno Pesery **PRODUCTION** Arena Films **CAST** Sophie Aubry (Tina), Judith Godrèche (Lise), Bernard Giraudeau (Constantin), Christine Boisson (Laurence), Philippe Torreton (Fred), Bernard Verley (Ludovic), Nelly Borgeaud (Nadine), Antoine Basler (Kléber), Roger Dumas (Martín), Nathalie Boutefeu (Brigitte), Richard Bean (Gérard), Maïté Maille (France)

35MM, COLOR, 117 MINUTES

L'EAU FROIDE (COLD WATER)

FRANCE 1994

DIRECTOR/WRITER Olivier Assayas **CINEMATOGRAPHER** Denis Lenoir **EDITOR** Luc Barnier **PRODUCTION DESIGNER** Gilbert Gagneux **COSTUME DESIGNER** Françoise Clavel **ASSISTANT DIRECTOR** François-Renaud Labarthe **SOUND** Hervé Chauvel, William Flageollet **MUSIC** "Me & Bobby Mc Gee" (Janis Joplin), "Up Around the Bend" (Creedence Clearwater Revival), "Janitor of Lunacy" (Nico), "Virginia Plain" (Roxy Music), "Avalanche" (Leonard Cohen), "Knockin' on Heaven's Door" (Bob Dylan), "School's Out" (Alice Cooper), "Easy Livin'" (Uriah Heap), "Cosmic Wheels" (Donovan) **PRODUCTION MANAGER** Sylvie Barthet **PRODUCERS** Georges Benayoun, Paul Rozenberg **PRODUCTION** IMA Films **CAST** Virginie Ledoyen (Christine), Cyprien Fouquet (Gilles), László Szabó (Gilles' father), Jean-Pierre Darroussin (inspector), Dominique Faysse (Christine's mother), Smaïl Mekki (Mourad), Jackie Berroyer (Christine's father), Jean-Christophe Bouvet (The Teacher), Ilona Györi (Marie, the nanny), Renée Amzallag, Jerôme Simonin, Laetitia Lemerle, Alexandra Yonnet, Caroline Doron, Laetitia Giraud

35MM, COLOR, 94 MINUTES

TV version: *La Page blanche* (part of the series *Tous les garçons et les filles de leur âge*), 67 minutes

IRMA VEP

FRANCE 1996

DIRECTOR/WRITER Olivier Assayas **CINEMATOGRAPHER** Éric Gautier **EDITOR** Luc Barnier **PRODUCTION DESIGNER** François-Renaud Labarthe **COSTUME DESIGNERS** Françoise Clavel, Jessica Doyle **ASSISTANT DIRECTOR** François-Renaud Labarthe **SOUND** Philippe Richard, William Flageollet **MUSIC** Philippe Richard & Yann Richard, "Bonnie and Clyde" (Luna), "Tunic (Song for Karen)" (Sonic Youth), "Soukora" (Ali Farka Touré & Ry Cooder) **PRODUCTION MANAGER** Sylvie Barthet **PRODUCERS** Georges Benayoun, Françoise Guglielmi **PRODUCTION** Dacia Films **CAST** Maggie Cheung (Maggie), Jean-Pierre Léaud (René Vidal), Nathalie Richard (Zoé), Nathalie Boutefeu (Laure), Alex Descas (Desormeaux), Dominique Faysse (Maïté), Arsinée Khanjian (The American), Bernard Nissilie (Markus), Olivier Torrès (Ferdinand/Moreno), Bulle Ogier (Maryelle), Lou Castel (José Murano), Antoine Basler (journalist), Jacques Fieschi (Roland), Estelle Larrivaz (publicist), Balthazar Clémenti (Robert), Lara Cowez (script supervisor), Dominique Cuny (grip), Jessica Doyle (Jessica), Maryel Ferraud (make-up woman), Filip Forgeau (camera operator), Valerie Guy (Valerie), Yann Richard (Kevin), Françoise Clavel (René's wife), Françoise Guglielmi (producer), François-Renaud Labarthe (TV cameraman), Sandra Faure, Catherine Ferny

35MM, COLOR, 99 MINUTES

MAN YUK

FRANCE 1997

DIRECTOR/CINEMATOGRAPHER Olivier Assayas **EDITOR** Luc Barnier **PRODUCTION** Fondation Cartier pour l'Art contemporain **WITH** Maggie Cheung

VIDEO, COLOR, 5 MINUTES, NO SOUND

HHH – PORTRAIT DE HOU HSIAO-HSIEN

FRANCE/TAIWAN 1997

DIRECTOR/WRITER Olivier Assayas **CINEMATOGRAPHER** Éric Gautier **EDITOR** Marie Lecœur **SOUND** Tu Du-Che, William Flageollet **PRODUCTION MANAGER** Elisabeth Marlangias **PRODUCERS** Xavier Carniaux, Peggy Chiao **PRODUCTION** La Sept-Arte, Arc Light Films, Hsu Hsiao-ming Film Corp., AMIP, INA **WITH** Hou Hsiao-hsien, Chen Kuo-fu, Chu T'ien-wen, Kao She, Lin Giang, Tu Du-che, Wu Nien-jen

35MM, COLOR, 90 MINUTES

Part of the series *Cinéma, de notre temps*

FIN AOÛT, DÉBUT SEPTEMBRE (LATE AUGUST, EARLY SEPTEMBER)

FRANCE 1998

DIRECTOR/WRITER Olivier Assayas **CINEMATOGRAPHER** Denis Lenoir **EDITOR** Luc Barnier **PRODUCTION DESIGNER** François-Renaud Labarthe **COSTUME DESIGNER** Françoise Clavel **ASSISTANT DIRECTOR** Marie-Jeanne Pascal **SOUND** François Waledisch, William Flageollet **MUSIC** "Contre Le Sexisme"

(Sonic Youth), "Altar" (Elli Medeiros), "Cinquante six, Goye Kur, Hawa Dolo" (Ali Farka Touré) **PRODUCTION MANAGER** Patrice Arrat **PRODUCERS** Georges Benayoun, Philippe Carcassonne, Françoise Guglielmi **PRODUCTION** Dacia Films **CAST** Mathieu Amalric (Gabriel), François Cluzet (Adrien), Virginie Ledoyen (Anne), Jeanne Balibar (Jenny), Alex Descas (Jérémie), Arsinée Khanjian (Lucie), Nathalie Richard (Maryelle), Mia Hansen-Løve (Véra), Éric Elmosnino (Thomas), Olivier Cruveiller (Axel), Jean-Baptiste Malartre (Vladimir, the editor) André Marcon (Hattou), Jean-Baptiste Montagut (Joseph Costa), Olivier Torrès (Marc Jobert), Jean-François Gallotte (Lucien Korner), Fejria Deliba (Maria), Bernard Nissille (Frédéric), Béatrice de Roaldès (Amie d'Alfonso), Elisabeth Mazev, Olivier Py, Joanna Preiss, Elli Medeiros, Catherine Mouchet
35MM, COLOR, 111 MINUTES

LES DESTINÉES SENTIMENTALES (LES DESTINÉES)

FRANCE / SWITZERLAND 2000
DIRECTOR Olivier Assayas **WRITERS** Jacques Fieschi, Olivier Assayas based on the novel by Jacques Chardonne **CINEMATOGRAPHER** Éric Gautier **EDITOR** Luc Barnier **PRODUCTION DESIGNER** Katia Wyskop **COSTUME DESIGNER** Anaïs Romand **ASSISTANT DIRECTOR** Marie-Jeanne Pascal **SOUND** Jean-Claude Laureux, William Flageollet **MUSIC** Pieces by Guillaume Lekeu interpreted by l'Ensemble de Musique Oblique, Waltzes by Emile Waldteufel and Olivier Metra interpreted by L'Ensemble Sorties d'Artistes **PRODUCTION MANAGER** Jean-Yves Asselin **PRODUCERS** Bruno Pesery, Jean-Louis Porchet, Gérard Ruey **PRODUCTION** Arena Films, CAB Prod., Arcade, Canal+, TF1, TSR **CAST** Emmanuelle Béart (Pauline), Charles Berling (Jean Barnery), Isabelle Huppert (Nathalie), Olivier Perrier (Philippe Pommerel), Dominique Reymond (Julie Desca), André Marcon (Paul Desca), Alexandra London (Louise Desca), Julie Depardieu (Marcelle), Louis-Do De Lencquesaing (Arthur Pommerel), Valérie Bonneton (Mme Pommerel), Pascal Bongard (Vouzelles), Didier Flamand (Guy Barnery), Jean-Baptiste Malartre (Fréderic Barnery), Nicolas Pignon (Bavouzet), Catherine Mouchet (Fernanda), Mia Hansen-Løve (Aline), Sophie Aubry (Dominique), Victor Garrivier (Paster Sabatier), Jerôme Huguet (René Fayet), Mathieu Genet (Max Barnery), Rémi Martin (Dahlias), Jean-Pierre Gos (Fayet), Saki Reid (Miss Howard), Claire Hammond (Madame Ducros), Roger Dumas
35MM, COLOR, 180 MINUTES

DEMONLOVER

FRANCE 2002
DIRECTOR / WRITER Olivier Assayas **CINEMATOGRAPHER** Denis Lenoir **EDITOR** Luc Barnier **PRODUCTION DESIGNER** François-Renaud Labarthe **ART DIRECTOR** James David Goldmark **COSTUME DESIGNER** Anaïs Romand **ASSISTANT DIRECTOR** Marie-Jeanne Pascal **SOUND** Philippe Richard, Olivier Goinard, Dominique Gaborieau **MUSIC** Sonic Youth, Jim O'Rourke **PRODUCTION MANAGER** Sylvie Barthet **PRODUCERS** Edouard Weil, Xavier Giannoli, Andrés Martín, Robin O'Hara, Jean Coulon, Claude Davy **PRODUCTION** Citizen Films, Elizabeth Films, M6 Films, Forensic Films **CAST** Connie Nielsen (Diane de Monx), Charles Berling (Hervé Le Millinec), Chloë Sevigny (Elise Lipsky), Gina Gershon (Elaine Si Gibril), Jean-Baptiste Malartre (Henri-Pierre Volf), Dominique Reymond (Karen), Edwin Gerard (Edward Gomez), Thomas M. Pollard (The American Lawyer), Abi Sakamoto (Kaori), Julie Brochen (Gina), Jürgen Doering (Stylist), Jean-Charles Dumay (Henri), Jean-Pierre Gos (Verkamp), Alexandre Lachaux (Erwan), Nao Omori (Shoji), Alexis Pivot (Frankie), Ludovic Schoendoerffer (Luis), Naoko Yamazaki (Eiko)
35MM, COLOR, 121 MINUTES

CLEAN

FRANCE / CANADA / UK 2004
DIRECTOR / WRITER Olivier Assayas **CINEMATOGRAPHER** Éric Gautier **EDITOR** Luc Barnier **PRODUCTION DESIGNERS** François-Renaud Labarthe, William Fleming **COSTUME DESIGNER** Anaïs Romand **ASSISTANT DIRECTOR** Matthew Gledhill **SOUND** Bill Flynn **MUSIC** Brian Eno, David Roback, Tricky, Elizabeth Densmore, Metric, Joey Ramone, Britta Phillips & Dean Wareham, The Notwist, z'Howndz **PRODUCTION MANAGER** Frédéric Sauvagnac **PRODUCERS** Edouard Weil, Niv Fichman, Xavier Giannoli, Xavier Marchand **PRODUCTION** Rectangle Prod., Rhombus Media, Haystack Prod., Arte, Forensic Films **CAST** Maggie Cheung (Emily Wang), Nick Nolte (Albrecht Hauser), Béatrice Dalle (Elena), Jeanne Balibar (Irene Paolini), Don McKellar (Vernon), Martha Henry (Rosemary Hauser), James Johnston (Lee Hauser), James Dennis (Jay), Rémi Martin (Jean-Pierre), Laetitia Spigarelli (Sandrine), Jodi Crawford (Gloria), Joana Preiss (Aline), Kurtys Kidd (The Detective), Régis Vidal (Alexis), David Salsedo (Jeff), Arnaud Churin, Man Kit Cheung, Emily Haines, David Roback, Tricky, Liz Densmore
35MM, COLOR, 110 MINUTES

HOTEL ATITHI

FRANCE 2005
A FILM BY Olivier Assayas, Luc Barnier
CINEMATOGRAPHER Olivier Assayas
MUSIC Mirror / Dash (Kim Gordon, Thurston Moore)
VIDEO, COLOR, 35 MINUTES

QUARTIER DES ENFANTS ROUGES

FRANCE / LIECHTENSTEIN / SWITZERLAND / GERMANY 2006
Segment *(3e arrondissement)* of the omnibus film *Paris, je t'aime*
DIRECTOR / WRITER Olivier Assayas **CINEMATOGRAPHER** Éric Gautier **EDITOR** Luc Barnier **PRODUCTION DESIGNER** Bettina von den Steinen **COSTUME DESIGNER** Olivier Bériot **ASSISTANT DIRECTOR** Matthew Gledhill **SOUND** Daniel Sobrino, Vincent Tulli **MUSIC** "Un elephant me regarde", "Petite fille ne crois pas" (Antoine) **PRODUCTION MANAGER** Philippe Delest **PRODUCERS** Emmanuel Benbihy, Claudie Ossard **PRODUCTION** Victoires Int., La Fabrique des Films, Pirol Stiftung, Filmazure, Canal+ **CAST** Maggie Gyllenhaal (Liz), Lionel Dray (Ken)
35MM, COLOR, 6 MINUTES +
VIDEO, COLOR, 10 MINUTES (DIRECTOR'S CUT)

NOISE

FRANCE 2006
DIRECTOR / WRITER Olivier Assayas **CINEMATOGRAPHERS** Michael Almereyda, Olivier Assayas, Éric Gautier, Léo Hinstin, Laurent Perrin, Olivier Torrès **EDITORS** Luc Barnier, Marion Monnier **SOUND** Jean-Baptiste Brunhes, Nicolas Cantin, Olivier Goinard **PRODUCTION MANAGER** Sylvie Barthet **PRODUCERS** Gérard Lacroix, Gérard Pont **PRODUCTION** Retro Active Films, Arsenal Associés, Assiciation Wild Rose, France 4 **WITH** Alla, Jeanne Balibar, Afel Bocoum, Rodolphe Burger, White Tahina (Vincent Epplay, Joana Preiss), Mirror/Dash (Kim Gordon, Thurston Moore), Emily Haines, Metric, Marie Modiano, Le Début de l'A (Kate Moran, Pascal Lambert), Jim O'Rourke, Text of Light (Lee Ranaldo, Steve Shelley)
DIGITAL, COLOR, 115 MINUTES

FOR YOU

FRANCE 2006
A MUSIC VIDEO BY Olivier Assayas
MUSIC Elli Medeiros
VIDEO, COLOR, 4 MINUTES

SCHENGEN

FRANCE 2006
A MUSIC VIDEO BY Olivier Assayas
MUSIC Raphaël
VIDEO, COLOR, 3 MINUTES

RECRUDESCENCE

FRANCE 2007
Segment of the omnibus film *Chacun son cinéma*
DIRECTOR / WRITER Olivier Assayas **CINEMATOGRAPHERS** Yorick Le Saux, Benoit Rizzotti, Léo Hinstin **EDITORS** Luc Barnier, Lise Courtès **COSTUME DESIGNER** Anaïs Romand **ASSISTANT DIRECTORS** Matthew Gledhill, Delphine Heude, Merryl Messaoudi **SOUND** Daniel Sobrino, Julien Sicart **PRODUCTION MANAGERS** Sylvie Barthet, Gaston Flores **PRODUCERS** Charles Gillibert, Sandrine Brauer, Denis Carot, Sergei Davidoff, Gilles Jacob, Marie Masmonteil **PRODUCTION** Cannes Film Festival, Elzévir Films, Studio Canal **CAST** George Babluani, Deniz Gamze Ergüven, Lionel Dray
DIGITAL, COLOR, 4 MINUTES

BOARDING GATE

FRANCE 2007
DIRECTOR / WRITER Olivier Assayas **CINEMATOGRAPHER** Yorick Le Saux **EDITOR** Luc Barnier **PRODUCTION DESIGNER** François-Renaud Labarthe **COSTUME DESIGNER** Anaïs Romand **ASSISTANT DIRECTOR** Matthew Gledhill **SOUND** Daniel Sobrino **MUSIC** "Music for airports: 2/2" (Brian Eno), "The Heavenly Music Corporation" (Robert Fripp & Brian Eno), "Deng zhe ni hui lai (waiting 4 u)" (Bai Kwong), "What Time is Love / LP Mix" (The KLF), "Lizard Point" (Brian Eno), "#1 Song in Heaven, Part 2" (Sparks), "Shi yi zhou mo (kelly chan)" (Lin Xi), "Younger Days" (Dickey Cheung), "Desire of Flying" (Al Jing) **PRODUCTION MANAGER** Sylvie Barthet **PRODUCER** François Margolin **PRODUCTION** Canal+, Margo Films, Samsa Films, Wild Bunch **CAST** Asia Argento (Sandra), Michael Madsen (Miles Rennberg), Kelly Lin (Sue Wang), Carl Ng (Lester Wang), Kim Gordon (Kay), Alex Descas (Andrew), Joana Preiss (Lisa), Raymond Tsang (Abacus Boss), Boss Mok (Mr. Ho), Régis Vidal (DJ at Vega), François-Renaud Labarthe (Night Watchman), Jim Ping Hei (Abacus Worker #1), Kim Lee Wing (Abacus Worker #2), Ricky Wong (Abacus Worker #3)
35MM, COLOR, 106 MINUTES

ELDORADO

FRANCE 2008

DIRECTOR/WRITER Olivier Assayas **CINEMATOGRAPHER** Yorick Le Saux **EDITOR** Marion Monnier **SOUND** David Rit, Martin Sadoux, Julien Sicart **MUSIC** Karlheinz Stockhausen **PRODUCTION MANAGER** Claire Dornoy **PRODUCTION** MK2 TV, Arte France, Ballet Preljocaj, Lithium Films **WITH** Angelin Preljocaj, Karlheinz Stockhausen

DIGITAL, COLOR

87 MINUTES *(Creation)* + **42 MINUTES** *(Sonntags Abschied)*

L'HEURE D'ÉTÉ (SUMMER HOURS)

FRANCE 2008

DIRECTOR/WRITER Olivier Assayas **CINEMATOGRAPHER** Éric Gautier **EDITOR** Luc Barnier **PRODUCTION DESIGNER** François-Renaud Labarthe **COSTUME DESIGNERS** Anaïs Romand, Jürgen Doering **ASSISTANT DIRECTOR** Matthew Gledhill **SOUND** Nicolas Cantin, Olivier Goinard **MUSIC** "Loftus Jones" (Turlogh O'Carolan & Robin Williamson), "Gwydion's Dream" (Robin Williamson), "Je Represente Paris" (Emotion La Foliiie), "Loser" (Plasticiens), "Little Cloud" (Incredible String Band) **PRODUCTION MANAGER** Sylvie Barthet **PRODUCERS** Marin Karmitz, Nathanael Karmitz, Charles Gillibert **PRODUCTION** MK2 **CAST** Juliette Binoche (Adrienne), Charles Berling (Frédéric), Jérémie Rénier (Jérémie), Edith Scob (Hélène), Dominique Reymond (Lisa), Valérie Bonneton (Angela), Isabelle Sadoyan (Eloïse), Kyle Eastwood (James), Alice de Lencquesaing (Sylvie), Emile Berling (Pierre), Jean-Baptiste Malartre (Michel Waldemar), Gilles Arbona (Maître Lambert), Éric Elmosnino, Marc Voinchet, Luc Bricault

35MM, COLOR, 102 MINUTES

CARLOS

FRANCE/GERMANY 2010

DIRECTOR Olivier Assayas **WRITERS** Olivier Assayas, Dan Franck **CINEMATOGRAPHERS** Denis Lenoir, Yorick Le Saux **EDITORS** Luc Barnier, Marion Monnier **PRODUCTION DESIGNER** François-Renaud Labarthe **COSTUME DESIGNER** Jürgen Doering **ASSISTANT DIRECTOR** Luc Bricault **SOUND** Nicolas Cantin **MUSIC** "Loveless Love" (The Feelies), "Sock it to me" (John O'Brien-Docker), "Dreams Never End" (New Order), "Basta Ya" (Atahualpa Yupanqui), "Yolanda" (Pablo Milanes), "All Night Party" (A Certain Ratio), "Amalia Rosa" (Carrasco), "El sueno Americano" (La Portuaria), "Feedback in Vienna" (Yarol Poupaud), "Ahead" (Wire), "Sea Magni" (Oumou Sangare), "Terebellum" (Robert Fripp & Brian Eno), "Hi'lawe" (Tia Carrere), "Contentement" (Marian McPartland), "Forces at Work" (The Feelies), "Sonic Reducer" (The Dead Boys), "Dot Dash" (Wire), "Ich will noch nicht nach Haus" (Cantus-Chor), "Drill" (Wire), "Sharing" (Satisfaction), "Sag ihr auch" (Gerd Christian), "The 15th" (Wire), "Pure" (The Lightning Seeds), "Jenra" (Davy Graham), "Duniya" (Tata Dindin), "Saa Magni" (Oumou Sangare), "Amir el-Hosn" (Mohammad Wardi), "Mwashah" (Hamza el-Din), "La Pistola y el Corazon" (Los Lobos) **PRODUCTION MANAGER** Sylvie Barthet **PRODUCERS** Daniel Leconte, Jens Meurer, Judy Tossell **PRODUCTION** Film en Stock, Egoli Tossell Film **CAST** Édgar Ramírez (Ilich Ramírez Sánchez/Carlos), Nora von Waldstätten (Magdalena Kopp), Alexander Scheer (Johannes Weinrich/Steve), Christoph Bach (Hans-Joachim Klein/Angie), Julia Hummer (Gabriele Kröcher-Tiedemann/Nada), Aljoscha Stadelmann (Wilfried Böse/Boni), Jule Böwe (Christa Margot Fröhlich/Heidi), Sylta Fee Wegmann (Juliane Plambeck), Katharina Schüttler (Brigitte Kuhlmann), Ahmad Kaabour (Wadi Haddad), Fadi Abi Samra (Michel Moukharbal/André), Rodney El-Haddad (Anis Naccache/Khalid), Talal Al-Jourdi (Ali Al-Issawe), Rami Farah (Joseph), Zeid Hamdan (Youssef), Juana Acosta (Nydia Tobon), Jean-Baptiste Malartre (Jacques Senard), Olivier Cruveiller (Jean Herranz), Pierre-François Dumeniaud (Raymond Dous), Simon-Pierre Boireau (Jean Donatini), André Marcon (Philippe Rondot), Jean-Baptiste Montagut (Luc Groven/Éric), Guillaume Saurrel (Bruno Breguet), Nicolas Briancon (Jacques Vergès), Vincent Jouan (Broussard), Belkacem Djemel Barek (Mohamed Boudia), Fabrice Jemfer (Colonel Choppin de Janvry), Samuel Achache (Guy Cavallo), Sarah Le Picard (Marie-Caroline Cavallo), Bibi Jacob (Angela Armstrong), Luise Berndt, Timo Jacobs, Olivia Ross, Hiraku Kawakami

DIGITAL, COLOR, 331 MINUTES +

35MM, COLOR, 187 MINUTES (theatrical version)

APRÈS-MAI (SOMETHING IN THE AIR)

FRANCE 2012

DIRECTOR/WRITERDIRECTOR/WRITER Olivier Assayas **CINEMATOGRAPHER** Éric Gautier **EDITOR** Luc Barnier **PRODUCTION DESIGNER** François-Renaud Labarthe **COSTUME DESIGNER** Jürgen Doering **ASSISTANT DIRECTORS** Delphine Heude, Valérie Roucher **SOUND** Nicolas Cantin **MUSIC** "Terrapin" (Syd Barrett); "Green Onions" (Booker T and the MG's); "Strings in the Earth and Air" (Dr Strangely Strange); "Ballad of William Worthy" (Johnny Flynn); "Queen of Scots" (Amazing Blondel); "Bransle For My Lady's Delight" (Amazing Blondel); "Know" (Nick Drake); "Abba Zaba" (Captain

Beefheart and his Magic Band); "Air" (Incredible String Band); "Why Are We Sleeping" (Soft Machine); "Sunrise in the Third System" (Tangerine Dream); "Fantasia Lindum / Celestial Light" (Amazing Blondel); "Fare Thee Well, Sweet Mally" (Robin Williamson); "Decadence" (Kevin Ayers); "After Me" (After Me) **PRODUCTION MANAGER** Benjamin Hess **PRODUCERS** Nathanaël Karmitz, Charles Gilbert, Sylvie Barthet, Marin Karmitz **PRODUCTION** MK2, France 2 Cinéma, Vortex Sutra **CAST** Clement Metayer (Gilles), Lola Créton (Christine), Felix Armand (Alain), Carole Combes (Laure), India Salvor Menuez (Leslie), Mathias Renoud (Vincent), André Marcon (Gilles' father), Hugo Conzelmann, Martin Loizillon
35MM, COLOR, 122 MINUTES

Screenplays

SCOPITONE

FRANCE 1977
DIRECTOR Laurent Perrin **WRITERS** Laurent Perrin, Olivier Assayas **CAST** Didier Sauvegrain, Martine Simonet, Jean-Claude Bouillon, Edwige Gruss, J.P. Fresqueline, Bibiane Kirby, Paquita
16MM, COLOR, 34 MINUTES

NUIT FÉLINE

FRANCE 1978
DIRECTOR Gérard Marx **WRITERS** Gérard Marx, Dominique Lancelot, Olivier Assayas **CAST** Marcel Delmotte, Philippe du Janerand
35MM, COLOR, 20 MINUTES

ÉTOILES ET TOILES – KIM BASINGER

FRANCE 1982
Episode for the TV programme *Étoiles et toiles* (1982–1986)
DIRECTOR Georges Bensoussan **WRITERS** Georges Bensoussan, Olivier Assayas (interactive dialogue)
VIDEO, COLOR, 10 MINUTES

PASSAGE SECRET

FRANCE 1984
DIRECTOR Laurent Perrin **WRITERS** Olivier Assayas, Laurent Perrin **CAST** Dominique Laffin, Franci Camus, François Siener, Ged Marlon, Michel Subor, Philippe Morier-Genoud, Julien Dubois, Léonard Smith
35MM, COLOR, 85 MINUTES

RENDEZ-VOUS

FRANCE 1985
DIRECTOR André Téchiné **WRITERS** André Téchiné, Olivier Assayas **CAST** Juliette Binoche, Lambert Wilson, Wadeck Stanczak, Jean-Louis Trintignant, Dominique Lavanant, Anne Wiazemsky, Jean-Louis Vitrac, Jacques Nolot
35MM, COLOR, 87 MINUTES

L'UNIQUE

FRANCE 1986
DIRECTOR Jérôme Diamant-Berger **WRITERS** Olivier Assayas, Jérôme Diamant-Berger, Jean-Claude Carrière, Jacques Dorfmann **CAST** Julia Migenes Johnson, Sami Frey, Charles Denner, Tchéky Karyo, Jezabel Carpi, Fabienne Babe
35MM, COLOR, 85 MINUTES

LE LIEU DU CRIME (SCENE OF THE CRIME)

FRANCE 1986
DIRECTOR André Téchiné **WRITERS** André Téchiné, Pascal Bonitzer, Olivier Assayas **CAST** Catherine Deneuve, Danielle Darrieux, Wadeck Stanczak, Nicolas Giraudi, Victor Lanoux, Jean Bousquet, Claire Nebout
35MM, COLOR, 90 MINUTES

AVRIL BRISÉ

FRANCE 1987
DIRECTOR Liria Begeja **WRITERS** Liria Begeja, Olivier Assayas, Vassilis Vassilikos based on the novel by Ismaïl Kadaré **CAST** Jean-Claude Adelin, Violetta Sanchez, Alexandre Arbatt, Sadri Sheta, Xhemil Vraniqi
35MM, COLOR, 100 MINUTES

FILHA DA MÃE (LOVELY CHILD)

PORTUGAL 1990
DIRECTOR João Canijo **WRITERS** Olivier Assayas, João Canijo, Manuel Mozos, Teresa Villaverde **PRODUCTION** Madragoa Filmes **CAST** José Wilker, Rita Blanco, Lídia Franco, Miguel Guilherme, Diogo Dória, João Cabral, Adriano Luz
35MM, COLOR, 105 MINUTES

ALICE ET MARTIN (ALICE AND MARTIN)

FRANCE/SPAIN 1998
DIRECTOR André Téchiné **WRITERS** Olivier Assayas, Gilles Taurand, André Téchiné **CAST** Juliette Binoche, Alexis Loret, Mathieu Amalric, Carmen Maura, Jean-Pierre Lorit, Marthe Villalonga, Roschdy Zem
35MM, COLOR, 120 MINUTES

Bibliography

Writings by Olivier Assayas

BOOKS

OLIVIER ASSAYAS & CHARLES TESSON, *Hong Kong cinéma*. Paris: Cahiers du cinéma, Editions l'Etoile, 1990. Reprint of the September 1984 Special Issue of *Cahiers du cinéma*, no. 362–363: *Made in Hong-Kong*. Includes, among other elements, O.A.'s essays "King Hu, géant exile," "Chang Cheh, l'ogre de Hong-Kong," "L'irrésistible ascension de Raymond Chow," "Mak Kar, la formule miracle" and "La génération de 1997," as well as interviews conducted by O.A. and/or Charles Tesson and Tony Rayns with King Hu, Xu Feng, Liu Chia-liang, Run Run Shaw, Raymond Chow, King Hu, Ann Hui, Michael Hui, Allen Fong and Tsui Hark.

OLIVIER ASSAYAS & STIG BJÖRKMAN, *Conversation avec Bergman*. Paris: Cahiers du cinéma, Editions l'Etoile, 1990
German edition: *Gespräche mit Ingmar Bergman*. Berlin: Alexander-Verlag, 2002; Italian edition: *Conversazione con Ingmar Bergman*. Torino: Lindau, 2008

OLIVIER ASSAYAS, *Éloge de Kenneth Anger. Vraie et fausse magie au cinéma*. Paris: Cahiers du cinéma. Collection Auteurs, 1999

OLIVIER ASSAYAS, *Une adolescence dans l'après-Mai. Lettre à Alice Debord*. Paris: Cahiers du cinéma, 2005. English edition: *A Post-May Adolescence. Letter to Alice Debord* and two essays on Guy Debord. Vienna: FilmmuseumSynemaPublikationen, 2012

OLIVIER ASSAYAS, *Présences. Écrits sur le cinema*. Préface de Laurence Schifano. Paris: Editions Gallimard, 2009
A rich selection of O.A.'s essays from 1980 to the present. Part I: *On marge des "Cahiers" (1980–1985)*. 1: on Visconti and *Ludwig;* Fassbinder and *Querelle*; *The King of Comedy*; Fellini and *E la nave va; Deep End*. 2: on Westerns and Road movies; *Raiders of the Lost Ark; The Empire Strikes Back*; *Honkytonk Man*; *White Dog; Body Double*. 3: on *A Passage to India; The Killing Fields;* King Hu; Chang Cheh; the Taiwanese New Wave. 4: on Truffaut; Godard and *Prénom Carmen*; Robbe-Grillet; "Du scénario achevé au scénario ouvert;" Clouzot's *Le Mystère Picasso* ("À propos des tableaux-séquences de Picasso," 1985, previously unpublished in French).
Part II: *En marge des mes films (1993–2008)*. "Le fil d'Ariane" (2008, previously unpublished); "Les images hantées" (1993, prev. unpubl.). 1: on Warhol; Debord; *Le Diable probablement* ("Permanence du Diable," prev. unpubl. in French); Cassavetes. 2: on Feuillade; Jean-Pierre Léaud; Maggie Cheung; "L'écriture et son scenario;" adapting *Les Destinées sentimentales*. 3: on Hou Hsiao-hsien; Edward Yang. 4: "Bergman, instantanés" (prev. publ. in *Télérama*, 2004); "La forme du cinema;" "Solitude d'être Godard" (prev. publ. in *Vogue*, 2006); "La voix de Johnny Cash" (prev. publ. in *Les Inrockuptibles*, 2002); Mark Power's photographs.

PUBLISHED SCREENPLAYS

OLIVIER ASSAYAS, *Fin août, début septembre*. Paris: Petite bibliothèque de Cahiers du cinéma, 1999
Includes an essay by O.A., "L'écriture et son scenario."

OLIVIER ASSAYAS & JACQUES FIESCHI, *Les Destinées sentimentales. Scénario d'après le roman de Jacques Chardonne*. Paris: Petite bibliothèque de Cahiers du cinéma, 2000
Includes an essay by O.A., "Tout et son contraire."

OLIVIER ASSAYAS, *L'Enfant de l'hiver*. La Madeleine: Editions LettMotif, 2011. Includes an introduction by O.A. and his 1989 conversation with Vincent Vallier.

OLIVIER ASSAYAS, *Une nouvelle vie*. La Madeleine: Editions LettMotif, 2012. Includes an introduction by O.A. and an expanded version of his 1993 conversation with Serge Grünberg.

SELECTED CONTRIBUTIONS TO CAHIERS DU CINÉMA, 1980–1985

OLIVIER ASSAYAS, "The Fog (John Carpenter)." No. 310, 1980

OLIVIER ASSAYAS, "Dark Star." No. 314, 1980

OLIVIER ASSAYAS, "Dennis Hopper revient à Cannes" [Interview]. No. 314, 1980

OLIVIER ASSAYAS, "SPFX News ou situation du cinéma de science-fiction envisage comme secteur de pointe". No. 315, 316, 317, 318, 1980. The four essays entitled "SPFX News," appearing in four consecutive issues of *Cahiers du cinéma*, are an extended reflection on the vogue for special effects in films, the complexity of elements involved in these films, the use of the storyboard, the relationship between comics and science-fiction films, journals specializing in SF cinema, and the parallel evolution of special sound effects and SF cinema. Including several interviews with technicians and producers.

OLIVIER ASSAYAS, "L'empire contre-attaque (Irvin Kershner)" [on *The Empire Strikes Back*]. No. 316, 1980

SERGE DANEY & OLIVIER ASSAYAS, "Entretien avec Wim Wenders" [Interview with Wim Wenders, on *Lightning Over Water*]. No. 318, 1980

OLIVIER ASSAYAS, "En attendant *Superman II:* La Lester 'touch'" [Interview with Richard Lester]. No. 318, 1980

OLIVIER ASSAYAS, "Vi amo, signor Allen" [on *Stardust Memories*]. No. 319, 1981

OLIVIER ASSAYAS, "La tribu et la loi" [on *Umarete wa mita keredo*, 1932]. No. 319, 1981

OLIVIER ASSAYAS, "Hurlements" [on *The Howling*]. No. 320, 1981

OLIVIER ASSAYAS, "L'esprit du temps" [on Michael Powell] and "Entretien avec Michael Powell" [Interview]. No. 321, 1981. English translation of the interview in: David Lazar (ed.), *Michael Powell: Interviews*. Jackson, Mississippi; London: University Press of Mississippi, 2003

OLIVIER ASSAYAS, "Le rock de la méthode" [on *Rude Boy*] and "Entretien avec Jack Hazan" [Interview]. No. 321, 1981

OLIVIER ASSAYAS & SERGE TOUBIANA, "Profession: monteuse. Entretien avec Thelma Schoonmaker" and "Profession: producteur. Entretien avec Irwin Winkler" [Interviews in relation to *Raging Bull*]. No. 321, 1981

OLIVIER ASSAYAS, "Berlin 81" [including a report on a retrospective of South East Asian cinema]. No. 322, 1981

OLIVIER ASSAYAS, "Jean-Pierre Mocky. Le malentendu." No. 323–324, 1981

OLIVIER ASSAYAS, "Le discours-Gaumont" and "Entretien avec Daniel Toscan du Plantier" [Interview, conducted together with Serge Toubiana]. No. 325, 1981

OLIVIER ASSAYAS, "L'Académie du cinéma" [on Cannes 1981]. No. 326, 1981

OLIVIER ASSAYAS, "New York 1997" [on *Escape From New York*]. No. 326, 1981

OLIVIER ASSAYAS & CHARLES TESSON, "Entretien avec Lino Brocka: La pointe de l'iceberg" [Interview]. No. 327, 1981

OLIVIER ASSAYAS, "George Lucas: Un cinéma conceptuel" and "La grâce perdue des aventuriers" [on *Raiders of the Lost Ark*]. No. 328, 1981

OLIVIER ASSAYAS, "Hyères 81. Cinéma d'aujourd'hui." No. 329, 1981

OLIVIER ASSAYAS, "La grande escroquerie du rock'n roll" [on *The Great Rock'n'Roll Swindle*]. No. 329, 1981

OLIVIER ASSAYAS & CHARLES TESSON, "Entretien avec Vincent Price" [Interview]. No. 331, 1982

***MADE IN USA*. SPECIAL ISSUE OF *CAHIERS DU CINÉMA*,** no. 334–335, 1982. This 145-page double issue was a collective endeavor by the editors and writers of the magazine and focussed on the current landscape of US cinema. Among several other elements, it includes O.A.'s essay "L'esprit de Belize" on special effects companies and the "electronic future" of cinema, his reviews of *Conan* and *Taps*, and several interviews he conducted: Douglas Trumbull, Peter Bogdanovich, Jon Davison, Budd Boetticher (the latter three with Bill Krohn), Francis Ford Coppola (with Lise Bloch-Morhange & Serge Toubiana), and Manny Farber (with Jean-Pierre Gorin, Serge Le Péron & Serge Toubiana). English translation of the Manny Farber conversation: "Manny Farber: Cinema's Painter-Critic," (re-)translated by Noel King, *Framework* 40, 1999

OLIVIER ASSAYAS, "Jean-Pierre Mocky: Un auteur-artisan" and "Entretien" [Interview with Mocky]. No. 336, 1982

OLIVIER ASSAYAS, "La ligne de fuite perdue" [on the Western and Road movies]. No. 337, 1982

OLIVIER ASSAYAS, "Le chien révélateur" [on *White Dog*]. No 339, 1982

OLIVIER ASSAYAS, SERGE LE PÉRON & SERGE TOUBIANA, "Entretien avec John Carpenter" [Interview]. No. 339, 1982

OLIVIER ASSAYAS & SERGE LE PÉRON, "Ridley Scott: Cineaste du décor" [Interview]. No. 339, 1982

OLIVIER ASSAYAS, "Fin d'été au Lido" [on Venice 1982]. No. 340, 1982

OLIVIER ASSAYAS, "L'enfer de Brest" [on Fassbinder and *Querelle*]. No. 340, 1982

OLIVIER ASSAYAS, "Eaux troubles" [on *Deep End*, 1970]. No. 346, 1983

OLIVIER ASSAYAS, "De l'autre côté des images" [on *The King of Comedy*]. No. 347, 1983

OLIVIER ASSAYAS, "Autoportrait du cinéaste en despote d'un autre siècle" [on Visconti and *Ludwig*]. No. 350, 1983

OLIVIER ASSAYAS, "La publicité, point aveugle du cinéma français" [on the aesthetics of advertising films and their influence on a certain kind of cinema, such as that of Jean-Jacques Beineix]. No. 351, 1983

CHARLES TESSON & OLIVIER ASSAYAS, "Entretien avec Ann Hui" [Interview]. No: 351, 1983

OLIVIER ASSAYAS, "Ici et maintenant", "Zig-zag vénitien" and "Que d'auteurs, que d'auteurs!" [on Venice 1983 and *Prénom Carmen*]. No. 352, 1983

OLIVIER ASSAYAS, "Sur un Politique" [on the position of the *auteur* today]. No. 353, 1983

OLIVIER ASSAYAS, "Eastwood in the country" [on *Honkytonk Man*]. No. 353, 1983

OLIVIER ASSAYAS, "Sic transit Gloria N." [on Fellini and *E la nave va*]. No. 355, 1984

OLIVIER ASSAYAS, "Les revenants de l'Empire céleste" [on a retrospective of Chinese cinema]. No. 355, 1984

OLIVIER ASSAYAS, ALAIN BERGALA, SERGE DANEY & SERGE TOUBIANA, "Le point critique" [Round table on the role of the critic and the crisis of criticism]. No. 356, 1984

OLIVIER ASSAYAS, "Voulez-vous jouer à 'Twilight zone' avec moi?" No. 356, 1984

OLIVIER ASSAYAS, "Itinéraire d'un 'grand pitre'" [Interview with Michel Serrault]. No. 357, 1984

OLIVIER ASSAYAS & CHARLES TESSON, *Made in Hong-Kong*. Special issue of *Cahiers du cinéma*, no. 362–363, 1984. See above (Books).

OLIVIER ASSAYAS, "De Truffaut à Doinel." No. 366, 1984

OLIVIER ASSAYAS, "Notre reporter en République de Chine" [a survey of Taiwanese cinema and its New Wave, including conversations with Sylvia Chang, Hou Hsiao-hsien and Edward Yang]. No. 366, 1984

OLIVIER ASSAYAS, "L'homme de l'ouest, le vrai" [Obituary and interview with Sam Peckinpah]. No. 368, 1985

CHARLES TESSON & OLIVIER ASSAYAS, "Le sourire 'off'. Entretien avec Clint Eastwood" [Interview]. No. 368, 1985

OLIVIER ASSAYAS, "La place du spectateur" [on *Body Double*]. No. 368, 1985

OLIVIER ASSAYAS, "Robbe-Grillet et le maniérisme" and "Le cinema, l'art et la manière" [Interview with author Patrick Mauriès, conducted together with Alain Bergala & Pascal Bonitzer]. No. 370, 1985

OLIVIER ASSAYAS, "Du scénario achevé au scénario ouvert" [on screenwriting]. No. 371–372, 1985

OLIVIER ASSAYAS, "L'empire et l'aventure" [on *A Passage to India*]. No. 373, 1985

OLIVIER ASSAYAS, "*Mishima*, de Paul Schrader." No. 373, 1985

OLIVIER ASSAYAS, "Octobre à New York" [on *After Hours*]. No. 377, 1985

SELECTED ESSAYS AND CONTRIBUTIONS TO BOOKS AND MAGAZINES SINCE 1986

OLIVIER ASSAYAS, "A proposito dei quadri-sequenza di Picasso." In: *Quaderno informativo*. Pesaro: Mostra Internazionale del Nuovo Cinema, 1989. French original in *Présences*, 2009 (see Books)

SERGE TOUBIANA & THIERRY JOUSSE, "Autour de *Pickpocket*. Table ronde acec Olivier Assayas, Jean-Claude Brisseau, Benoît Jacquot, André Téchiné" [Round table discussion]. *Cahiers du cinéma*, no. 416, 1989

OLIVIER ASSAYAS, "Juste une chose" [on Serge Daney]. *Cahiers du cinéma*, no. 458, 1992

OLIVIER ASSAYAS, "Andy Warhol." *Positif*, no. 400, 1994. English translation in: John Boorman & Walter Donohue (eds.), *Projections 4½*. London: Faber & Faber, 1995

OLIVIER ASSAYAS, "Dans des circonstances éternelles / Du fonds d'un naufrage" [on Guy Debord]. *Cahiers du cinéma*, no. 487, 1995. English translation: "'Under circumstances eternal / From the depths of a shipwreck,'" in: Olivier Assayas, *A Post-May Adolescence. Letter to Alice Debord* and two essays on Guy Debord. Vienna: FilmmuseumSynemaPublikationen, 2012.

OLIVIER ASSAYAS, "Vers les bruits du monde" [on rock music and cinema]. *Cahiers du cinéma* Special issue no. 18: *Musiques au cinema*, 1995

MARTIN SCORSESE & CAHIERS DU CINÉMA (EDS.), "Cinq questions de Martin Scorsese à John Carpenter, Abel Ferrara, Alain Resnais, John Woo, Takeshi Kitano, Wu Nien-Jen et Olivier Assayas." *Cahiers du cinéma*, Special Issue edited by Martin Scorsese, no. 500, 1996. English translation: "Five Questions," in: John Boorman & Walter Donohue (eds.), *Projections 7*. London: Faber & Faber, 1997

OLIVIER ASSAYAS & BÉRÉNICE REYNAUD, "Tarkovsky: Seeing Is Believing" [Conversation]. *Sight and Sound*, no. 1/1997

OLIVIER ASSAYAS, "HHH, portrait de Hou Hsiao-hsien" and "Journal de tournage" [Recollections and a production diary, related to O.A.'s film of the same title]. *Cahiers du cinéma*, no. 512, 1997

OLIVIER ASSAYAS, "A propos of Maggie." *Metro*, Melbourne, no. 113–114, 1997. German translation, "Apropos Maggie," in: *Meteor*, Vienna, no. 7, 1997. Italian translation in: Giona A. Nazarro & Andrea Tagliacozzo (eds.), *Il cinema di Hong Kong. Spade, kung fu, pistole, fantasmi*. Genova: Le Mani, 1997

OLIVIER ASSAYAS, "Cassavetes, posthume." In: *Supplement d'Ame. Hors série 1: Régards sur Cassavetes*, La Madeleine: LettMotif, 1997; new edition 2010. English translation: "Cassavetes, posthumously," in: Tom Charity, *John Cassavetes, lifeworks*. London: Omnibus Press, 2001

CHARLES TESSON & OLIVIER JOYARD, "De Hong-Kong à la Chine. Dialogue avec Olivier Assayas" [Interview with O. A. about Chinese cinemas]. *Cahiers du cinéma* Special Issue no. 24: *Made in China*, 1999

OLIVIER ASSAYAS, "Préface. Hou Hsiao-hsien: en Chine et ailleurs." In: Jean-Michel Frodon (ed.), *Hou Hsiao-hsien*. Paris: Cahiers du cinéma, 1999; expanded edition 2005

OLIVIER ASSAYAS, "Le vent de la vie: Conversation avec Catherine Deneuve." *Cahiers du cinéma*, no. 535, 1999

OLIVIER ASSAYAS, "The Devil Probably" [on Bresson's *Le Diable probablement*]. *Film Comment*, no. 4/1999

OLIVIER ASSAYAS, "L'opera nascosta" [from a conversation on Guy Debord and his films]. In: Enrico Ghezzi & Robert Turigliatto (eds.), *Guy Debord (contro) il cinema*. Milano, Venezia: Editrice Il Castoro / La Biennale di Venezia, 2001.

Expanded and rewritten in 2002, and published in English: "The Hidden Oeuvre," in: Olivier Assayas, *A Post-May Adolescence. Letter to Alice Debord* and two essays on Guy Debord. Vienna: FilmmuseumSynemaPublikationen, 2012

OLIVIER ASSAYAS, "Ils nous ont appris à réinventer le cinema" [Comments on the American experimental cinema of the 1960s]. *Cahiers du cinéma*, no. 558, 2001

CHARLES TESSON, CLAUDINE PAQUOT & ROGER GARCIA (EDS.), *L'Asie à Hollywood* [Chapter: Round table with Olivier Assayas, Christophe Gans and Charles Tesson on the Asian New Wave]. Locarno, Paris: Cahiers du cinéma, Festival International du Film de Locarno, 2001.

L'EXCEPTION, GROUPE DE REFLEXION SUR LE CINEMA (ED.), *Le Banquet imaginaire* [O.A. contributes to this wide-ranging debate between several participants about current changes in cinema]. Paris: Gallimard, 2002

OLIVIER ASSAYAS, "La forme cinema." In: Thierry Jousse, *Pendant les travaux, le cinéma reste ouvert*. Paris: Cahiers du cinéma, 2003

OLIVIER ASSAYAS, "My Generation. Breaking the sound barrier: A director's take on movies, music, adolescence, and politics." *The Village Voice*, August 17, 2004

TAKESHI KITANO & CAHIERS DU CINÉMA (EDS.), "Ciné-Manga par Takeshi Kitano" [with contributions by Olivier Assayas, Bertrand Bonello, Catherine Breillat, Arnaud des Pallières, Arnaud Desplechin, Jacques Doillon, Yervant Gianikian & Angela Ricci Lucchi, Hong Sang-soo, Kyoshi Kurosawa, Claude Lanzmann, Rithy Panh, Gus Van Sant and Apichatpong Weerasethakul]. Supplement to *Cahiers du cinema*, no. 600, 2005

OLIVIER ASSAYAS, "Le flue" [on Mark Power's photographs]. In: Serge Toubiana, Dominique Dufour (eds.), *L'Image d'après: le cinéma dans l'imaginaire de la photographie*. Göttingen, Paris: Steidl / Magnum / La Cinémathèque française, 2007

OLIVIER ASSAYAS, "Modern Time" [Essay on Edward Yang]. *Film Comment*, no. 1/2008. Reprinted in French, in *Le cinéma d'Edward Yang*, ed. Jean-Michel Frodon. Paris: Editions de l'éclat, 2010.

OLIVIER ASSAYAS, "Laurent Perrin, été 1976" [Obituary of filmmaker and friend Laurent Perrin]. *Cahiers du cinéma*, no. 676, 2012

About Olivier Assayas

BOOKS

BRUNO FORNARA & ANGELO SIGNORELLI (EDS.), *Olivier Assayas*. Bergamo: Bergamo Film Meeting, 1995. Includes essays by Kent Jones and Bruno Fornara, an interview conducted by Bruno Fornara and Angelo Signorelli, O.A.'s lists of favourite films and records, Italian translations of his essays on George Lucas, on the Western and Road movies, and on screenwriting, as well as an annotated filmography.

ÁNGEL QUINTANA, *Olivier Assayas. Líneas de fuga*. Gijón: Festival Internacional de Cine de Gijón, 2003. Includes the author's analysis of O.A.'s oeuvre, several of his conversations with O.A., and Spanish translations of O.A.'s essays "La forme cinéma," "La grace perdue des aventuriers," "Sic transit Gloria N.," "La place du spectateur," "Robbe-Grillet et le maniérisme" and "L'écriture et son scenario."

STEFANO BONI & MASSIMO QUAGLIA (EDS.), *Olivier Assayas*. Torre Boldone: Edizioni di Cineforum, 2006. Includes essays by Adriano Piccardi, Carlo Chatrian, Giona A. Nazzaro, Michele Marangi and Umberto Mosca, an interview conducted by Jean-Michel Frodon, and an annotated filmography.

SELECTED INTERVIEWS, ARTICLES, AND BOOK CHAPTERS

Note: The following selection mainly focuses on French- and English-language film magazines and books, with very few German, Italian, Dutch and Spanish entries added. Articles in weekly and daily newspapers were mostly not considered.

THIERRY CAZALS "L'orage des sentiments" [*Désordre*] and Thierry Cazals & Alain Philippon, "L'émotion pure" [Interview]. *Cahiers du cinéma*, no. 389, 1986

FRANÇOIS RAMASSE, "Adam et Eve on rate le precedent" [*Désordre*]. *Positif*, no. 312, 1987

CLAUDE RACINE, "Olivier Assayas: nouvelle 'nouvelle vague' du côté de Cahiers...?" [Interview, *Désordre*]. *24 Images*, Montréal, no. 34–35, Fall 1987

HEINER GASSEN, "Lebenswut" [*Désordre*]. *EPD Film*, no. 5/1987

SAMRA BONVOISIN & MARY-ANNE BRAULT, *L'Aventure du premier film* [Chapter: Interview on *Désordre*]. Paris: Editions Bernard Barrault, 1989

HERVÉ LE ROUX, "L'avancée belle" [*L'Enfant de l'hiver*]. *Cahiers du cinéma*, no. 418, 1989

FRANÇOIS RAMASSE, "Lorsque l'enfant paraît" [*L'Enfant de l'hiver*]. *Positif*, no. 340, 1989

VINCENT VALLIER, "Intervista con Olivier Assayas." *Quaderno Informativo*. Pesaro: Mostra Internazionale del Nuovo Cinema, 1989

RAINER GANSERA, "Leben aber ohne Liebe sei Tod. Zu den ersten Filmen von Olivier Assayas" [*Désordre* and *L'Enfant de l'hiver*]. *Steadycam*, Cologne, no. 14, 1989

MART DOMINICUS & JOS DE PUTTER, "Afstandelijkheid is een foute opvatting van de realiteit" [Interview, *L'Enfant de l'hiver]*. *Skrien*, no. 172, 1990

NICOLAS SAADA, "Les ombres," and Marie-Anne Guérin, "Intra-muros," and Serge Toubiana, "En quête de personnages" [*Paris s'éveille*]. *Cahiers du cinéma*, no. 450, 1991

OLIVIER KOHN, "Olivier, Louise et l'air du temps" [*Paris s'éveille*]. *Positif*, no. 370, 1991

BERNARD BENOLIEL, "Histoire d'Adrien," and Jacques Zimmer, "Le plaisir et la nécessité" [*Paris s'éveille*]. *Revue du cinéma*, no. 477, 1991

MART DOMINICUS & MIEKE BERNINK, "Olivier Assayas: acrobat of poppenspeler?" [*Paris s'éveille*]. *Skrien*, no. 186, 1992

FRÉDÉRIC SABOURAUD, "Crisi del punto di vista" [*Paris s'éveille*]. *Filmcritica*, no. 423, 1992

MARIE-CLAUDE LOISELLE, "Mouvement et tourments" and "Entretien avec Olivier Assayas" [Interview, *Paris s'éveille*]. *24 Images*, Montréal, no. 59, Winter 1992

JACQUES VALOT & YVES ALION, "Une nouvelle vie: Désordre" and "Olivier Assayas: 'cette part obscure de soi.'" *Mensuel du cinéma*, no. 10/1993

FRÉDÉRIC SABOURAUD, "Les somnambules," "14 images pour une sequence" and "Autour de la fiction" [*Une nouvelle vie*, essays and an interview]. *Cahiers du cinéma*, no. 472, 1993

FRANÇOIS RAMASSE, "La mise en scène des sentiments" [*Une nouvelle vie*]. *Positif*, no. 393, 1993

JACQUES MORICE, "Les chants magnétiques" [*L'Eau froide*]. *Cahiers du cinéma*, no. 481, 1994

THIERRY JOUSSE & FRÉDÉRIC STRAUSS "La fiction c'est les femmes" [Interview, *L'Eau froide*] and Jacques Morice, "Dans le juke-box de L'Eau froide." *Cahiers du cinéma*, no. 482, 1994

OLIVIER DE BRUYN, "Désordre" [*L'Eau froide*]. *Positif*, no. 401–402, 1994

ADRIANO PICCARDI, "Un autore tra scrittura e sentimenti." *Cineforum*, no. 345, 1995

KENT JONES, "Tangled Up in Blue" [on O.A.'s work so far]. *Film Comment* , no. 1/1996

OLAF MÖLLER, "Die Erziehung des Herzens" [on the work of O.A. and André Téchiné]. In: *Viennale 1996*. Vienna: Vienna International Film Festival, 1996

KENT JONES, "Burn This" [on the work of O.A. and André Téchiné]. In: *Viennale 1996*. Vienna: Vienna International Film Festival, 1996

FEDERICO CHIACCHARI, "Irma Vep / Intervista a Olivier Assayas." *Cineforum*, no. 358, 1996

NOËL HERPE, "Irma Vep. On dirait qu'on jouerait aux vampires." *Positif*, no. 429, 1996

SERGE GRÜNBERG, "L'acrobate" [*Irma Vep*] and Frédéric Strauss, "Le vol des bijoux" [Conversation between O.A. and Èric Gautier]. *Cahiers du cinéma*, no. 507, 1996

FABIO BO, "Giuventú." *Filmcritica*, no. 553–554, 1996

SUSAN MORRISON, "Irma Vep." *CineAction*, no. 42, 1997

GAVIN SMITH, "The Grand Illusion" [*Irma Vep*]. *Frieze*, no. 34, 1997

JONATHAN ROSENBAUM, "Life Intimidates Art" [*Irma Vep*]. *Chicago Reader*, June 13, 1997. Reprinted in: Rosenbaum, *Essential Cinema. On the Necessity of Film Canons*. Baltimore, London: The Johns Hopkins University Press, 2004

STEVE ERICKSON, "Making a connection between the cinema, politics and real life: an interview with Olivier Assayas." *Cineaste*, no. 4, 1997

MARIE-CLAUDE LOISELLE, "Regard sur le corps poétique. Échange avec Olivier Assayas" [Interview]. *24 Images*, Montréal, no. 86, 1997

ERNIE TEE, "Van Les Vampires tot Irma Vep. In latex verpakte bespiegelingene". *Skrien*, no. 218, 1997

RAFFAELLE CAPUTO, ROLANDO CAPUTO & CLAIRE STEWART, "Irma Vep: Le femme d'Est". *Metro*, Melbourne, no. 113–114, 1997

ADRIANO PICCARDI, "Olivier Assayas. Energia/movimento: riprendere le forze." *Cineforum*, no. 367, 1997

TIM LUCAS, "Irma Vep." *Video Watchdog*, no. 46, 1998

ALEXANDER HORWATH, "Song for Maggie" [*Irma Vep*]. *Die Zeit*, June 18, 1998

ANTOINE DE BAECQUE, "HHH: paroles, gestes, musiques" [*HHH*]. *Cahiers du cinéma*, no. 529, 1998

HELEN BANDIS & ADRIAN MARTIN, "The Cinema According to Olivier Assayas." *Cinema Papers*, Melbourne, no. 126, 1998

JACQUES RANCIÈRE, "De la difficulté d'être un personage de cinéma" [*Fin août* and other films]. *Cahiers du cinéma*, no. 529, 1998. German translation, "Von der Schwierigkeit, eine Filmfigur zu sein," in: Rancière, *Und das Kino geht weiter*. Berlin: August Verlag, 2012

KRISTIN M. JONES, "Weight in Measure" [Interview, *Fin âout*]. *Artforum*, no. 10/1999

JEAN-MARC LALANNE, "La mémoire d'Adrien" [*Fin août*]. *Cahiers du cinéma*, no. 532, 1999

NOËL HERPE, "Un roman est un miroir qui se promène sur une grande route" [*Fin août*]. *Positif*, no. 456, 1999

MARK PERANSON, "A conversation with Olivier Assayas on 'Fin août, début septembre'" [Review and interview]. *CineAction*, no. 48, 1999

ROBERT HORTON, "Late August, Early September." *Film Comment*, no. 5/1999

CHRIS DARKE, "Late August, Early September." *Sight and Sound*, no. 9/1999

SERGE TOUBIANA & CHARLES TESSON, "Quelques vagues plus tard. Table ronde avec Olivier Assayas, Claire Denis, Cédric Kahn et Noemie Lvovsky." *Cahiers du cinéma* Special Issue: *La Nouvelle Vague. Une légende en question*, 1999

FERGUS DALY, "Critical instinct: Olivier Assayas" [Interview]. *Film West*, Dublin, no. 37, 1999

OLIVIER KOHN, "Olivier Assayas" [Interview]. In: Michel Ciment & Noël Herpe (eds.), *Projections 9. French Film-makers on Film-making*. London: Faber & Faber, 1999

OLIVIA KHOO, "Anagrammatical Translations: Latex Performance and Asian Femininity Unbounded in Olivier Assayas's *Irma Vep*." *Continuum: Journal of Media and Cultural Studies*, no. 3/1999. Also in: Khoo, *The Chinese Exotic: Modern Diasporic Femininity*. Hong Kong: Hong Kong University Press, 2007

FRÉDÉRIC BAS, "Les grandes espérances" [Set report, *Les Destinées*]. *Cahiers du cinéma*, no. 541, 1999

PHIL POWRIE, *French cinema in the 1990s: continuity and difference* [Chapter on *Irma Vep*]. Oxford: Oxford University Press, 1999

DOMINIQUE BLUHER, "Histoire de raconteur: décentrement, elision et fragmentation dans *Nénette et Boni, La Vie de Jésus, Fin août, début septembre* et *Peau neuve*." *Iris*, no. 29, 2000

DAVID THOMPSON, "Industrial light and magic" [Set report, *Les Destinées*]. *Sight & Sound*, no. 4/2000

STÉPHANE BOUQUET, "Le temps modernes," and Marie-Anne Guérin, "Trajets et ellipses," and Michel Crépu, Marie-Anne Guerin, Baptiste Piegay & Charles Tesson, "Le passé devait trouver sa place au coeur de ma vision du cinema" [Essays and interview, *Les Destinées*]. *Cahiers du cinéma*, no. 548, 2000

JEAN-PHILIPPE GRAVEL, "Les meilleures intentions" [Review and interview, *Les Destinées*]. *Ciné-Bulles*, Montréal, no. 1/2000

KEITH READER "Les Destinées sentimentales." *Sight and Sound*, no. 1/2001

NICO DE KLERK, "Kwaliteit tot elke prijs: Les Destinées sentimentales." *Skrien*, no. 7/2001

WALTER METZ, "From Jean-Paul Belmondo to Stan Brakhage: romanticism and intertexuality in Irma Vep and Les misérables." *Film Criticism*, no. 1/2002

KRISTIN M. JONES, "Les Destinées." *Film Comment*, no. 2/2002

CLÉLIA COHEN, "Fantasme interrompu" [*demonlover*]. *Cahiers du cinéma*, no. 569, 2002

NICOLAS AZALBERT, "Connected people" [*demonlover*]. *Cahiers du cinéma*, no. 573, 2002

KENT JONES, "World Gone Wrong" [*demonlover*]. *Cinema Scope* no. 11, 2002

GIONA A. NAZZARO, "Olivier Assayas, una violenza profetica" [*demonlover*]. *Filmcritica*, no. 526–527, 2002

MARK PERANSON, "Reattaching the Broken Thread: Olivier Assayas on Filmmaking and Film Theory" [Interview]. *Cinema Scope*, no. 14, 2003

SERGE KAGANSKI, "Movie of the moment: *Demonlover*," and Howard Hampton, "Sound and vision: *Demonlover*" [soundtrack]. *Film Comment*, no. 5/2003

JASON SHAWHAN, "Qui Est Sylvie Braghier?": Identity and Narrative in Olivier Assayas' Demonlover." *thefilmjournal.com* (online), no.6, 2003 [www.thefilmjournal.com/issue6/demonlover.html]

JOHN CALHOUN, "Techno lust" [*demonlover*, Denis Lenoir]. *American Cinematographer*, no. 9/2003

DENNIS LIM, "The Rise of the Machines" [*demonlover*]. *The Village Voice*, September 16, 2003

NEAL BLOCK, MICHAEL KORESKY, JEFF REICHERT & ERIK SYNGLE (EDS.), "Olivier Assayas: Interview & Symposium" [an extensive dossier on O.A., including several reviews of *demonlover*, as well as the earlier films, and an interview]. *Reverse Shot online*, 2003 [www.reverseshot.com/legacy/septoct03/index.html]

JONATHAN ROMNEY & KATE STABLES, "Stop making sense" [*demonlover*, including an interview]. *Sight and Sound*, no. 5/2004

JEAN-MICHEL FRODON, "Où vas-tu, Emily?" and "'La musique de Brian Eno pose des questions de cinéma'" [*Clean*, review and interview]. *Cahiers du cinéma*, no. 593, 2004

KENT JONES, "Our Music" [*Clean*]. *Cinema Scope*, no. 19, 2004

JEAN-CHRISTOPHE BERJON, "Olivier Assayas: le glace et le feu" [*Clean*]. *Avant-Scène Cinéma*, no. 534, 2004

MAYA KCKECHNEAY & MICHAEL OMASTA, "'Der Realität vertrauen'" [Interview, *Clean*]. *Falter*, Vienna, no. 47/2004

JOSÉ ANTONIO GARCÍA JUÁREZ, "Olivier Assayas: Teoría del vacío." *Lettras de Cine*, no. 8, 2004

JEAN-MICHEL FRODON, "Les perruques de la gratitude" [Interview with O.A. on Guy Debord]. *Cahiers du cinéma*, no. 605, 2005

ELIZABETH WALDEN, "'You want to torture Zora?' Olivier Assayas's *Demonlover* as critique." *New Cinemas: Journal of Contemporary Film*, Leeds, no. 1/2005

JONATHAN ROMNEY & ROGER CLARKE, "Less than Zero" [*Clean*, interview and review]. *Sight and Sound*, no. 7/2005

JONNY COSTANTINO, "Giro di vite allo stato liquido" [*Clean*]. *Cineforum*, no. 446, 2005

OLIVER FAHLE, *Bilder der Zweiten Moderne* [Chapter on *Irma Vep*]. Weimar: VDG – Verlag und Datenbank für Geisteswissenschaften, 2005

ÀNGEL QUINTANA, "*Demonlover:* el estado de las cosas." *Dirigido por…*, Barcelona, no. 344, 2005

ANITA SCHILLHORN VAN VEEN, "The floating world: representations of Japan in *Lost in Translation* and *Demonlover*." *Asian Cinema*, no. 1/2006

HOWARD HAMPTON, "Clean." *Film Comment*, no. 2/2006

DALE HUDSON, "Just play yourself, 'Maggie Cheung': *Irma Vep*, rethinking transnational stardom and unthinking national cinemas." *Screen*, no. 2/2006

FRANCK LE GAC, "Olivier Assayas" [Overview essay]. *Senses of Cinema* (online), no. 39, 2006 [http://sensesofcinema.com/2006/great-directors/assayas]

GIONA A. NAZZARRO & MARINA DELVECCHIO, "Vivere oggi quello che hai fatto ieri" [Interview]. *Filmcritica*, no. 573, 2007

SAUL SYMONDS, "Way Out East" [Set report, *Boarding Gate*]. *Film Comment*, no. 3/2007

MARION POIRSON-DECHONNE, "*Irma Vep* d'Assayas: de l'anagramme à la mise en abîme". *CinémAction*, no. 124, 2007

JEAN-MICHEL FRODON, "Un geste" [*Boarding Gate*]. *Cahiers du cinéma*, no. 625, 2007

ALEX HUGHES, *France/China: Intercultural Imaginings* [Chapter on *Irma Vep*]. London: Legenda, 2007

MARTINE BEUGNET, *Cinema and Sensation: French Film and the Art of Transgression* [Chapter on *demonlover*]. Edinburgh: Edinburgh University Press, 2007

MAJA MANOJLOVIC, "*Demonlover:* Interval, Affect and the Aesthetics of Digital Dislocation." In: Bruce Bennett, Marc Furstenau & Adrian Mackenzie (eds.), *Cinema and Technology: Cultures, Theories, Practices*. London: Palgrave Macmillan, 2008

AARON HILLIS, "Olivier Assayas on 'Boarding Gate'" [Interview]. *IFC.com*, 2008 [www.ifc.com/fix/2008/03/oliver-assayas-on-boarding-gate]

JESSICA WINTER, "Boarding Gate." *Film Comment*, no. 2/2008

JOSHUA CLOVER, "The New World System" [*Boarding Gate* and other films]. *Film Quarterly*, no. 4/2008

STÉPHANE BOUQUET, "Portrait de l'artiste en artiste" [*Eldorado*]. *Cahiers du cinéma*, no. 634, 2008

MARC CERISUELO, "*L'Heure d'été:* le temps des cerises." *Positif*, no. 565, 2008

CYRIL NEYRAT, "Changement d'adresse" [*L'Heure d'été*]. *Cahiers du cinéma*, no. 632, 2008

GINETTE VINCENDEAU, "Family ties" [*L'Heure d'été* and other films], and Nick James, "Polishing off" [Interview], and Tony Rayns, "Summer Hours" [Review]. *Sight and Sound*, no. 8/2008

SIMONE EMILIANI, "Tornando a casa" [*L'Heure d'été*]. *Filmcritica*, no. 590, 2008

DAVID PHELPS, "Bringing Down the House, Part I: Summer Hours" and Daniel Kasman, "Bringing Down the House, Part II: a conversation with Olivier Assayas." *MUBI Notebook*, 2008 [http://mubi.com/notebook/posts/bringing-down-the-house-part-i-summer-hours-assayas-france and http://mubi.com/notebook/posts/bringing-down-the-house-part-ii-a-conversation-with-olivier-assayas]

KATE INCE, *Five Directors: Auteurism from Assayas to Ozon* [Chapter: "Olivier Assayas and The Cinema of Catastrophe"]. Manchester: Manchester University Press, 2008

ROSANNA MAULE, *Beyond Auteurism: New Directions in Authorial Film Practices in France, Italy and Spain Since the 1980s*. Bristol: Intellect Books, 2008

BRIAN PRICE AND MEGHAN SUTHERLAND, "On Debord, Then and Now: An Interview with Olivier Assayas," *World Picture* (online), no. 1, 2008 [www.worldpicturejournal.com/World%20Picture/WP_1.1/Assayas.html]

CLAIRE PERKINS, "Lost in Decryption: Female Subjectivity in the Films of Olivier Assayas." *www.cinemascope.it*, no. 12, 2009 [www.cinemascope.it/Issue%2012/PDF/CLAIRE%20PERKINS.pdf]

FRÉDÉRIC BONNAUD, "Summer Hours." *Film Comment*, no. 2/2009

STÉPHANE DEFOY, "Parfait éclectisme" [on O.A.'s work and *L'Heure d'été*]. *Ciné-Bulles*, Montréal, no. 3/2009

EKKEHARD KNÖRER & SIMON ROTHÖHLER, "Der letzte Debordianer. Der französische Filmemacher Olivier Assayas über sein Carlos-Projekt, seine politische Biografie und Guy Debord" [Interview]. *Cargo*, Berlin, no. 2, 2009

JEAN-PHILIPPE TESSÉ, "Série d'attentats" [*Carlos*] and Stéphane Delorme & Jean-Philippe Tessé, "'Impossible au cinema, possible à la télé': entretien avec Olivier Assayas" [Interview]. *Cahiers du cinéma*, no. 656, 2010

NICOLAS BAUCHE, "Carlos: Commandante abandonné" and Philippe Rouyer & Yann Tobin, "Entretien avec Olivier Assayas: Une enterprise hors norms" [Interview]. *Positif*, no. 592, 2010

KENT JONES, "Recent history" [*Carlos* and other films]. *Film Comment*, no. 4/2010

SIMON ROTHÖHLER, "Zeit des Handelns" [*Carlos*]. *Cargo*, Berlin, no. 7, 2010

J. HOBERMAN, "Sympathy for the Devil" [*Carlos*]. *Film Comment*, no. 5/2010

DAVID THOMPSON, "Five hours of the Jackal" [*Carlos*, interview]. *Sight and Sound*, no. 11/2010

ESTHER BUSS, "Die Ausweitung des Raums" [on O.A.'s work], *Film-Dienst*, no. 22/2010

ANDREAS BUSCHE, "Erst die Libido, dann die Revolution" [*Carlos* and other films]. *EPD Film*, no. 11/2010

ROB WHITE, "Interview with Olivier Assayas" [*Carlos*]. *Film Quarterly*, no. 2/2010

BENJAMIN B., "The world's most wanted man" [*Carlos*, Yorick Le Saux, Denis Lenoir]. *American Cinematographer*, no. 11/2010

RICHARD PORTON, "Demystifying Carlos: an interview with Olivier Assayas." *Cineaste*, no. 1/2010

A.O. SCOTT, "A New Kind of Cineaste" [on O.A.'s work]. *The New York Times*, September 24, 2010

JOACHIM SCHÄTZ, "You may have heard of me." [*Carlos*]. *Kolik Film*, Vienna, no. 14, 2010.

LUCA BANDIRALI & ENRICO TERRONE, "Carlos" [comparison of versions]. *Segnocinema*, no. 170, 2011

ELENA OUMANO, *Cinema Today: A Conversation With Thirty-nine Filmmakers from Around the World*. New Brunswick: Rutgers University Press, 2010

STEVEN SHAVIRO, *Post Cinematic Affect* [Chapter on *Boarding Gate*]. Winchester: Zero Books, 2010

OKSANA BULGAKOWA & ROMAN MAUER, "Im Zeichen von Krise und Utopie. Olivier Assayas und Christian Petzold im Gespräch" [Conversation between O.A. and Ch.P.]. *Film-Dienst*, no. 16/2010

TIM PALMER, *Brutal Intimacy: Analyzing Contemporary French Cinema* [Chapter on O.A.]. Middletown, Connecticut: Wesleyan University Press, 2011

Contributors

The Editor

KENT JONES (b. 1960) is an internationally recognized writer and filmmaker. He writes regularly for *Film Comment* and his work has appeared in many magazines, newspapers, anthologies, and catalogues. In 2007, Wesleyan University Press published *Physical Evidence*, a selection of his writings. In 2009, he was appointed Executive Director of The World Cinema Foundation. He has worked with Martin Scorsese on numerous projects and several documentaries including *My Voyage to Italy* (1999), *Val Lewton: The Man in the Shadows* (2007) which he wrote and directed, and the Emmy-nominated and Peabody Award-winning film *A Letter to Elia* (2010) which he and Scorsese co-wrote and co-directed. He is preparing a feature film, *It Never Entered My Mind*, for the winter of 2012.

Contributors

CHRIS CHANG (b. 1961) is the author of *Va-Va-Voom! Classic Hollywood Pin-Ups* and *Reel Work: Artists' Film and Video of the 1970s* and has contributed to *James Casebere: The Spatial Uncanny* and *Philip Brophy: Hyper Material for Our Very Brain*. He is currently a contributing editor to *Film Comment* and *BOMB* magazines.

LARRY GROSS (b. 1953) is a screenwriter (*48 Hrs.*, *Streets of Fire*, *Geronimo: An American Legend*, *True Crime*, among many others) and a semi-regular contributor to *Film Comment* magazine.

HOWARD HAMPTON (b. 1958) is the author of *Born in Flames: Termite Dreams, Dialectical Fairy Tales, and Pop Apocalypses* (2007), a collection on movies, music, and the thing we call "culture." He has written for *Artforum*, *The Believer*, *Film Comment*, *The Village Voice*, *The New York Times*, *the Boston Globe*, *LA Weekly*, and *Black Clock*. He was born in St. Thomas, Virgin Islands, raised in Skull Valley, Arizona and Hollywood, and resides in Apple Valley, California.

KRISTIN M. JONES (b. 1964) is a writer and editor living in New York. She has written about art and film for *Artforum*, *Film Comment*, *Frieze*, *The Wall Street Journal*, and other publications.

GLENN KENNY (b. 1959) is the chief film critic for the website MSN Movies; from 1998 to 2007 he was the chief film critic for *Premiere* magazine. His writing has appeared in *Rolling Stone*, *The New York Times*, *The New York Daily*

News, *Film Comment*, and other publications. He is a member of the rock band Artificial Intelligence which is preparing its first album as of this writing.

B. KITE has written for a number of periodicals and other publiations, including *Sight & Sound*, *The Believer*, *La Furia Umana*, *Trafic*, *Masters of Cinema*, and *The Criterion Collection*. Also makes little movies. He lives in Brooklyn, NY.

MICHAEL KORESKY (b. 1979) is the staff writer of The Criterion Collection, as well as the co-founder and editor of the online film journal *Reverse Shot*. His writings have appeared in *Cinema Scope*, *Film Comment*, *indieWIRE*, *Moving Image Source*, and *The Village Voice*.

ALICE LOVEJOY (b. 1979) is Assistant Professor in the Department of Cultural Studies and Comparative Literature at the University of Minnesota. Her recent publications include essays in *Screen*, *The Moving Image*, and the anthology *Opening Bazin: Postwar Film Theory and its Afterlife*. She is currently writing a book about Czechoslovakia's Army Film studio.

GREIL MARCUS (b. 1945) is the author of *Mystery Train: Images of America in Rock 'n' Roll Music* (1975), *Lipstick Traces: A Secret History of the 20th Century* (1989), *Dead Elvis* (1991), *The Dustbin of History* (1995), *Invisible Republic: Bob Dylan's Basement Tapes* (1997), *The Manchurian Candidate* (2002), *The Doors* (2011), and other books. With Werner Sollors, he is the editor of *A New Literary History of America*, published by Harvard University Press in 2009.

GEOFFREY O'BRIEN (b. 1948) is the author of fifteen books including *The Fall of the House of Walworth* (2010), *Sonata for Jukebox* (2004), *Castaways of the Image Planet* (2002), *The Browser's Ecstasy* (2000), *The Phantom Empire* (1993), and *Dream Time: Chapters from the Sixties* (1988). His poetry has been collected most recently in *Early Autumn* (2010). He is editor-in-chief of The Library of America.

DAVID PHELPS is a writer, translator, programmer, and an editor at *La Furia Umana*. He was born in September, 1986: conceived by a love affair of horses, and an unlikely alliance of fertility drugs and senior citizen coupons, his cradle to be guarded by a Yorkie, his bed by a Russian Blue. He works in New York as a private tutor.

NICK PINKERTON, born 1980 in Cincinnati, is a Brooklyn-based film critic. He writes regularly for *The Village Voice* and *Sight & Sound* magazine.

JEFF REICHERT (b. 1978) is co-founder and editor of the online film journal *Reverse Shot*. He also wrote and directed the 2010 feature documentary *Gerrymandering*, which explored American democracy and the method through which it allows politicians to control electoral outcomes; his second film is in post-production as of this writing.

RICHARD SUCHENSKI (b. 1982) is a film historian who has curated and organized several film retrospectives and interdisciplinary conferences. He is a frequent contributor to *The Moving Image* and *Senses of Cinema*. Among his recent publications are articles on Robert Bresson, Pedro Costa, and Robert Beavers. He has taught at Bard College since 2010.

GINA TELAROLI was born in 1982, into the lap of Reagan. She started living in 1997, and is a contributor to *La Furia Umana*; *Traveling Light* is her second feature.

List of Illustrations

PRIVATE COLLECTION OF OLIVIER ASSAYAS Pages 13, 15 [3], 17 [2], 19, 23 (above left), 27, 47 (above right, below), 48, 56–59, 88, 100, 179 [16], 197 (below)
BUREAU ASSAYAS PAGES 21 (above), 37 (above), 39 (below), 45 [2], 49, 53 [2], 64, 90 [2], 106, 115 [2], 119, 123 [2], 163 [2], 165, 169 [4], 181 (© JC Carbonne), 182 (above), 185, 188, 193 [2], 201 [2], 202, 203, 205 [2]
RÉGIS D'AUDEVILLE Cover image
FALTER ARCHIVE Page 8 (© Katharina Gossow)
FRANÇOIS-RENAUD LABARTHE Page 55
CHARLES TESSON Page 47 (above right)
ISABELLE WEINGARTEN Pages 23 (above right, below), 25, 26 (below), 29 [2], 31 (above), 33 [2], 35 [2], 41 (above), 69 [2], 71, 73, 77 [2], 78, 81, 83, 85, 86, 91 [2], 93 [2], 97, 99, 103, 105 [2], 107, 109 [2], 110, 113, 210, 226

ASCOT ELITE FILMVERLEIH Pages 37 (below), 171, 177 [3]
AUSTRIAN FILM MUSEUM 39 (above), 47 (above left), 51 (middle, below: frame enlargement by Roland Fischer-Briand), 116–117 (frame enlargements by Roland Fischer-Briand), 127 (above, middle), 141, 145 [2], 146, 151 ([2]), 152, 157 (above), 182 (below), 187, 207 ([4], below: frame enlargements by Florian Wrobel]), 208 ([2], frame enlargements by Florian Wrobel), 209 [2], 211 [4], 227, 229, 230, 231 (frame enlargement by Georg Wasner), 232
BRITISH FILM INSTITUTE Page 234
CINÉMATHÈQUE SUISSE Pages 61 [2], 67, 125, 127 (below), 129, 228, 233
KINOTEKA SLOVENSKA Page 225
POLYFILM FILMVERLEIH Pages 21 (below), 43 (above), 191 [2], 195 [2], 197 (above), back cover
RAY FILMMAGAZIN Page 173 [2]
STADTKINO FILMVERLEIH 26 (above), 41 (below), 43 (below), 51 (above), 65 [2], 130 [2], 137 [2], 139 [2], 155 [2], 157 (middle, below), 159 [2], 161 [2]
WILD BUNCH 31 (below)

Acknowledgments

Apart from Olivier Assayas without whose generosity and support this book would not exist, and apart from the writers whose wonderful work we are able to present here, we want to express our gratitude to many other individuals and institutions: to Gabi Adébisi-Schuster, Jean-Brice Assemat, Sylvie Barthet, Regina Schlagnitweit and Isabelle Weingarten, who were all instrumental in defining the visual shape of the book and supplying most of its illustrations; to Bérénice Guidat and the PAP Programme of the Institut français in Paris for supporting the acquisition of publishing rights for some materials in this volume and its companion book; and to Jean-Claude Crespy and the Institut français in Austria for their general support of and help with the "Vienna Assayas Project."

Thanks are also due to many staff members of the Austrian Film Museum for their help during the production of the book: to Roland Fischer-Briand for his 'hands-on engagement' with the final passage of *Irma Vep* (pp. 116–117); to Florian Widegger for his work on the bibliography; and to Andrea Glawogger, Marcus Eberhardt, Richard Hartenberger, Eszter Kondor, Elisabeth Streit, and Florian Wrobel. Rainer Dempf came to our rescue during an analog/digital impasse. Our search for illustrations was warmly supported by Thomas Bissegger (Cinémathèque suisse), Metka Dariš (Kinoteka Slovenska), Lisl Hajdu (Viennale), Birgit Kohler (Arsenal – Institut für Film- und Videokunst), Gabi Mühlberger (Stadtkino Wien), Andrea Mühlwisch (SKIP), Robert Newald, Frank Robert (Der Standard), Paul Taylor (BFI), Alexander Tuma, and Markus Zabinski (Ascot Elite Filmverleih). *The publishers*

KENT JONES WISHES TO THANK all the writers who agreed to contribute to this book; Ryan Werner of IFC Films and Charles Gillibert from MK2; Paul Brunick; Denis Lenoir, Éric Gautier, Luc Barnier and Sylvie Barthet, for their time and their reflections; Gina Telaroli, for making certain hard-to-find titles available; Arnaud Desplechin, for helping me to clarify my thoughts about Olivier's place in French cinema; and Alex Horwath, Regina Schlagnitweit and Olivier Assayas – "Our intellectual and active powers increase with our affection" (Emerson, *Friendship*).

FilmmuseumSynemaPublikationen

Volume 15
SCREEN DYNAMICS
MAPPING THE BORDERS OF CINEMA
Edited by Gertrud Koch, Volker Pantenburh, and Simon Rothöhler
Vienna 2012, 184 pages.
ISBN 978-3-901644-39-9. In English

This volume attempts to reconsider the limits and specifics of film and the traditional movie theater. It analyzes notions of spectatorship, the relationship between cinema and the "uncinematic", the contested place of installation art in the history of experimental cinema, and the characteristics of the high definition image. Contributors include Raymond Bellour, Victor Burgin, Vinzenz Hediger, Tom Gunning, Ute Holl, Ekkehard Knörer, Thomas Morsch, Jonathan Rosenbaum and the editors.

Volume 14
WAS IST FILM. PETER KUBELKAS ZYKLISCHES PROGRAMM IM ÖSTERREICHISCHEN FILMMUSEUM
Edited by Stefan Grissemann, Alexander Horwath, and Regina Schlagnitweit
Vienna 2010, 208 pages. ISBN 978-3-901644-36-8
In German

Volume 13
ROMUALD KARMAKAR
Edited by Olaf Möller and Michael Omasta
Vienna 2010, 256 pages, ISBN 978-3-901644-34-4
In German

Volume 12
APICHATPONG WEERASETHAKUL
Edited by James Quandt
Vienna 2009, 256 pages.
ISBN 978-3-901644-31-3. In English

Apichatpong Weerasethakul is widely praised as one of *the* central figures in contemporary cinema. This first English-language volume on the Thai filmmaker looks at his works from a variety of angles and is extensively illustrated. With contributions by James Quandt, Benedict Anderson, Mark Cousins, Karen Newman, Tony Rayns, Kong Rithdee, and Tilda Swinton. With two interviews and personal essays the filmmaker's own voice is also a strong presence in the book.

Volume 11
GUSTAV DEUTSCH
Edited by Wilbirg Brainin-Donnenberg and Michael Loebenstein
Vienna 2009, 252 pages.
ISBN 978-3-901644-30-6
In English and German

According to Viennese filmmaker Gustav Deutsch, "film is more than film." His own career proves that point. In addition to being an internationally acclaimed creator of found footage films, he is also a visual artist, an architect, a researcher, an educator, an archaeologist, and a traveler. This volume traces the way in which the cinema of Gustav Deutsch transcends our common notion of film. Essays by Nico de Klerk, Stefan Grissemann, Tom Gunning, Beate Hofstadler, Alexander Horwath, Wolfgang Kos, Scott MacDonald, Burkhard Stangl, and the editors.

Volume 10
MICHAEL PILZ. AUGE KAMERA HERZ
Edited by Olaf Möller and Michael Omasta
Vienna 2008, 288 pages, ISBN 978-3-901644-29-0
In German

Volume 9
FILM CURATORSHIP. ARCHIVES, MUSEUMS, AND THE DIGITAL MARKETPLACE
Edited by Paolo Cherchi Usai, David Francis, Alexander Horwath, and Michael Loebenstein
Vienna 2008, 240 pages.
ISBN 978-3-901644-24-5. In English

This volume deals with the rarely-discussed discipline of film curatorship and with the major issues and challenges that film museums and cinémathèques are bound to face in the Digital Age. *Film Curatorship* is an experiment: a collective text, a montage of dialogues, conversations, and exchanges among four professionals representing three generations of film archivists and curators.

Volume 8
LACHENDE KÖRPER. KOMIKERINNEN IM KINO DER 1910ER JAHRE
Claudia Preschl
Vienna 2008, 208 pages, ISBN 978-3-901644-27-6
In German

Volume 7
JEAN EPSTEIN
BONJOUR CINÉMA UND ANDERE SCHRIFTEN ZUM KINO
Edited by Nicole Brenez and Ralph Eue,
translated from French by Ralph Eue
Vienna 2008, 160 pages, ISBN 978-3-901644-25-2
In German

Volume 6
JAMES BENNING
Edited by Barbara Pichler
and Claudia Slanar
Vienna 2007, 264 pages.
ISBN 978-3-901644-23-8. In English
James Benning's films are among the most fascinating works in American cinema. He explores the relationship between image, text and sound while paying expansive attention to the "vernacular landscapes" of American life. This volume traces Benning's artistic career as well as his biographical journey through the United States. With contributions by James Benning, Sharon Lockhart, Allan Sekula, Dick Hebdige, Scott MacDonald, Volker Pantenburg, Nils Plath, Michael Pisaro, Amanda Yates, Sadie Benning, Julie Ault, Claudia Slanar and Barbara Pichler.

Volume 5
JOSEF VON STERNBERG
THE CASE OF LENA SMITH
Edited by Alexander Horwath
and Michael Omasta
Vienna 2007, 304 pages.
ISBN 978-3-901644-22-1
In English and German
The Case of Lena Smith, directed by Josef von Sternberg, is one of the legendary lost masterpieces of the American cinema. Assembling 150 original stills and set designs, numerous script and production documents as well as essays by eminent film historians, the book reconstructs Sternberg's dramatic film about a young woman fighting the oppressive class system of Imperial Vienna. The book also includes essays by Janet Bergstrom, Gero Gandert, Franz Grafl, Alexander Horwath, Hiroshi Komatsu and Michael Omasta, a preface by Meri von Sternberg, as well as contemporary reviews and excerpts from Viennese literature of the era.

Volume 4
DZIGA VERTOV. DIE VERTOV-SAMMLUNG IM ÖSTERREICHISCHEN FILMMUSEUM THE VERTOV COLLECTION AT THE AUSTRIAN FILM MUSEUM
Edited by the Austrian Film Museum,
Thomas Tode, and Barbara Wurm
Vienna 2006, 288 pages.
ISBN 3-901644-19-9. In English and German
For the Russian filmmaker and film theorist Dziga Vertov *KINO* was both a bold aesthetic experiment and a document of contemporary life. This book presents the Austrian Film Museum's comprehensive Vertov Collection: films, photographs, posters, letters as well as a large number of previously unpublished sketches, drawings and writings by Vertov including his extensive autobiographical "Calling Card" from 1947.

Volume 3
JOHN COOK. VIENNESE BY CHOICE, FILMEMACHER VON BERUF
Edited by Michael Omasta and Olaf Möller
Vienna 2006, 252 pages. ISBN 3-901644-17-2
In German (part 1) and English (part 2). OUT OF PRINT

Volume 2
PETER TSCHERKASSKY
Edited by Alexander Horwath and Michael Loebenstein
Vienna 2005, 256 pages. ISBN 3-901644-16-4
In English and German. OUT OF PRINT

Volume 1
CLAIRE DENIS. TROUBLE EVERY DAY
Edited by Michael Omasta and Isabella Reicher
Vienna 2005, 160 pages. ISBN 3-901644-15-6
In German. OUT OF PRINT

All bilingual or English-language publications produced by the Austrian Film Museum are distributed internationally by Columbia University Press (**cup.columbia.edu**).
For German-language titles please see **www.filmmuseum.at** or **www.synema.at**